STILL BURNING

Half a Century of Chicago, from the Streets
to the Corridors of Power: A Memoir

JEREMIAH JOYCE

LITTLE CREEK PRESS®
AND BOOK DESIGN
MINERAL POINT, WISCONSIN

Little Creek Press®
A Division of Kristin Mitchell Design, Inc.
5341 Sunny Ridge Road
Mineral Point, Wisconsin 53565

Book Design and Project Coordination:
Little Creek Press and Book Design

First Printing
September 2021

Printed in the United States of America

For more information or to order books,
www.littlecreekpress.com

Library of Congress Control Number: 2021914603

ISBN-13: 978-1-955656-03-0

INTRODUCTION

On the summery Monday evening of August 16, 1965, I gathered with several of my friends in the parking lot behind Chris Quinn's Tavern on West 79th Street on Chicago's South Side, just down the street from the anchoring presence of St. Sabina Church and its adjacent community center. I was 22, and with Quinn's permission, my friends and I took our seven-ounce beers outside. Looking back, it's not hard to assume what was on our minds—and, for that matter, on the minds of most Americans that night over half a century ago. In Los Angeles, African Americans in the Watts neighborhood had been rioting for five days, a shocking rampage set off by the arrest of a Black motorist. At the same time, Chicago had been reeling from its own disturbances—three nights of violence on the West Side that had already injured at least 62 people, including 11 policemen. The trouble had ignited when a careening fire truck, responding to a false alarm in the West Garfield Park neighborhood, struck and killed a woman on the sidewalk. The angry mood in that African American neighborhood, however, had almost certainly been kindled by what was going on in Watts.

A story in the Sunday *Chicago Tribune* the day before had reported that the West Side rioting and a request from Police Superintendent O.W. Wilson had prompted Governor Otto Kerner to send 2,000 National Guardsmen "with full battle equipment" to Chicago. A paragraph buried in the *Tribune* story noted, "The last time the national guard was called to suppress racial violence was in 1951, when rioting broke out in Cicero after a Negro family rented an apartment in a building at 6139 19th Street."

The *Tribune* didn't bother pointing out that the rampage in that 1951 incident was led by Cicero whites trying to chase the Black family from the neighborhood. Indeed, in the years after World War II, reported "racial violence" by white people was almost commonplace in Chicago, as the city lurchingly responded to its changing population. Between 1946 and 1953, for example, there were at least five riots in response to Black people moving into a neighborhood— six if you count the November 1949 South Peoria Street violence set off by a visit of Black friends to a Jewish household. Those were major outbreaks—the list doesn't track the countless smaller episodes of firebombs, rocks thrown, and beatings. Chicago's Black population was bursting out of its narrow geographical confines, and whites were responding with hostility. White racism drove some of the fury, of course, but I think white people worried about the safety of their families and the value of their homes. Panic-peddling, block-busting real estate agents soon exploited all these factors.

The responses of elected officials and community leaders to these neighborhood changes were similar and clearly ineffective. The officials and leaders mistakenly assumed that the new arrivals were crusading for the American right to reside where they chose. In fact, the newcomers were really seeking safer neighborhoods and better schools for their families—a truth the officials and leaders downplayed. Even more significant, these authorities underestimated the role and power of the panic-peddlers, the contract sales promoters, the shady mortgage brokers and the redlining insurance operators.

St. Sabina Parish, however, promised to be different. After watching other South Side neighborhoods turn from white to Black like falling dominoes, the St. Sabina community, led by a forward-thinking priest, had taken a new approach. The church, residents, and businesses had come together to promote orderly integration. Blacks were moving in, aided by a strong community organization, but whites weren't fleeing. Craven block busters were held at bay. Religious leaders, both Catholic and Protestant, preached the necessity of getting along. And it seemed to be working. Many residents had the vision that the neighborhood could be a model of urban integration.

And then, on that August evening, as my friends and I drank our beers and talked, the sound of gunshots interrupted our gathering. We ran down Racine Avenue and saw a young white man, Frank Kelly, lying on the sidewalk in front of the church's community center. We could see that he was dying. Someone said he'd been shot by a group of Black teens. I'd known Frank for years. He was a nice kid, four years younger than I. When he was in the fourth grade, I supervised him and three other St. Sabina students in the annual Christmas card sale. As he lay bleeding, one of the parish priests ran up and administered the last rites. An angry crowd of neighborhood teenagers had gathered in the street, and the priest told my friends and me to quiet them. A gunshot had also hit a girl who'd been with Frank, and she was lying nearby. An ambulance took her to the hospital, and she survived. Frank died on the sidewalk.

The shooting had grown from a glancing but typical teenage confrontation, probably a show of bravado. But it shattered the goodwill carefully built in the parish, destroying what one thoughtful observer called the last best hope for integration on the South Side. Almost immediately, white families started moving out, the fearmongers worked their cruel sorcery, and within a few years, the neighborhood was almost all Black.

By 1969, I had lived in five different neighborhoods that had been completely resegregated. Frequently, when friends from the former neighborhoods or church parishes would meet, they would speak of what might been done differently to deal with block-by-block turnover. In 1973, it seemed the people in Chicago's South Side 19th Ward community were facing a stay-or-move decision, and that became the sole reason I ran for office.

After a long life in politics and a career largely spent focusing on the issues facing Chicago, I often think of the remarks made by the Columbia University historian Barbara Fields at the close of Ken Burns's great documentary, *The Civil War*. Fields asks who won the war and acknowledges that if you are talking about battles, then of course the Northern soldiers and generals did. The union was restored, slavery was abolished. But, she adds, the men, women, and children who were slaves hardly achieved the freedom they anticipated. In that sense, Fields says, "The Civil War is in the present as well as in the past .... It's still being fought, and, regrettably, it can still be lost."

One measure of the Civil War's duration stands out if you drive around Washington and see the names adorning three monumental government buildings: the Russell Senate Office Building, named for Richard Russell, the long-time Democratic senator from Georgia; the Rayburn House Office Building, named for Sam Rayburn, the Texas congressman who was speaker of the House for 17 years; and the J. Edgar Hoover Building, headquarters of the FBI, named for the man who headed the law enforcement agency for almost half a century. Two Southerners and the third, Hoover, a native of Washington, D.C., a segregated city during his childhood. Three lifelong single men (well, Rayburn married once for a few months) who, without families to distract them, devoted themselves to amassing power and steering the country in directions they desired. Those directions redounded to the advantage of the South, financially and socially, and punished Northern cities and the country's Black citizens.

Richard Russell, for years an outspoken segregationist, earned a legendary reputation as a master of procedural manipulation during his years in the Senate, from 1933 to 1971. Along with his cohort of Southern Democratic senators, he did all in his power to block civil rights legislation, from voting rights to integrated schools to anti-lynching measures. As long-time chairman of the Senate Armed Services Committee and a member of the Appropriations Committee, he wielded enormous influence over federal spending. That meant that funds poured into the South for military bases, defense manufacturing, research facilities, and roads. The post-war economic recovery of the South and the rise of the Sunbelt were built in large part on spending by the Pentagon.

Sam Rayburn carries a more moderate record on race relations—for example, refusing to sign the so-called Southern Manifesto, the racist denunciation of *Brown vs. Board of Education* signed by more than 100 Southern politicians and drafted in part by Richard Russell. What's more, during his long service in the House (1913-1961), he championed New Deal legislation and worked closely with Presidents Truman and Eisenhower. Still, he used his role as speaker and his control of committee chairmanships to shepherd his preferred agenda, which included going slow on civil rights and providing federal financial support to Texas and the South.

J. Edgar Hoover rightly gets credited with founding the Federal Bureau of Investigation and introducing many modern police procedures. But as his long tenure atop the agency proceeded, his abuses of power increased along with his deep prejudices. By various accounts, agents under his direction gathered information illegally, invented and planted evidence, and maintained secret dossiers on well-known people in and out of government. Many officials are said to have resisted challenging him out of fear that he would retaliate by exposing their foibles and indiscretions. At the same time, he developed an almost obsessive fear of so-called subversives around the country, which grew into the surveillance of civil rights workers and of Black people generally. In short, Hoover used his power in Washington to impart his two-tier view of American life, white people on the top tier and Black people on the bottom.

The post-war economic bounce in the South, of course, wasn't distributed evenly. Times remained hard for African Americans, many of them tenant farmers and most handicapped by decrepit, segregated schools. Add the humiliations of Jim Crow and the outright dangers Black people faced at the hands of whites, and it's small wonder that millions moved North, crowding into cities in the Northeast and Midwest and West Coast.

Paradoxically, the jobs were going the other way. Particularly after the introduction of air-conditioning made Southern summers more bearable, a lot of Northern manufacturing businesses moved South, taking advantage of the region's low taxes and antagonism to unions. Meantime, global competition and technological advances buried some traditional Midwest manufacturing strengths, notably Chicago's steel industry. The harsh combination of factors increasingly left African Americans in the North with declining prospects for finding good employment while being jammed together into crumbling city neighborhoods that were segregated by tradition and discriminatory housing laws.

Meantime, as Daniel Patrick Moynihan argued in his famous 1965 report, *The Black Family: The Case for National Action*, ghetto living aggravated strains in African American families tracing back to the years of slavery. The report forecast a rapid dissolution of the two-parent household in American inner cities and argued that a single-parent child growing up poor has a difficult time acquiring the values needed to thrive.

The troubled inner-city dynamic exacerbated existing divisions in most Northern cities, highlighting the unresolved legacy of the Civil War that I think was in the mind of Barbara Fields. Sometimes as the conflicts unfolded, it was easy to tell right from wrong. In many instances, however, the moral questions were nuanced and intimately touched on families and homes. For a time, during the middle of the last century, the forces of division were tamped down in most cities by a triumvirate of interlocked institutional powers— the Roman Catholic Church, labor unions, and the Democratic Party. The triumvirate began to disintegrate in the 1950s and 1960s, though Mayor Richard J. Daley held it together somewhat longer in Chicago. Once the lid was off, however, a kind of chaos descended, sometimes in slow motion, sometimes devastatingly fast and ugly.

Over my lifetime in Chicago, I was a firsthand witness to much of this history. I grew up on the South Side and saw neighborhoods turn from all white to virtually all Black with astonishing speed.

To my wife, Mairsey,
and our four sons

I taught for several years in some of Chicago's most troubled public schools, and later I spent almost seven years as a policeman on the South Side during an era, like today, when the relationship between officers and the communities they patrolled was often terribly raw. For most of that time, I was on the street as a detective in the Gang Intelligence Unit as part of an initiative to slow the ravages of street gangs on neighborhoods and schools.

My political career stretched from four years as an alderman to 14 years as a state senator, all during a period of extraordinary turmoil in Chicago city government. Harsh feuds and fragile alliances constantly played out against the backdrop of changing demographics. Always, my focus was on doing what I thought was best for Chicago. Nationally, I worked or consulted with at least a dozen presidents or presidential contenders—I never volunteered, but only became involved when the candidate would personally request my help. But when asked, I would offer the political insights and skills I'd picked up over the years and always looking for candidates whose visions touched directly on help for the cities. Watching Barack Obama's remarkable rise to the White House became one of the interesting experiences of my later years.

Other major American cities have gone through cycles of transformation similar to Chicago's. My roles as a teacher, policeman, politician, and businessman have provided the vantage for a particularly close view.

This book obviously draws on my life, but through that, I hope it tells in part the story of Chicago over the last half century. That's a story with many painful elements, but also featuring a stirring revival, as the city rose from the economic losses and divisions of the 1970s and 1980s to a fresh vitality in the 1990s and into the new millennium. Urban life was vibrant again, and Chicago became a magnet for both young and old. Crime was down, attractions and greenery were up, and the economy bubbled along helpfully. Sadly, the brighter outlook covered over some of the enduring weaknesses and conflicts, which became apparent in the aftermath of the financial meltdown of 2008. The COVID-19 pandemic has further aggravated the divisions.

Today, Chicago remains vital and potent, an anchor of the Midwest and a contributor in countless ways to the well-being of the country. But an observer doesn't have to cast his gaze much beyond Lake Michigan to the east to see that even one-time thriving cities are fragile bodies. Chicago saw that with tragic results in the summer of 2020, when the streets erupted in uncontrolled chaos, leaving North Michigan Avenue, among other neighborhoods, deeply scared.

I hope my experience contributes in some small way to keeping our cities great. ◼

"Nobody rose in Packingtown by doing good work. You could lay that down for a rule—if you met a man who was rising in Packingtown, you met a knave."

Upton Sinclair, The Jungle

When I was about five, I buried what someone would call a treasure in the backyard of my family's home—a tin can of silver dollars given to me by my grandfather. To this day, I cannot figure what was going through my mind. We lived at 75th and South Prairie Avenue on Chicago's South Side, in a brick bungalow that featured a large backyard. It was summer, the ground was soft, and I dug deep. Regrettably, I didn't draw a map. Around nine months later, my father noticed and asked why the can of silver dollars no longer sat on the shelf in my bedroom closet. I told him what I had done, and I tried to show him the burial spot. By now it was March, but spring had barely begun. The top layer of earth was muddy from the melting snow, but below the surface, the ground remained frozen. Nonetheless, my gentle and calm father took the shovel and dug. No luck. I suggested another spot. Still nothing. In the end, the can of silver dollars never appeared. It probably remains buried there today, in the backyard of a bungalow that still stands in a neighborhood that has long since vastly changed.

I joined my family in that bungalow just after New Year's in 1943. With me, we made four: my father, Daniel; my mother, Rita; and my sister, Pat, two-and-a-half years older. In time, three more siblings would crowd that little house, and two more would join us after we moved to larger quarters.

That bungalow, though, sat in the heart of my first neighborhood, Park Manor, a little north and west of better-known Chatham and about 10 miles south of the Loop. Park Manor was typical Chicago middle-class in those days: all white, with an interesting cross-section of ethnic groups—Irish, Italian, some Jewish families. Our most famous neighbor was Mrs. Alphonse Capone—Mae, the wife of the infamous gangster. She lived down the street with her mother-in-law, Teresa, at 7244 South Prairie. Capone had bought the solid, two-story brick building in the early 1920s as a family residence. As he rose to the top of Chicago's underworld, the mobster preferred to stay at the Lexington Hotel on South Michigan Avenue while in Chicago. His mother and various family members remained in the house on Prairie, however, and Mae joined her after Capone's death in Miami in 1947. I recall seeing the two women in church at St. Columbanus—they attended regularly and garnered the same respect as every other parishioner.

Only once did I ever witness anything unusual at that location. A street photographer with a pony was using the residence as a backdrop as he shot posed photos of kids. A man came out and told the photographer to move his tripod and camera down the street.

Another memory of Sunday Mass at St. Columbanus stands out— one ominous in retrospect. A uniformed Chicago policeman entered the church one Sunday on the heels of a lone African American woman attending the service. He followed her down the church aisle and sat in the row of pews directly behind her. He shadowed her for the rest of the Mass, and flanked her as she proceeded out the back of the church and down the street. I later learned that this lady had encountered some racial trouble upon her recent move into the parish—perhaps related to a racial disturbance in the summer of 1949, when Roscoe Johnson, a Black postal worker, and his wife bought and moved into a two-flat in the neighborhood and endured several nights of protests and violence. The crowd heaved rocks, breaking windows, and lit gasoline on the lawn. Though I only saw the officer once with the churchwoman inside St. Columbanus, he continued to meet her outside and escort her home.

Developers had laid out Park Manor in the 1870s with unusually wide streets for Chicago. Because many families didn't own cars, those streets became extensions of the lawns, and for kids, the entire neighborhood was a kind of playground. My sister Pat palled around with four or five kids on the block, including two boys who lived in a foster home across the street. By the time I was four or five, I would tag along. Since I was by far the youngest, the older kids would find ways to amaze me and use me. Once, one of the foster boys placed me at the basement window of a house to watch as he chopped off the head of a Thanksgiving turkey. A Coca-Cola plant sat on a corner a few blocks down, and on hot summer afternoons, Pat's friends would stand me out front, looking miserable and thirsty, so one of the drivers returning from his run would take pity and give me a Coke—which, of course, I had to share.

Just down the street from the Coke plant sat the Swift Ice Cream factory, a naturally enticing place for a group of young kids. My sister and several of the older boys figured out how to climb to the roof and discovered a trapdoor they could open. One day, they led me up there and, using my jacket as a rope, lowered me through the opening into a refrigerated room and onto a pallet of ice cream stacked 30 feet high. As instructed, I threw up a dozen or so cups of the cold treat. After they hauled me back up, my jacket fell back down onto the pallet. We had to leave it there.

We enjoyed the ice cream, but when I got home, my mother immediately wanted to know what had happened to my jacket. Eventually, I confessed. She was upset with me but also furious that the plant had an attractive nuisance like an open trapdoor in the roof that was tempting to the children that swarmed the neighborhood. So she marched me over to the plant and confronted the Swift manager. He didn't believe my story, but finally he sent a man up on a lift and, sure enough, there was my jacket, thoroughly chilled by then. I don't exactly recall my punishment—my mother probably confined me to the backyard for a period of time. Equally painful, though, Pat wouldn't speak to me for days because I had told on us.

Perhaps I picked it up from my sister, perhaps it was there from the start, but early on I displayed an anti-authoritarian streak that has stayed with me in assorted manifestations throughout my life. The first consequential sign of this trait appeared when I was six. A group of older children were playing baseball down the block, and I wanted to join in. They wouldn't let me, so I stood on home base and wouldn't move. An older boy—Jack Wakefield, who was probably 10 or so—warned he would hit me with the bat if I didn't move. When I refused, he conked me on the head and knocked me out. I ended up in the hospital. When I was older and messed up, my mom would comment to my dad, "That Wakefield boy may have done more damage than we thought."

In October of the same year, not long after the baseball incident, I was walking to St. Dorothy School, where I was in second grade. A patrol boy at a school crossing ordered me to stand away from the curb and gently pushed me back. My sister told him not to touch me, and I picked up a pile of wet leaves and threw them at his face. He reported me, and the school's student court made me write "I will not disobey the rules" a countless number of times.

My tireless mother was the disciplinarian in our family. My father was often away for several days at work, but occasionally my mother would rely on him to mete out corporal punishment when he got home. Inevitably, he would march one of us into the bedroom, close the door, and make an ominous ceremony of removing his belt. Then he would noisily slap it against his hand several times, warning us never to commit the offense again—whatever it was. But he never hit any of us. The bedroom routine was all a charade worked out between my mom and dad.

In another era, my mother would have gone to college and on to a professional career—she was an A+ student throughout high school years at Visitation High and later an astute business person. Instead, she married my dad in 1939 and devoted her life to keeping house and tending to the needs of her seven children. When she was in her mid-40s, she contracted multiple sclerosis and spent most of her last years in a leg brace and a wheelchair, but that hardly slowed her down.

My father and his twin sister, Eileen, were the youngest of 13 children. With that large a family, the offspring could head off in all sorts of directions. One older brother, James, returned from World War I in Europe to pursue a bootlegging career on the South Side. Though Uncle Jim was arrested several times, he remained a friendly presence when I was growing up, dapper and cigar-smoking, a man who still seemed to be living in the 1920s. (More about him later.)

Another uncle, Ed, went from being a bricklayer to a Chicago police detective back to being a bricklayer and an official in the Bricklayers' Union. One evening in 1954, someone shot him in a tavern on South Ashland, a place said to be a favorite hangout for union officials. Though hospitalized in critical condition, he survived. Authorities found a .32 caliber revolver at the scene, but Uncle Ed didn't cooperate with the investigation, according to the *Tribune*, and his assailant was never arrested. The newspaper picture of him being carried out of the tavern came as a terrible shock to my sister and me.

Uncles Ed and Jim carried their own sense of justice. One of my aunts made an unfortunate marriage to a man who beat her. Years before I was born, Ed and Jim took the man for a ride to Ohio, and he never returned. As far as the family was concerned, he had simply absconded.

My father was a far cry in disposition from those two older brothers. Though he started at Mount Carmel High School, the same school my grandson Christian will enter in the fall of 2021, he graduated from St. Rita High School, the same school from which my grandson Sam graduated in 2017, 90 years later. My father had been an outstanding high school basketball player and earned a college scholarship. Though he enrolled, he was away from home and on a poor team, so he came back and went to work. Eventually, he would succeed his own father, becoming the international auditor of the Amalgamated Meat Cutters and Butcher Workmen of North America, a job that required him to travel around the country. He'd arrange his schedule to be away mostly mid-week, so he'd have as much time as possible for his family, and as the years went by, he turned down numerous promotions. He was twice offered the vice presidency of the international, but it would have required moving to California. He didn't think relocating was the best thing for his family, and he lived for his family.

As a young child, I abhorred being called by my given name, Jeremiah—to children, the name sounded funny. Early on, I was told that I was named for my great-grandfather. Perhaps indirectly, that is true. But as a young adult, I learned that in fact I was named for an uncle. According to my mother, her father-in-law visited her at the hospital after my birth. He told her I would be the last grandson born in his life who could carry the name. His son Jeremiah—another of my father's older brothers and a successful businessman—had been a victim of the Chicago cab wars and was beaten to death on a downtown street in the 1930s.

It's hard to say whether knowing any of this background would have mitigated the aversion I had for the name. At school, I insisted that my parents tell the authorities that I was to be called Jerry. By the time I came to the point where it didn't matter to me, everyone who knew me, knew me as Jerry. But in 1974, when I first ran for office as an alderman, another Jerry Joyce was running in Illinois for a state Senate seat. To avoid confusion, I ran as Jeremiah, the name that I have used on ballots ever since. Incidentally, the other Jerry Joyce, also a Democrat, was elected to the Illinois Senate, where later I would serve with him. He represented a rural area south of

Chicago, and colleagues would often refer to us as Farmer Joyce and City Joyce.

At a state dinner for the president of Ireland at the White House in 1980, I was seated at a table next to the conductor Leonard Bernstein, and we introduced ourselves. I said I was Jerry Joyce from Chicago. Apparently reading from the place card, he said he thought my name was Jeremiah. I explained that growing up, I had preferred being called Jerry.

"Tell me, Jerry, when were you born?"

"1943," I replied.

"That was the year I was working on my composition *Jeremiah*! I think you made a bad choice when you rejected your real name!"

I was going to respond that I now had a son named Jeremiah, but I let it pass. Today my wife and I have both a son and grandson named Jeremiah.

By the fall of 1950, when I was in second grade, our family had grown to five children. The opportunity came to move to my father's parents' house at 5632 South Morgan in Visitation Parish in the north Englewood neighborhood. Old, wood, and labyrinthine, the house belonged to my grandmother Mary, who still lived there as a widow. My father and his twin sister, Eileen, had grown up in the house. Their parents, John T. and Mary Joyce, had been married in Visitation Catholic Church in 1888. Visitation also represented a return home for my mother, whose family extended back decades in the parish. Her maternal grandfather had started a broom factory that became successful, and he later prospered from investing in residential buildings in the area. My mother was raised in the parish and graduated from Visitation grade school and high school.

The church and the school complex straddled Garfield Boulevard, a gracious street of broad trees and comfortable homes. Sherman Park, a large, inviting oasis designed by Frederick Law Olmstead and his brother John and featuring a circular lagoon, sat just a few blocks west. The parish, which was largely Irish and working-class, thrived.

In the months before my family moved in, Visitation had a

discouraging brush with racial and ethnic housing issues. Two Jewish families, both with far-left politics and union affiliations, moved into a house at 5643 South Peoria Street. The house was just down the street from the church and a couple of streets over from the homes of both of my grandmothers.

At a social event one night, the new families invited several African American friends. A rowdy crowd from the neighborhood gathered outside. The disturbance that night dissipated, but on the following evening, neighbors came back and turned violent. Rocks shattered windows. The crowd eventually grew to 10,000, according to a Chicago newspaper, and 21 people ended up hospitalized, all but one white. What started as anger over Black people entering the white enclave shifted to outbreaks of anti-Semitism and charges that the new neighbors were communists. Police got called out repeatedly, and the tumult didn't calm for months. I was puzzled by the antagonism directed at Jews because my Aunt Eileen was married to a Jewish man, Ernie Rubel, and after the war, they occasionally visited at my grandmother's home just a block away from the disturbances.

The week after the riots started, my mother's mother, Grandmother Lynch, died. Her funeral was held at Visitation, and a large number of police remained on Peoria. The officers were still there when I entered second grade at Visitation in February 1950.

I knew my Grandmother Lynch quite well. She stayed with us often, and we celebrated every holiday together. After her husband died suddenly in 1927, his brother Tom Lynch, a Chicago police sergeant, stepped in to help, and her father, J.P. Cahill, the broom factory owner, provided financial aid. Tragically, later that same year, both Tom and her father died. Sergeant Lynch was killed in a police shootout, and J.P. Cahill suffered a fatal stroke.

Visitation Catholic School was one of the oldest and largest Catholic schools in the city. In fact, the kindergarten enjoyed its own building and featured—in a triumph of good intentions over sound judgment—a fishpond on the floor in the classroom. As Alice Halpin

Collins writes in her book, *Vis Revisited,* "[W]hat began as innocent curiosity soon became a daily dunking as one by one brave little souls would edge nearer and nearer to the pond only to find themselves, in the blink of an eye, amongst the fishies." The inevitable cry: "Somebody pushed me!" (That building is no longer there.)

In those days, as the oldest boy in a family whose father was away often, I assumed a special relationship with my mother. She assigned me tasks—actually, we all had tasks—and mine included shopping. Twice a week, my mother's list neatly folded and firmly placed in my front pants pocket, I would tug a red wagon four blocks to the National Tea grocery store. I had discretion as to price and brand. I'd pick the goods out and truck them home, quite a load, given the size of our family.

Burning coal kept our house warm in the frigid Chicago winters. When my father was away, another of my tasks was to shovel coal into the basement furnace. I performed this gritty task with all the concentration and effort an eight-year-old could muster, knowing that if the fire died, we would freeze. Later, in our next home, we got an automatic stoker and, later yet, we moved to gas, but in those days the waiting list to convert to gas stretched forever.

The unpretentious two-story house on Morgan Street had a spacious attic with stacked boxes and trunks containing the history of the Joyce family. On late winter afternoons, I would browse through the containers, creating a Joyce ancestry suited to my own comfort— one enhanced, perhaps, yet retained intact in my present memory. After these sessions, I would often seek to verify my discoveries, only to be told, "Don't concern yourself with the stuff in the attic."

I found an 1886 photo of my grandfather, John T. Joyce, speaking to an enormous crowd prior to a strike at the Union Stockyards. There was a 1923 letter from national Republican leader Roy O. West to fellow Republicans urging the candidacy of John T. Joyce for U.S. senator. A picture showed my Uncle Jeremiah wearing a fez with the word "Medina" printed on it. A newspaper story recounted my Uncle John being cited for walking two lions on a leash down Michigan

Avenue in front of the Art Institute of Chicago (it was a publicity stunt for his business, the Lion Oil Company). Uncle Jim appeared on his horse in a cavalry uniform, looking to be about 12 years old (he was actually 16). In a photo of my dad's baseball team taken in 1933, he appeared to be about 12 (he was 22).

Sometimes an attic discovery connected to current events. In April 1951, the Visitation Community and my third-grade class stood on Garfield Boulevard holding plaster statues of General Douglas MacArthur as the general's motorcade passed by. MacArthur had recently been fired by President Truman for trying to expand the Korean War. In the attic, I'd already found an Army photo of my Uncle Ernie Rubel and 50 or so other officers posing with the renowned general. A handwritten notation on the back identified Ernie standing in the back row.

An attorney, Ernie Rubel met my dad's twin, Eileen, when they were students at the University of Illinois, and they later united in what the church termed a mixed marriage. Having enlisted in the mid-1930s, Uncle Ernie remained a career military officer, and he, Eileen, and their family lived in Germany and Japan before settling back in the States. A few months after that MacArthur visit to Garfield Boulevard, my cousin Joyce Ruble sat in our living room and recited the Lord's prayer in Japanese.

Hour after hour, day after day, as a young boy, I consumed all of this information and later passed it on to my children and grandchildren without caveat.

Grandfather John T. Joyce was born in Newport, County Tipperary, Ireland, in 1863. For the time and the place, John's father, my great-grandfather Jeremiah, was relatively prosperous. He raised cattle on a farm in Newport, six miles outside of Limerick. He also raced horses from a racing stable in Limerick, where their home was. One of his horses, Liberator, won the English Grand National Steeple Chase in

1879. At the time, though he had sold the horse, he remained its trainer.

In Ireland, John attended school and worked on the family farm. Early on, his father and the workers on the farm taught him how to dress cattle, and by 15, he was considered proficient.

John's mother, Ann, had four older sisters who had emigrated to the United States before the Civil War and settled in upstate New York. They all prospered, and several married into prominent families. Ann Joyce died around 1879, and John's father sent him to America to go to school and live with one of his aunts in Watertown, New York. At some point, he went to live with another aunt and uncle, Mary and John Owens, who owned a large farm 40 or so miles away. John T. Joyce had plans to start a farm nearby, but while his father was arranging the financing, John went to work as a manager of sorts for the Owens' farming operation. This lasted six months and ended when John started complaining that the workers on the farm deserved better conditions and wages. The Owens sent him packing.

John set out for Kansas City, a meat-packing center, where he found work as a cattle butcher. While there, he reached out to the Knights of Labor for advice. Four or five months later, he headed for Chicago, a hotbed of labor strife centered around the growing stockyards. On the way, he stopped off in Wichita, Kansas, and East St. Louis, Illinois, working for a few months at each place, honing his skills—not as a butcher but as a labor organizer. He arrived in Chicago determined to help organize the butchers and packinghouse workers.

After a few years of organizing, he joined a half-dozen friends and in 1886 called a strike at the Union Stockyards over the right for an eight-hour day, down from the current 10-hour day. The walkout of 40,000 workers led the major employers to settle. But the victory was short-lived. Armour, Swift, and the other big packers joined forces and successfully reimposed the 10-hour day in the fall. The eight-hour day wouldn't become solidly established in the stockyards for more than three decades. Nonetheless, in a 1930 article, the *Chicago Tribune* cited the brief strike in calling John T. Joyce the "Father of the Eight Hour Day."

John took enough time out from organizing to court and marry a Chicago girl, Mary Barrett. Their marriage was among the first recorded in Visitation Parish.

Because of his union activities, John was blacklisted by the packers, yet he continued to assist with organizing efforts in the stockyards. In 1897, a group of butchers formed a groundbreaking national union, the Amalgamated Meat Cutters and Butcher Workmen of North America (AMC), and the organization soon hired John to be international auditor, a position he held for decades, eventually to be succeeded by my dad. John T. Joyce became a kind of paterfamilias to the labor movement. When Upton Sinclair came to Chicago to research *The Jungle,* his incendiary 1906 novel about the horrid conditions in the packinghouses, he drew on Joyce as a major source. Reportedly, Sinclair wrote much of his novel while sitting on the Joyce back porch.

The AMC built a tumultuous record in its early years, losing several major strikes, seeing its membership plummet before rising again. Nonetheless, it holds a significant place in labor history as one of the first unions to include both skilled and unskilled workers. The skilled workers were principally butchers, while the unskilled were the so-called packinghouse workers, the men and some women who labored in a business that was increasingly moving to mass production. The union welcomed women and Black members, and though the Chicago branch included many Irish, other ethnic groups—Lithuanians, Poles, and Germans, among them—also joined in large numbers.

Sometime during this period—the mid 1890s—John T. Joyce met Roy O. West, an attorney who lived in the town of Lake, soon to become Chicago's 30th Ward. They both became active in Republican politics. West eventually became head of the Illinois Republican Party and secretary of Interior in the Coolidge Administration. He encouraged my grandfather to go into politics, even to seek a U.S. Senate seat. I was told my grandfather demurred because he didn't think it would be practical with a large family. West and Joyce remained close friends throughout their lives.

In the early years, AMC's membership was famously fractious, owing largely to the divide between skilled and unskilled workers. The union also had a complicated history with African Americans. Though its earliest membership included Blacks, the packinghouse employers often brought in Black workers as strikebreakers, sometimes keeping them on after the strike ended. During World War I, at a high point of the Great Migration, when tens of thousands of Black people moved to Chicago from the deep South, many of the newcomers went to work in the packinghouses. Resentments festered, often pitting the new arrivals against slightly more established immigrant groups, particularly the Irish. Still, Black workers continued to play a substantial role in the AMC, and after World War II, the union allied closely with the United Packinghouse Workers of America, which included many Black members. Later, the two unions merged and today are part of the 1.3-million-member United Food & Commercial Workers International Union.

The AMC had a strong liberal tilt beyond its focus on labor. The attitude was encouraged by Patrick E. Gorman, a Louisville native who led the union for a half century, starting in the early 1920s. My grandfather knew Pat Gorman's family from Ireland and was instrumental in persuading Gorman to move to Chicago and accept the stewardship of the union. Though a socialist follower of Eugene Debs, Gorman kept communists out of the union. He strongly supported civil rights and spoke out aggressively against the Vietnam War. *The Nation* magazine once called him "one of the most enlightened leaders of American organized labor."

It seemed as if I always knew Pat Gorman. Over the years, when I happened to be near the international offices at 2800 North Sheridan Road, I would often stop in to see him. He once told me that in the spring of 1963 President Kennedy asked him to discourage participation by organized labor in Martin Luther King Jr.'s march on Washington. Gorman declined to do it.

While I don't have strong memories of Grandfather Joyce—I was five when he died in 1948—I do recall his funeral at Visitation, the church in which he had been married in 1888. It was the first time I had seen a large number of Black people in the same setting with a large number of whites. The African American men wore ribbons and medals and clustered together in the back corner of the church. Many of them had known John T. Joyce from his early days with the union.

As it turned out, my residence in Visitation Parish didn't last long, only 28 months. The brevity of our stay owed to two terrible events— well, one terrible event and one act of childish stupidity. On a Sunday, in the spring of 1952, my mother and I went to 6 a.m. Mass. On our way home, we stopped at the bakery to pick up an order of dinner rolls for my cousin's First Communion party later that day. As we walked together, I dropped the bag of rolls, and several collected bits of dirt. Picking them up, I said to my mom, "We'll let the others eat these." We laughed uproariously. I'll never forget: While we shared this fit of laughter, my mother said, "Laugh before seven, cry before eleven"—an antique folk saying. As we approached our house, we saw people running up and down our front stairs.

My sister Maureen, who was six at the time, had climbed out of bed and retrieved the Sunday *Tribune* from our yard. She took it into the kitchen, pulled out the funnies section, and set the rest of the paper on the stove. She was sitting nearby when the pilot light ignited the newspaper, and the flames jumped to her bathrobe. She ran screaming through the house. My father came bounding down the stairs from the top floor and tried to beat out the flames with his hands and then rolled her back and forth on the carpet. By the time my mother and I arrived, the fire was out, but Maureen was screaming in pain and terror. Luckily, the flames never touched her face, but when I recall that moment, my mind always trips forward to that infamous picture from Vietnam of the little girl running down the road after being hit by napalm. My father was hurt, too. He had collapsed on the floor. Ashes covered his white shirt, and his hands and arms were badly burned.

Both Maureen and my father were taken to German Evangelical Deaconess Hospital a few blocks away. My father recovered relatively quickly, but Maureen stayed for months at Deaconess and later the University of Chicago Hospital. Happily, she eventually recovered.

That was the terrible event. The childish stupidity followed just a few months later at a time when my parents were preoccupied with Maureen. That spring, I had taken to reckless behavior—flipping moving freight trains above the viaduct at 58th and Morgan, leaping off garage roofs, hang-jumping from branches of tall trees. It was July, and as in the earlier incident that sent me to a hospital, baseball and older kids supplied the context.

The neighborhood children used to play on a gravelly schoolyard next to Holmes Elementary, the public school just up the block from our house. On this day, a group of older boys had commandeered the schoolyard for a softball game, so my friends and I opted for a far corner of the yard to play a game with a rubber ball. As it turned out, our ball kept flying off, disrupting the other game. The older boys got annoyed, and finally one of them pitched our ball up onto the roof of the school.

The old Holmes school—since replaced—stood three stories high. I was nine, small and thin, but agile. I decided to see if I could climb up and retrieve the ball. In fact, the climb turned into a lark. I shimmied up a gutter, scooted along a ledge, and then shimmied up another gutter. I not only retrieved our ball but discovered dozens of balls that I heaved down to my friends below. I started back down, but when I got to the ledge, about 25 feet above ground, I stopped. Someone below dared me to jump. Someone else offered a wager that led to a lot of shouting back and forth. Some kids, including friends, dared me to do it. Others—including the older kids—warned me to climb down.

An area of concrete bordered the gravel schoolyard and extended out from the school building for about 10 feet. I had jumped from heights before, but never onto concrete or gravel, always grass. I thought it would be better to land on gravel, so instead of hanging and dropping, I leapt off the ledge, figuring at worst I would end up with a bruise or two. I landed on the concrete in sort of a fetal position, which probably saved me. I sustained a broken arm, broken leg, broken wrist, and a concussion. I was carried across the street to a neighbor's house and then taken to German Evangelical Hospital.

My leg and arms were in casts for the next few months.

Toward the end of August, the nun I'd had for fourth grade the year before, Sister Ursula, stopped by to check on my recovery with the nun who would teach me in fifth grade. After Maureen's accident, Sister Ursula had taken a special interest in me—fast-tracking me through Latin to become an altar boy, convincing me to continue with piano lessons, and finding reasons to send me on errands in the school. The two visiting sisters spoke with me for a little bit, gave me a holy card, and said they would see me when school started. That wasn't to be.

A few days later, my mom said we were leaving Visitation. The recent events had taken their toll. She determined that the neighborhood was jinxed, and there was no turning her back. She talked to the school principals at Little Flower and St. Sabina parish schools, and then went house hunting. We were all surprised. Our extended family *was* Visitation. Both sets of my grandparents had been married at the church. My parents had gone to school at Vis and had been married there. Most of my aunts and uncles lived in Vis. I was baptized and made my First Holy Communion at the church. Ultimately, though, my parents chose a house in St. Sabina Parish.

When school began that fall, instead of seeing Sister Ursula and the rest of the nuns and classmates at Visitation, I started fifth grade as a new student at St. Sabina. It would be 35 years before I saw Sister Ursula again. In February 1987, I was in downtown Chicago and received a phone call from my wife. She told me that my father's health was rapidly deteriorating and he had been taken by ambulance to St. Francis Hospital in Blue Island. The year before, my dad had suffered a massive stroke and never recovered. He had been cared for at home, but my mother and siblings had decided to take him off life support, and they were awaiting my arrival and concurrence. At the hospital, I was directed to the office of the chaplain. She greeted me with what seemed to be an understanding, compassionate, almost half smile. Struck by sadness and engulfed in a sort of solemn trance, I was startled by the words I heard the chaplain speak. "Jerry, I am Sister Ursula. Do you have any questions?"

I was so shaken by the loss of my father that I could only answer, "No, I really don't, Sister." ■

"... like old times ... we are alumni of a corner
of fellowship in Chicago."

*Letter from Carl Sandburg to Robert Hardy Andrews
of the* Chicago Daily News

Because of the people and events that have touched St. Sabina
in the last century, the parish has assumed what's perhaps an
outsized role in Chicago history, particularly in relation to race in
the city. When my family moved there in 1952, the neighborhood
was overwhelmingly white and predominantly Irish, and my long-
ago classmates and friends speak and write of the parish as if it had
been a kind of urban paradise, an ideal place where the "rain may
never fall till after sundown," in the words of Alan Jay Lerner. This is
unfair to the largely African American parishioners who make their
lives in the community today. The longtime pastor, Father Michael
Pfleger, a white man, guided the mostly Black congregation for four
decades and became an outspoken, sometimes divisive civil rights
leader. (In January 2021, the Chicago archbishop, Cardinal Blase
Cupich, asked Father Pfleger, 71, to relinquish his position pending
an investigation of decades-old sex-abuse allegations against him
raised by two brothers. The priest denied the allegations and in May
Cardinal Cupich reinstated Pfleger, saying an investigation had

found there is "insufficient reason to suspect Father Pfleger is guilty of these allegations.")

Chicago is famously known as a checkerboard of neighborhoods, many anchored by particular ethnic groups. But almost none of those neighborhoods stands immutable. Like any great city, Chicago evolves constantly—residents move out, new residents move in, sometimes the progeny of former residents return. The character and landscape of any Chicago neighborhood is almost certain to change over time.

What's unquestionably true about St. Sabina, though, is that a great many people who lived in the parish in the early and middle decades of the 20th century have extraordinarily fond memories of their time there.

The St. Sabina Catholic Church complex occupies a square half block at 78th Street between South Racine Avenue and South Troop Street. When church leaders founded the parish in 1916, the neighborhood, Auburn Gresham, was only partially settled, and muddy fields occupied much of the area. As the city built streetcar lines, developers started putting up bungalows, three-flats, and small apartment buildings, attracting residents from older, grittier neighborhoods to the north and east. Many of the newcomers were second-generation Irish looking for more space and eager to enjoy such modern conveniences as indoor plumbing. Working- and middle-class families predominated, with a sizable population of policemen, teachers, and white-collar workers from the stockyards.

In those early years in the parish, the general attitude was aspirational. "Although many parishioners were primarily employed in technically blue-collar occupations and the lower rungs of the middle class, they generally considered themselves middle class," writes Eileen M. McMahon, a history professor at Lewis University, who focuses on St. Sabina in her excellent 1995 book, *What Parish Are You From? A Chicago Irish Community and Race Relations*. "The newness of the area, good homes, and being removed from industrial neighborhoods no doubt contributed to their optimism."

After opening in a storefront, the parish put up buildings over the course of several decades, including—despite the Depression—a splendid gray limestone Gothic cathedral in 1933 and a huge community center with a cavernous gym in 1937. Under the supervision of an enterprising young priest, Father Thomas McMahon, the community center became a magnet for Catholics from all over the South Side. They flocked to basketball tournaments and dances, which sometimes attracted more than 1,000 people a night. In one of the more curious twists, Father McMahon introduced roller skating in the gym after recoiling at what he thought were the sorry conditions at the local rink, according to Professor McMahon. The sport caught on and became a signature of St. Sabina School. Students grew so proficient that they would put on an elaborate annual variety show, performing dance numbers and tricks, throughout the 1940s, 1950s, and early 1960s. Thousands of spectators from around the city came out to watch shows that stretched over a week. A 1955 *Tribune* article, complemented by a full page of pictures, crowed that 400 students would skate in that year's show, while another 300 would crew backstage. Those acts would include "scenes from *The Wizard of Oz*, a kicking chorus, ballet numbers and Irish minstrels," the paper reported.

Like most Sabina kids, I grew proficient at roller skating and participated in the annual Roller Skating Varieties. One year, I performed with an older boy named Peter Casey, who had learned to skate on stilts, a skill that was not only unique and difficult but dangerous. My role was to skate through his legs at high speed without knocking him over. At the end, we would both skate backwards, and just before we left the stage, he'd lift me above his head. The stagehands had to catch us when we got out of sight. We pulled off seven or eight performances flawlessly, though years later, Pete told me I'd caused him severe discomfort during our pre-show practice runs. That year's show included my younger brother Dan and his third-grade classmate John Gilhooley. A little more than a decade later, John, working as a Chicago police officer, would get killed on duty in a shootout on the South Side with a Black Panther.

My family, now with six children and still growing—my brothers Dan and Jim and my sister Robin had joined us by then, and Jack would come along in 1954—moved into a brick house at 8245 South Elizabeth Street. The previous owner had run a business out of the front bedroom, and he'd sunk a combination safe in the wall, which always fascinated my siblings and me. I still remember the combination. A stretch of 79th Street served as the neighborhood's commercial center. With everything from groceries to butchers to drug stores to clothing emporia to an Ace Hardware, plus a wide range of service providers, you hardly needed to leave the area. Restaurants abounded, and a movie theater and bowling alley offered entertainment. In his book, *The Guys in the Gang*, my friend James T. Joyce (not related) says he counted 15 Irish taverns in the neighborhood. "The place was, if you were a parochial, idyllic," he writes.

I arrived for the fifth grade at St. Sabina elementary still wearing casts on my arm and leg from the Holmes school jump. For a while, I had to sit away from others in a separate desk. St. Sabina fifth-graders numbered over 150, and our individual room had more than 50 students, presided over by one nun. (The total grade school enrollment numbered more than 1,000.) Given those numbers, it's perhaps not surprising that some of the nuns believed in corporal punishment. Typically, one infraction would get you a painful slap across the knuckles with a ruler, though sometimes you'd get a slap in the back of the head. This type of punishment was reserved for boys only. My classmates from those days agree that the school principal paid close attention to teacher assignments and classroom make-up to provide the right balance and equal exposure to the best teachers.

The nuns could be tough, but I've been interested recently to come across articles on training teachers. Almost all refute the notion that great teachers are born, not made, and most say that teaching techniques can themselves be taught. It turns out that the advised methods of instruction closely resemble the way nuns taught us in the Catholic grade schools of Chicago. For example, studies show that teachers should instruct from one set position; walking around while instructing can be distracting to students. That brought back memories of the nuns perched like statues in the chair behind the desk. Another recommended technique: "cold-calling" when asking questions. That is, rather than waiting for a student to raise a hand, pick a student and ask the question. I recall working to be prepared in case the sister called on me.

As a grade school student, I did fine academically, but, like many of my friends, I was more interested in baseball than anything else. The neighborhood fanned excitement. In the 1953 World Series, Jim Hughes, the older brother of one of my friends, pitched for the Brooklyn Dodgers. Despite being one of the smaller players in my age group, I played well enough to make a number of good teams. I was somewhat slow afoot, but I could make contact with the ball. If I wasn't playing baseball, I was reading about it endlessly, most particularly about the South Side home team, the Chicago White Sox, and their American League rivals.

As part of his auditing responsibilities, my father took an occasional long trip visiting union locals around the country, and sometimes he would bring a sibling or me along. The summer I was 10, he enlisted me on a nine-week trip to the far Northwest, Washington and Oregon. We flew out and then traveled by bus, mostly from one small town to another. My father would spend the day auditing the books at the union local, but before he started, we would share a big breakfast. Then he would drop me off at the town library. I'd head straight for the sports section and pull down the books on baseball. Sometimes the librarians would take an interest and suggest things to read. And I always carried a pencil and paper with me, so when I got tired of reading, I would compile and try to memorize lists of players and their stats. Some were vertical—say, the lineup for every American League team. Others were horizontal— every shortstop I could name. I don't recall ever being bored. My father would drop me off with a soda and a snack, so I held up for the day. When he finished his audit, he'd pick me up, and we'd go out to dinner. Then maybe we'd take in a movie or a minor league baseball game in the town we were in, before retiring for the night to a hotel.

At the time, I had somewhat mixed feelings about the trip. I missed my friends and playing ball—the Little League season had ended before we left, but the neighborhood featured constant pickup games. Still, getting to spend that much time with my father was a gift. I vaguely recognized it at 10, but see it vividly today.

St. Sabina provided its grammar school students with a heavy overlay of Catholicism. You prayed in the morning. In some classes, you prayed before you went home for lunch. When you returned after lunch, you prayed again. You'd have religion class for an hour or so a day. And sometimes you even prayed before you went home. Though I remain a believer to this day, some of the more dogmatic rules and overly strict authority figures slowly chipped away at my reliance on the word of the Church.

I took my first confession at Visitation Church when I had just turned seven. All week, my parents helped prepare me. I wrote my sins down on a piece of paper—the back of a paper coin roller used for collecting nickels. My only real sins came from failing to honor my father and mother and perhaps using a few bad words, but I wrote down everything that a just-turned–seven-year-old could think of. The confessional, however, had no lights. The priest said, "Go ahead, son." I knew enough to say, "Bless me, Father, for I have sinned." But when I looked down at my list of sins, I couldn't read it. For a moment, I froze and considered escaping out the door. But that option would require navigating the gauntlet of classmates still waiting their turn to be cleansed of their sins. In the end, I stumbled through, but the memory of that experience overshadowed my confessions for years to come.

The Catholic fear factor motivated me for a long time—the pains of Hell and the whole fire and brimstone thing. At the same time, the parade of Old Testament horrors led me to question many things. I clearly remember reading the story of Abraham and Isaac. A picture in our religion book showed Abraham about to chop off the head of his beloved son because God had ordered the boy's sacrifice. I studied that picture for a long time. God would never be that cruel, even if, as it turned out, the order only served as a test. I didn't believe it. Someone had made this stuff up.

Many of our local parish rules grated. We were not allowed to enter a non-Catholic church. If a friend got married in a Protestant church, you were not supposed to attend the wedding. And forget about setting foot in a YMCA. James T. Joyce recalls in his book that one priest devoted a sermon to the evils of playing basketball on the outdoor court at the Y at 81st and Racine. Doing so would be a sin. As Joyce puts it, "At St. Sabina, four hundred years after the Reformation, we remained pissed at the Protestants."

About the time I was 13, the school separated the boys and girls for a retreat. The subject of discussion was adolescence and the occasion of sin. The school brought in a priest who specialized in the material. He traveled around to Catholic grade schools with a big trailer full of God gadgets and gimmicks. Among his treasures was a supply of what used to be called eight-pagers—suggestive comic books that were around in the 1940s and 1950s. He'd toss a bundle of the comics in a bucket—his smut bucket, he called it—and set them on fire. Perhaps he added another substance for effect, because the smoke had a nauseating odor. The foul conflagration served as a warning that if you looked at those comics, you'd go to Hell. It got worse. He also traveled with a full-size human skeleton that for some unstated reason he crowned with an Indian chief's headdress. When his lecture heated up, he'd pull out the skeleton. The priest would yell and scream and wave his arms and predict the world was about to end—even citing the exact year, a time not too distant from that moment. After I returned from that eighth-grade retreat, one of the nuns asked me what I had learned. I said that until then I didn't know there were crazy people in the priesthood. That remark earned me a trip to the principal's office and a note to my parents from the school priest.

Overall, though, while my friends and I may have chafed under some of the church's strictures, we faithfully attended Mass on Sundays and on all the Holy Days of Obligation. St. Sabina stood at the center of our lives, and the 3,500 families in the parish were considered a particularly devoted group. The church held 11 Masses on Sundays to accommodate the crowds. Parishioners filled a wide array of charitable organizations, societies, and clubs. In the early 1950s, St. Sabina's leaders created a parish credit union, further connecting their community to the church. By this time, Chicago's geography had famously come to be identified through its parishes, a reference system used by students, politicians, and real estate agents, Catholic and non-Catholic alike. Everyone knew where St. Sabina was.

Together with Catholicism, an overlay of Irish pride pervaded the neighborhood. "Local stores stocked Irish products," writes Professor McMahon. "The neighborhood record store claimed to have the most complete set of Irish music available in the city. Many parents sent their children to learn the intricacies of Irish step dance, while teens gathered at the Shamrock Corner for the all-American hamburger."

McMahon writes that in 1953, Father Tom McMahon, the same priest who pioneered roller skating in the parish, helped organize a parade celebrating St. Patrick's Day. The parade wound through Auburn Gresham and in front of a review stand on 79th Street. By the next year, the *Tribune* reported that 80,000 spectators lined the parade route. The 13,000 marchers included bands from the Great Lakes Naval Training Station and Notre Dame University, and the paper made a point of mentioning that one of the dozens of floats featured a stuffed "kilaloo" bird from Ireland, apparently a mythical creature that could fly backwards. By 1960, McMahon says, the parade had outgrown the South Side and become an annual attraction in the Loop. (South Siders reclaimed their own version of it again in the late 1970s.)

After World War II, a number of new Irish immigrants settled in St. Sabina Parish, and some of the younger men loved to fight, particularly after they had been drinking. My most vivid memory was midnight Mass on Christmas Eve. St. Sabina produced a beautiful service, and the church would be mobbed. Families began arriving an hour early just to get a good seat. At two minutes to midnight, a group of the Irish guys, who would never miss Mass, would spill out of the 79th Street bars and head to the packed church. They would stride down the main aisle toward the front and glare at someone who had been seated patiently for an hour, a signal to squeeze over. Failure to move would create a scene, so the parishioners jammed and bore it. This annual seating event was my favorite part of the St. Sabina Christmas Eve ritual.

Irish politics, here and in the old country, held a major place in the life of Grandfather Joyce. In 1896, he was part of a delegation sent to Ohio to arrange a deal with powerbroker Mark Hanna: Republican presidential candidate William McKinley would promise to name an Irishman to his cabinet in exchange for support from Chicago's Irish. McKinley won, handily beating William Jennings Bryan, and indeed named as his attorney general Joseph McKenna, the son of Irish immigrants.

Like many second- and later-generation Irish, however, my parents didn't press Irish heritage on their children. Our Irish roots were always a presence—my parents had met on St. Patrick's Day one year and married two years later, also on St. Patrick's Day. But in our family the day was mostly an occasion for celebration and a parade—my parents did little to instill a sense of Irish culture or history. Far more than Irish pride, my family exercised union pride. In the 1960 Democratic primary, for example, my father supported Hubert Humphrey over John Kennedy because of Humphrey's strong stand for labor.

Because I grew up in an Irish neighborhood, however, most of my friends were Irish. James T. Joyce, the author of *Guys in the Gang*, and his collaborator, confusingly also named James T. Joyce, were both friends of mine. Much of the book describes the pleasures of hanging with our gang. This was a loosely connected roster of friends who attended St. Sabina School, made faces at each other in church, played sports constantly, shared triumphs and trials, and, as the book puts it, "became more like brothers than friends."

The pleasures of hanging with the gang would not be on my calendar for the summers of 1956 and 1957, however. After the baseball season ended and with a couple of weeks left before school resumed, I was shuttled out to my Aunt Anna's farm in southwestern Cook County. Aunt Anna, my father's older sister, was a well-educated, well-spoken widow. She had owned and operated a millinery shop and also gave piano lessons in the decades before she moved to the farm. Now, her routine was hard work and a lot of church praying.

To deem her property a farm required some license—no crops had been planted in half a century. Her house, a recruiting station for Union soldiers during the Civil War and subsequently the local public school, stood alone a half mile away from anything but farmland. The house reflected her lifestyle—no television, no cooling fans, and no sweets in the pantry. For entertainment, a child guest could read a book, listen to a baseball game on the radio, listen to Aunt Anna play the piano, walk a mile on a dusty, gravel road to pray in a convent chapel, or walk a further distance in the opposite direction on the same road to buy a bottle of pop at a gas station. The pop had to be consumed before returning to the farm. The only reprieve I had from this pattern came with an occasional visit by my Uncle Jim, the older brother to Aunt Anna and my dad.

Uncle Jim had a history—he was a rough, Chicago version of a Damon Runyon character. At 16, he misrepresented his age to join the Army cavalry under General John J. Pershing and chase after Pancho Villa in Mexico. My grandfather tracked him down and arranged to have him sent home. Jim re-enlisted when the U.S.

entered World War I and shipped with his unit to Europe. After the war, he bided his time in various ventures, but with the arrival of Prohibition, he partnered with the energetic John "Dingbat" Oberta, and the two hooked up with the South Side beer chief, "Polack Joe" Soltis. Dingbat was the Republican committeeman of Chicago's 13th Ward, and he had once run for Chicago alderman and Illinois state Senate. He and Uncle Jim became an integral part of Polack Joe's bootlegging operation. Just prior to being assassinated at age 29 in 1930, Dingbat boasted of his popularity. True to his boast, more than 20,000 people showed up at his wake. His killing remains another of the many unsolved murders from the Chicago Prohibition era. I always suspected that Uncle Jim popped him.

Uncle Jim was Irish-handsome, with a friendly presence. He would show up at the farm with candy, baseball magazines, and comic books, which I would leave unread until he left because he was so entertaining. Though he had a reputation for being close-mouthed, he happily talked to me, particularly on the topic of our family history—about which he was remarkably candid. I would ask about matters I had overheard or had read about in my grandmother's attic, curious for verification or elaboration:

What had the priests at Visitation said about Aunt Eileen's marriage to Uncle Ernie, a Jew?

"They didn't bless it."

Did he ever see Uncle John's pet lions?

"No. If I wanted to see lions, I would go to the zoo."

Why did Uncle Jerry wear a fez in those parades?

"He was trying to help his business connections."

What about the time Uncle Ed was shot in a bar?

"The shooter apologized, and everything was okay."

Invariably, Aunt Anna would interrupt these conversations with the stern directive, "Time to go to bed!" The Saturday before Labor Day in 1957, my sister Pat and I were talking with Uncle Jim while Pat flipped through pages of a photo album. She came upon a picture of Uncle Jim in uniform on a horse. This prompted Pat to ask if he had ever killed anyone. "A few," Uncle Jim responded.

Pat pressed, "Were they all Germans?"

"No," he replied. "They were mostly Irish and Italians."

That response prompted my final reprieve from the farm. Aunt Anna, who was within earshot, rushed in. Uncle Jim left and three hours later, my sister and I were on the Rock Island train, heading home to Chicago. Not with complete regret though, for Jim had secretly given me a book I would begin reading, *Studs Lonigan,* by James T. Farrell.

Later when I was in college, I met Jim for a milkshake at an ice cream parlor on 59th Street, not far from where he had owned a flower shop. In the course of our conversation, his bootlegging activities came up. I asked if it had shamed him to be in that business. He explained: "Some of the guys in the neighborhood put on a policeman uniform and walked a beat. Some of the guys put on an Army uniform and marched through France. When the war was over, we came home, took off our Army uniforms, and many went into bootlegging. The coppers on the beat kept their police uniforms on and went into bootlegging." Likening it to Bingo, he said it was against the law, but nobody cared—the guy calling the numbers was usually the president of the school's men's club. (Bingo made an interesting analogy, I thought—the guy calling the numbers wasn't likely to get shot if he made a mistake.)

Uncle Jim said that even before the end of Prohibition, he had switched out of bootlegging and into providing security against outfit guys trying to take over union elections. He boasted that his activities resulted in winners who went on to become great labor leaders.

The next summer, freed from the farm visits, I hung out with my friends on the corner of 79th and Racine, next to a busy newsstand and Chris Quinn's Tavern—even though we were only 15 or 16 and not allowed inside. The newsstand on the corner was operated by a man named Spike, whose last name we never knew. Most of us considered him somewhat loony, as he talked to himself and sporadically waved his arms. He voiced a deep dislike for politicians, reserving his loudest loathing for FDR. The number 158 was permanently sketched in small, bold letters on the inside of his forearm. He told us this was his assigned number in the World War II draft lottery—the number announced by President Roosevelt as the first number picked.

Spike was far from loony in some matters—as evidenced by the rules of his small baseball betting operation. You won by selecting three players on the same team who would together get at least five hits in the game. Extra innings did not count; games shortened by rain did. Spike wouldn't accept bets on the Yankees (the Mantle-Berra combo was too strong) or the Braves (ditto Aaron and Matthews). All bets had to be placed with silver half-dollars, wrapped with the bettor's selections. It took us half a summer and lots of half-dollars to learn how hard it was to win this wager.

Chris Quinn, who owned the tavern, was a wonderful man. Long ago, he'd been an engineer on a freight train, and he had made some money on real estate investments in the late 1930s. He ran the tavern mostly to give himself something to do. Women were not allowed inside. A seven-ounce beer cost 15 cents. That never changed.

The Chicago police commissioner, Timothy J. O'Connor, lived in our neighborhood, and on weekday evenings around eight o'clock, he would walk his dog, stop for a newspaper, and then have a glass of beer at Chris Quinn's. The local police commander, the affable Captain William J. Hennessey, didn't want the commissioner to find a noisy clump of boys gathered on a street corner in his district, so he issued an edict: no loitering on the corner of 79th and Racine. The order was ignored until one evening a paddy wagon collected five or six older boys and drove them a mile or so away, dropping them off to walk back.

We learned to avoid that corner for the rest of the summer and retreated west to the White Castle parking lot at 79th and Loomis.

There, we met another Spike, the infamous and flamboyant gangster Spike O'Donnell. Through the years of the Chicago gang wars, he had been a bootlegger, and his gang had engaged in a running battle with Al Capone. In those days, Spike's gang used to hang out in front of a Walgreens drug store at 79th and Ashland. Spike was shot at so often that Walgreens once went to court to prevent him from standing in front of the store.

Years later, Spike and his four or five cronies used to sit on folding chairs in the southeast corner of the White Castle parking lot and tell us about their various shootouts, fondly reminiscing about loading up and going out to hunt for a gang rival. In the middle of a story, Spike would tell one of us to take an order for coffee, and then he would continue the tale. The stories seemed pure fantasy—the idea that these raging gun battles had occurred at locations so near and so familiar to us. One evening, one of the friends in our group gave Spike a copy of the book *The Untouchables*, a story about federal agent Eliot Ness enforcing the Prohibition laws in Chicago. A week or so later, Spike announced that he had read the book and that "most of the agents were crooked."

Once in a while, Spike would laugh about the irony of the situation—both his gang and ours had been chased off corners on 79th Street a few blocks apart. Unnoticed by us, Spike died in 1962. Three decades later, I read that what had been the White Castle parking lot (the restaurant has been relocated to the north side of the street) sat in the middle of a police beat in the Gresham District, described as the most murderous place in Chicago.

In those days, our horizons didn't stretch much beyond the parish. "Most of the guys in the gang planned to keep living in the parish into adulthood and then raise their own kids there," James T. Joyce wrote. That was not to happen, but almost all of us have remained friends through the past six decades.

As for me, those early teenage summers provided an education not readily available elsewhere. From the newsstand, I learned never to make a bet unless you understand the odds. In the parking lot at 79th and Loomis, I observed little remorse on the part of those who brought violence and lawlessness to Chicago streets in the 1920s and 1930s. I also learned that a convivial, friendly fellow might still put a bullet in you, if you pushed him the wrong way.

As I moved toward adulthood, I returned occasionally to Aunt Anna's farm and even came to enjoy those visits. I found the atmosphere relaxing. Aunt Anna's conversation was interesting, her piano playing excellent, and after I bought a large cooling fan from Sears, my hours with a book in hand turned most pleasant. Sometimes I would sit on her front porch and—to borrow a thought from Mark Twain—muse over how Aunt Anna had become so engaging and wise in such a short period of time.

For high school, I headed with most of my friends a few blocks east on 79th Street to Leo Catholic High School, an all-male institution run under the fierce discipline of the Irish Christian Brothers. The school had a mission to educate students for advanced degrees and leadership roles and train others to enter the world of business and commerce. Graduates included leaders of international corporations—General Motors, McDonald's, Waste Management, American Can, and numerous others.

A strong emphasis on sports buttressed Leo, and the football and basketball teams often dominated in city play. For some reason, with a school full of outstanding baseball players, Leo didn't field a baseball team. For me, it didn't matter. By age 15 or 16, I realized that my playing days were coming to an end.

I did fine academically as a freshman, but I left Leo five weeks into my sophomore year over a contest of wills that today seems ludicrous. The school believed in dividing its classes according to academic achievement, and in my second year, I remained in the top section. But that section followed a different schedule than the other sophomore classes—which meant that the friends I had journeyed with through St. Sabina and Leo now started and ended school at different times from me. Suddenly, I saw less of my pals.

One day during the second week that fall, I ran into our hard-nosed principal, Brother Reagan, in the hallway and had the nerve to ask if I could transfer to a different section. I quickly explained my reason. "Absolutely not!" he pronounced. And that was that. But he mentioned my request to my homeroom brother, who viewed my conduct as impudent and assigned me a one-hour after-school detention.

I'd never before received a detention at Leo, and I chose not to serve this one, so the sentence was doubled. I held fast, and a third hour was added. I continued to stay away, and the sentence was extended indefinitely. As the battle of wills continued, my father was summoned, and he and I sat down with the principal. My father was mild-mannered, but he made it clear that he thought I had been treated unfairly. Things got edgy. The principal said students couldn't choose their sections, and if I didn't like it at Leo, maybe I should go someplace else. And so I headed over to Calumet High School, the well-regarded public school in the neighborhood. But it was the fourth or fifth week of classes, and the administration at Calumet insisted I belonged at Leo because I had started the year there.

Fifty years later, at a Leo alumni banquet honoring the class of 1958, I had a brief conversation with that homeroom brother with whom I'd run afoul. He said Leo thought I was having a tantrum and so had told Calumet that the school would not forward any of my records and that Calumet should refer me back to Leo. Though Leo had anticipated my return, the whole situation was a watershed for my discontinuous high school career.

At age 14, I enrolled in Beverly Business College, a training school now closed. At the time, I was rather pleased. I never enjoyed school. I was too rambunctious or antsy to sit in a desk for long. In retrospect, I realize that some of my grade school nuns recognized this restlessness and assigned me little chores or enlisted me to help other students with their reading. Other nuns let me fidget away, ignoring the minor distraction I likely was creating. Beverly Business College offered a pleasing alternative to my school experiences up to that date. My classmates consisted mainly of 18- and 19-year-old girls who had finished high school and enjoyed letting me hang around, even if their older boyfriends, some home on leave from the military, groused at my presence. In the meantime, I learned to type over 60 words a minute and excelled at bookkeeping.

I did eventually enroll at Calumet High School, but I also attended Fenger and Lindbloom, two other Chicago public high schools. I twice dropped out in the spring semester to work as a bricklayer, a trade introduced to me by my Uncle Tom, who had a small bricklaying crew. Though I wasn't highly skilled, I could work fast on the wall, and I carried my own, particularly on bungalow jobs. In 1961 and 1962, I continued my apprenticeship, working on the construction of Cabrini Green and the Robert Taylor Homes, two massive public housing projects. Strange today, but all the tradesmen working on the projects thought they were building something great, a terrific alternative to typically decrepit ghetto housing.

After completing high school, I stayed with bricklaying, living at home and hanging out with my friends during my free time. In many ways, the early '60s were dandy for St. Sabina's Irish-American parishioners. John F. Kennedy, an Irish Catholic, occupied the White House. In Chicago, the robust economy had raised wages for many in the working- and middle-classes, and by then, St. Sabina Parish contained almost as many white-collar as blue-collar residents. Richard J. Daley marked the third Irishman in a row to sit at the mayor's desk at City Hall, a sequence that went back three decades.

I never had any particular interest in politics, though my friends and I once helped out an older friend, Leo McAvoy, and distributed literature for a successful legislative candidate he supported. The political attitudes of most neighborhood Chicagoans in those days is best described by Mayor Frank Skeffington in Edwin O'Connor's novel *The Last Hurrah*: a tolerance of unworthy means to achieve worthy results.

When we were teenagers, the only politician we really knew about was Mayor Daley, whom many of us had met when he came to the grand reopening of a Chevrolet dealership near St. Sabina. The business was owned by a man named William Hartigan, who was well-liked by the neighborhood kids because he allowed us to play baseball in vacant land adjacent to his dealership. Years later, I asked Mayor Daley if he remembered the occasion. He smiled and said, "Oh, sure, I remember it," and he laughed.

I first met Rich Daley, the mayor's eldest son in high school. He played on the De La Salle Institute basketball team. One of his teammates was dating my sister Pat—they later married—so I attended a number of De La Salle games. I would bump into Rich at these games or at St. Sabina functions. Every now and then, I'd also see him in Michigan. My parents had bought a small cottage in Grand Beach, and the Daleys owned a home there, too. I didn't spend much time in Michigan, but on occasion, I would see Rich and the group he hung out with. In those days, we were acquaintances more than friends.

Working as a bricklayer in the early 1960s, I was fairly content and had no interest in pursuing a more formal education. As a bricklayer, you would put your trowel down at 4:30, clean up your tools, and head home. The certainty and finality of a tradesman's workday appealed to me. The money was good, and the hours still afforded me the opportunity to pursue other interests. I even spent some time at the track. Yes, laying brick had its benefits.

Then one cold, late November afternoon, an older bricklayer whom I'd befriended was working on the wall next to me. Knowing the winter layoff was coming, he had been searching for off-season work to support his family. He talked about the difficulty and uncertainty of this routine. He said it was fine when you were young and didn't have a family to support. He advised me to start thinking about what I would do in the winters when I got older or even in season when the work slowed. The advice struck home. I decided I needed something to fall back on, maybe teaching.

In those days, Northern Illinois University primarily educated future teachers. Its faculty had an excellent reputation and included some top-flight professors who had been dropped by elite universities during the red scare of the early 1950s. Just 70 miles west of Chicago, in rural DeKalb, Illinois, the school offered a convenient route to a degree, as I could attend and continue to work. So I enrolled at NIU, and soon my St. Sabina friends accompanied me there. Six of us ended up renting a house in DeKalb.

I only attended classes on Tuesdays, Wednesdays, and Thursdays. I spent the rest of the days in Chicago working full time in the merchandise and marketing department of United Vintners. The producers of Swiss Colony, United Vintners was the largest wine company in the world at the time.

In the spring of 1965, attending a party in Chicago, I was introduced to my wife to be, Mairsey Carey. She'd grown up in Longwood Manor on the far South Side and attended Longwood Academy and at the time was working as an administrator at a construction supply company. Within a little more than a year, I finished college, got married, and embarked on a teaching career. My life was headed in a new direction—just as St. Sabina Parish was undergoing its own tumultuous change. ◼

A racially integrated community is a chronological term
timed from the entrance of the first Black family to
the exit of the last white family.

Saul Alinsky

Though history credits a Black man, Jean Baptiste Point du Sable,
as the founder of Chicago—in the 1790s, he lived in a cabin at the
mouth of the Chicago River—the city's Black population remained
small for more than a century, reaching about 44,000 by 1910,
around 2 percent of the population. Then the population of Black
Chicagoans grew dramatically in two waves of the Great Migration.
The first arrived during World War I, when thousands fled the Jim
Crow South to answer the call of jobs at the stockyards and at
factories, businesses that had been energized by the war economy.
The Black population doubled to 100,000 during the war, making it
about 4 percent of the total population in 1920. The great majority
of the newcomers moved into what came to be known as the Black
Belt—despite its name, a vertical strip of blocks that ran along
State Street between Wentworth and Cottage Grove avenues from
22nd Street to 51st Street and beyond. A smaller, horizontal band of
Black neighborhoods ran due west from the far edge of downtown.
White hostility backed by restrictive covenants in property deeds

confined African American Chicagoans almost exclusively to these increasingly overcrowded corridors.

The Depression slowed the Great Migration, but the movement picked up again as the economy fired up in World War II, and this second wave continued through the 1940s and 1950s. By 1960, the Black population of Chicago had swelled to 813,000, almost 25 percent of the total. Isabel Wilkerson reports in her excellent book on the Great Migration, *The Warmth of Other Sons,* that the migrants—contrary to stereotype—tended to be of higher socioeconomic status than the Black population they joined, and the newcomers brought educational achievements that compared well with the educational levels of the white residents. Still, these new arrivals were shunted into the cramped and dilapidated housing in the Black Belt and on the West Side. Soon, those overburdened areas couldn't contain the numbers, and Black people began moving to other neighborhoods on the South and West sides.

A number of commentators have pointed out that government policies, both national and local, worked to continue the concentration of Blacks. "After World War II, ... government urban redevelopment and renewal policies, as well as a massive public housing program, had a direct and enormous impact on the evolution of the ghetto," writes Arnold R. Hirsch in *Making the Second Ghetto: Race and Housing in Chicago 1940-1960.* Some of the policies were well-meaning but misguided: In *The Promised Land,* another excellent book on the Great Migration, Nicholas Lemann explains that almost everyone thought high-rise buildings surrounded by open space offered the most livable alternative to tenements—a prescription that followed the precepts of the great architect and urban planner Le Corbusier. Other policies were similarly shortsighted: In 1947, Illinois gave the Chicago City Council the right to determine where federally funded public housing would go in Chicago, and the largely white council made sure the new units stayed in Black neighborhoods.

Commentators have also pointed out that the Catholic Church—which had enormous influence on the South and West sides through the parish system—played at best an ambiguous role in dealing with the spread of Blacks into white neighborhoods. By several accounts, the archbishops of the Chicago Archdiocese in the years after World War II, Samuel Cardinal Stritch and Albert Gregory Cardinal Meyer, while supporting integration, hesitated to take aggressive leadership roles in encouraging it. Both prelates, however, strongly backed Monsignor John J. "Jack" Egan, an outspoken social activist who led the Archdiocesan Office of Urban Affairs and devoted his career to promoting civil rights and fighting poverty. Among other things, Egan clashed with elected officials over housing issues and marched with Martin Luther King Jr. at Selma.

Much of the opposition to integration within the church came at the parish level, where many of the pastors worried about the fate of their congregations. St. Leo Parish, for example, just to the east of St. Sabina, was ruled by a hard-nosed priest named Patrick J. Molloy who would respond to a Black family moving into St. Leo by slicing that block out of the parish boundaries. In *The Guys in the Gang*, James T. Joyce recounts being at a Sunday Mass at St. Leo and watching Molloy walk up and down the aisle. When he came to a Black family sitting in a pew, he stopped, put his arms behind his back and glared at them, sending an unmistakable message. Professor McMahon explains that another South Side priest, Father Francis X. Lawlor, outspokenly campaigned against integration, and she argues that his considerable media attention helped shape the "mostly negative" public perception of Catholic-Black relations.

St. Sabina, however, was led by a liberal priest who spent half a decade helping to build an organization that would promote orderly integration. Tall, cerebral, autocratic, and somewhat socially awkward, John A. McMahon saw what was happening on the South Side and knew the Church had to get out in front of it. (He was no relation to the parish's roller-skating impresario, Thomas McMahon.) Father McMahon believed that Christian principles required the parish to respond generously to Black people. "Our goal is not to induce Negroes to move in or to force integration," he once told a reporter. "But if they do move in, it is their right, and they should be treated like anyone else."

While other South Side neighborhoods were forming block clubs and protective associations that worked to keep Black people out, McMahon helped create the Organization for the Southwest Communities (OSC), bringing together merchants, bankers, real estate businesses, neighborhood groups, and churches, both Catholic and Protestant. To help guide the organization, McMahon enlisted Saul Alinsky, the community organizer famous for his work in the gritty Back of the Yards neighborhood (and a colleague of Monsignor Jack Egan). Over the course of several years, OSC put together an array of programs designed to preserve neighborhood stability even as some Black families moved in. The organization fought aggressively against blockbusting, cracking down on speculators who tried to induce panic selling. A loan program helped families keep up their homes, part of an effort to eliminate any hint of blight. Working through local banks, OSC encouraged the issuance of low down-payment mortgages, making home ownership easier for Black families as well as for young white people who had grown up in St. Sabina. Donald O'Toole, president of Standard State Bank, one of the major banks on the South Side, headed OSC for a time and actively tuned bank policies to discourage panic selling and encourage stable ownership. Around the time of OSC's founding, the *Tribune* quoted one South Side civic leader as saying the organization would act as a dike to stem the flow of residents to the suburbs by stopping neighborhood deterioration before it starts.

Robert McClory, at the time a young priest assigned to St. Sabina, suggests that the OSC was perhaps too broad-based, including so many groups with varying agendas that the organization often sank into conflict. But in addition to the quite public actions of OSC, McMahon and others worked from the pulpit and behind the scenes to encourage the friendly transition to an integrated neighborhood. Almost every sermon delivered at St. Sabina discussed what was happening, and McMahon railed continually against hateful gossip and rumors. Church and community leaders were candid about what was happening—telling white residents that if they didn't want to live in an integrated neighborhood, they should leave. Other members of McMahon's inner circle kept a list of Black families who were interested in moving in and helped steer them to blocks that would likely be welcoming. In the introduction to *Radical Disciple,* his biography of Father Michael Pfleger, the longtime St. Sabina pastor, McClory recalls that the parish in those days "was determined to become a successful interracial community. It was to stand as a model for large urban cities everywhere—Blacks and whites living in harmony, proof that rational planning and common sense could overcome what seemed inevitable."

The net result was a comfortable transition. Whereas some South Side communities went from white to Black almost overnight in an ugly spiral of fear mongering and panic selling, St. Sabina held steady. Some white families moved out, some Black families moved in, but the parish seemed to be accommodating change. There may have been some taunting or squabbling among the younger teenagers, but the priests always stepped in to calm things. The neighborhood had so much to offer, and so many people were involved in making the transition work, that many people hoped and expected the population would stabilize.

That's where things stood on the evening of Monday, August 16, 1965, when riots were ravaging Watts, Los Angeles, and Chicago's West Side, and white teenager Frank Kelly was shot down by several Black teens in front of the St. Sabina community center. Oddly enough, the next day the *Tribune* ran just a short, four-paragraph story on the shooting, with a three-paragraph follow-up the next day after the suspects were arrested. I always presumed that editors played down the case out of concern for inflaming passions, but I don't know. People who were with Frank Kelly that night later told me what had happened: Frank and his friends had been on Racine when they crossed paths with three African American boys. The groups tossed glares back and forth and exchanged words. One or two of the Black teens drew guns and started firing, hitting Frank in the chest and a girl who was with Frank in the hip. Frank staggered across the street to the front of the community center and collapsed. Within a day, the police had arrested three suspects, 14, 15, and 16 years old, and they were eventually convicted. (Six or seven years later, one of the convicted youths—by now back on the streets—was shot and killed by a policeman while burglarizing a gas station in the neighborhood. Coincidentally, the officer was the older brother of one of the kids who had been with Frank Kelly the night of the murder.)

The shooting had a devastating impact on St. Sabina—as if the well-constructed veneer of tolerance and order had suddenly been shattered. "Instantly, instantly, everybody knew that name—Frank Kelly," said Father Daniel Sullivan, a St. Sabina priest who recalled the aftermath years later for Professor McMahon. Kelly's funeral service overflowed the church. "The horror that spread! The fear that it engendered! Up to that time, people were figuring they were going to buck it out," Sullivan said. Because some of the community's anger focused on Father McMahon, the architect of the orderly integration program, the church decided that he shouldn't preside at Frank Kelly's funeral, and another priest, Father Tom White, took on the painful assignment.

The church closed the community center for the remainder of the summer out of concern that it might become a crucible for anger. When the school opened in September, a quarter of the students who had been registered the previous spring didn't show up—their parents were in the process of moving out. The for-sale signs started appearing. The three-flats and six-flats were the first to go, but soon the signs cropped up as if they'd been planted like trees up and down the blocks. The unsolicited calls came in from speculators and real estate agents: "Six houses on your block are already on sale or about to be listed; we've got a bunch of good buyers who can get financing; you can still get a nice price, but if you don't act now, the value of your house will plummet." All the symptoms of panic selling that had been resisted before now swept through St. Sabina. The church fathers and the block clubs tried to push back, but the forces of fear overwhelmed the neighborhood. By the end of 1965, the number of families enrolled in St. Sabina Parish had dropped by 1,000 from the year before to 1,900, according to figures in *What Parish Are You From?* By the end of 1966, parish enrollment had dropped by another thousand. By the early 1970s, the parish, the school, and the neighborhood were almost all Black.

My family stayed for a year or so after Frank's murder. They put the house up for sale around August 1966, when three-fourths of the houses on the block had been sold to Black people. A month or two later, a Black family bought it. Several years previously, my parents had bought a year-round house in Grand Beach, not far from our beach cottage, and my family moved there. My two younger brothers had yet to finish school, and they enrolled in parochial schools in nearby Michigan City, Indiana. That spring, I had graduated from college and married Mairsey. With the Vietnam War heating up, I expected to enter the military at any moment, so my wife and I moved into the Grand Beach cottage while I waited to get summoned. My friends from St. Sabina had scattered to the winds.

Over the years, Father Pfleger presided over St. Sabina Church, serving an overwhelmingly Black congregation. The church appears to be thriving. Father Pfleger has turned the Mass and even the appearance of the church interior to reflect the African American culture of his parishioners. He's added music and dancing to services, and he preaches, as one *Tribune* reporter put it, "as if he were a Black Baptist minister." A depiction of an African Jesus hangs at the altar, and a bust of Martin Luther King Jr. stands in the front. From the pulpit and outside the church, he has taken on a variety of causes, from racism to drugs and violence in the community to Hillary Clinton's purported sense of entitlement to higher office during her

2008 campaign for president. He has clashed often with the Catholic Church hierarchy and faced several suspensions even before the abuse allegations arose.

Father Pfleger has also clashed with some of the former white parishioners of St. Sabina. Over the years after my family moved out, I continued to go back to the church for Mass every couple of months. A number of former parishioners did the same—among other things, it offered a nice chance to catch up with old friends. In 1988, my graduating class of 160 or so from grade school planned an informal reunion. I was one of the organizers. Then several of the neighboring classes got wind of it and asked to be included. Because the event started as a small affair, we mistakenly didn't reach out to later classes that included many Black students. As the planning unfolded, Father Pfleger offended many of the organizers by seeming to express the attitude that anyone who moved from the neighborhood in the 1960s must have been racist. The reunion turned controversial, and finally Archbishop Cardinal Joseph Bernardin stepped in. The reunion went forward and turned into a big success, though the bitterness lingered.

Father Pfleger has done a good job maintaining a parish, and a few years ago, he gave a group of us a thoughtful tour of the church campus. St. Sabina's neighborhood has not fared as well. Poverty and crime afflict Auburn Gresham. Median household income for residents, recently at $32,470, sits at almost $20,000 below the level for Chicago generally. A quarter of Auburn Gresham households stagger along below the poverty level, and unemployment recently stood at almost 25 percent, even before the COVID-19 pandemic. Auburn Gresham remains one of the city's most violent neighborhoods. Residents have kept up my family's old house on Elizabeth Street, and the block looks tidy. But the strip of 79th Street that once featured lively stores and businesses now looks bleak—low buildings broken by empty lots.

For many long-ago white residents of the neighborhood, the physical deterioration and the reports of crime and poverty can't help but be painful, even if we are cheered by the continued survival of the church. Still, the fate of Auburn Gresham can't be separated from the fates of hundreds of other urban neighborhoods around the country—communities paying the price for three centuries of deplorable laws, policies, and people. To me, what sets St. Sabina apart is that brief, shining moment just over half a century ago when so many people and factions joined to try to make history.

Years later, I met the brilliant and forward-thinking churchman Jack Egan at the Cliff Dwellers Club. Over what turned out to be a four-hour lunch, Monsignor Egan confided to me that the effort around St. Sabina was the closest that any community in the country ever came in that era to creating a truly integrated urban neighborhood in America. ◼

"When I was growing up, the most popular guy in our
neighborhood was the policeman walking his beat.
I don't think we will see that again."

Father Andrew Greeley, speaking to a
gathering of Chicago police

By the fall of 1968, I was both a cop, working a beat in the Third
District—the Grand Crossing neighborhood—and a history
teacher, working as a regular substitute at Parker High School at
6800 South Stewart Avenue.

The school shared a name—honoring the education theorist F.W.
Parker—with an elite private school on the North Side. But the name
was almost all the two institutions had in common. The population
of the South Side Parker was almost all African American. Violence
plagued the campus. The local street gangs both recruited students
and preyed on them. On the first day of school that fall, gangbangers
shot three students in the hallway. Student arsonists regularly set
fires throughout the building.

The police department didn't object to me holding down a second
job, but all Chicago police are considered on duty 24 hours a day
and required to have their weapon with them at all times. At school,
I preferred that the students didn't know I was an officer, so I kept

my gun in a secured case behind my desk chair. But one day during class changes, I noticed one student pulling a gun on another. I approached the kid and talked him into putting the gun away. After he sauntered off, I ran to my classroom, retrieved my own weapon, and raced back to find the armed student. When he came sashaying down the south stairwell, I came up behind him and, keeping my gun in my jacket pocket, jabbed him in his ribs and ordered him to hand over his weapon. As I marched him to the principal's office, a crowd of students milled around us, even though they were supposed to be in class.

The principal was an older white man who rarely left his first-floor office. He clearly wasn't happy to face this problem, but we called the local police district, and the commander came to the school. He and the principal talked it over and decided that the gun incident should be treated as a school matter, not a crime. I suspect that neither man wanted the bad publicity. I told them that was crazy—the police had to step in if guns were involved. Still, the commander refused to fill out a report, so I filled one out myself.

I don't know whatever happened to that student, but the incident exposed me as a cop, and in a matter of days, students started boycotting my class. I'd wait in the classroom, and no one would show up. A couple of students told me the gangs were behind it— they ordered the kids to stay away. I kept on for two weeks, but the situation didn't make sense, so I transferred to a position at Calumet High School in Auburn Gresham. (Neither Parker nor Calumet still exist.) Not long after the gun incident, the Parker principal retired.

That incident at Parker probably encapsulates as well as anything the tenor of the times that I witnessed firsthand in the late 1960s and early 1970s—an era of terrible violence and confusion in Chicago. Street gangs were devastating entire neighborhoods. Unchecked gangbangers—whether 15 strong or 50—could destroy a city school of 2,000 students in a matter of months. Outside the schools, ordinary protests turned into riots. Opposition to the Vietnam War warped into a general distrust of any authority. The schools and the police—

two of the institutions that, for better or worse, had helped stabilize urban life—were being threatened as never before.

My journey through those times started mildly enough. I knew that after I graduated from college I would be drafted into the military, so in February of 1966, I applied to the Marine Corps officers program. But paperwork confusion caused a delay, and I decided to wait to be drafted into the Army. Mairsey and I had been married in May 1966, and she quickly got pregnant. As it turned out, draft officials announced in August that year that they would continue to defer men with children or children on the way. So I took a teaching job in Chicago Heights, and our oldest son, Dan, was born on February 25, 1967. Meantime, I enrolled in the master's program at Chicago Teachers College (now Chicago State) and eventually earned a master's in teaching reading to disadvantaged children.

One day, I happened to run into a teacher who was also a youth officer in the Chicago Police Department. He explained that his primary role was to corral wayward kids and steer them away from a life of crime. Youth Division officers, he added, were selected on the basis of a history of working with kids and included a lot of teachers and coaches. The police department had no real concern about officers also working as teachers or coaches, but that would mean having to pull a straight night shift on the police job. Also, before joining the Youth Division, you had to put in a couple of years as a patrolman.

With a family to support and graduate school to pay for, I thought a police job sounded promising, so I applied to the police academy. I had never before considered being a policeman—telling someone he or she was under arrest hadn't come up in my imaginative plans. I didn't hold any ill feelings towards the profession—growing up, many of my friends' fathers were officers, and they always seemed available to help or offer good advice. My Uncle Grover Mulvaney was a Chicago police sergeant, and my grandfather's brother, my great uncle Tom Lynch, was a Chicago sergeant killed in the line of duty.

I passed the department's written exam and managed the physical fitness test easily. But there was a problem. I was six feet tall, but several pounds under the required 148-pound weight limit. The examiner who weighed me told me to go home and drink a lot of milk shakes and come back in a month. I did, but milk shakes really didn't move the needle. On the day of my return, I drank a gallon of water just before the weigh-in. The scale still showed I was light. But the man in charge of the weigh-in, sitting across the room from where I stood on the scale, bellowed, "148, right?" So be it.

That fall, I put my teaching career temporarily on hold and spent 14 weeks at the police academy, based in those days in a well-polished, late 19th-century ex-school building on O'Brien Street in the Maxwell Street market area. The sign outside announcing the academy was crudely painted on metal—the sort of thing you'd see at the auto pound. Inside, the gym was a narrow, rectangular basement room with an eight-foot ceiling and fire extinguishers everywhere. The lunchroom contained a few wooden tables and a handful of vending machines offering cigarettes, pop, gum, and candy bars. Though the building was an antique, the curriculum reflected the impact of Superintendent O.W. Wilson, an academic from the University of California at Berkeley, brought in as a reformer following a police scandal in 1960. On his arrival, he convened the entire department in two sessions at the International Amphitheatre and announced that the past is the past, go and sin no more, and know that in the future all department promotions will be based on merit.

My police academy class numbered 34 and included a good mix—a number of veterans, six or seven African Americans, and a recruit named Dennis Farina, who would put in 18 years as a cop before finding success as an actor in Hollywood. The training included classes in report writing, criminal law, police procedure, firearms use, and defensive tactics. The lesson plan for every class contained a reference to personal integrity—a warning not to trade your honor and reputation for material gain.

The most unpopular course taught defensive tactics, a class conducted in the low-ceilinged basement, where the instructors, unobserved, could fashion programs suited to each individual. Some recruits thought that the instructors delighted in roughing them up, getting pleasure from breaking fingers or spraining joints. In the 14-week program, every class would send three or four members for medical treatment, and there was always a recruit walking the halls with a neck brace. In later years, officials changed the course, due in part to the inclusion of women as regular police officers but also to the cost of worker's compensation claims. Eventually, I learned that the real function of the defensive tactics course in my era was to weed out the psychologically unfit—those too aggressive and those too hesitant.

The most tested matter at the academy addressed the proper use of deadly force, the awesome power the law was entrusting to each prospective officer. In Chicago, as in most major police departments, officers are instructed to shoot to kill, not to wound, though an officer can only shoot if he believes an offender is likely to cause death or great bodily harm to the officer or to another. As recruits, we often heard conflicting points of view on the matter. At the gun range, the rangemasters advised: "Shoot or be shot. Hesitate and you die. We are not here to create police widows and orphans." The classroom instructors cautioned differently: "Shoot, and if you are mistaken, you may go to prison. That fleeing offender with a gun better have that gun when he goes down."

The real difficulty comes in a confusing situation when an officer's moral code runs up against his legal authority—the 14-year-old with a gun who looks to be 21 or vice-versa. Life-or-death decisions have to be made in split seconds. Malcolm Gladwell provides a good examination of this dilemma in his book *Blink* when discussing the 1999 shooting of Amadou Diallo, a Guinean immigrant killed by the New York City police.

The one subject not listed in the academy curriculum, but learned at every training school, is the Code of Silence, the unofficial and largely unacknowledged agreement that one policeman will not report the misdeeds of another. Undefined and subjective, it is something that each officer sorts out for himself. On any given day, before the watch is over, the officer standing next to you at roll call may put his life on the line for you. What behavior will you tolerate from your colleagues? At what point would you break the silence and report an infraction? Ultimately, it comes down to the individual's moral code.

At the conclusion of our 14 weeks, 33 of the original 34 candidates were sworn in. The one hopeful weeded out by the defensive tactics course became a city dogcatcher.

Police officers had to furnish their own firearms. Because I never cared about guns, I was happy to rely on a used revolver given to me by a friend. The department rejected the weapon as too old. So I went into a gun store and requested the least expensive, department-approved four-inch barrel Smith & Wesson in the store. As it turned out, in almost six years on the street, I only fired my weapon one time. Here's how that unfolded:

In July 1969, I was working the day shift in a car with my partner when the dispatcher announced a robbery in progress a block away at a real estate office on East 79th and Philips Street. One of the two armed offenders was wearing a police uniform. When we arrived, I went in the front, and my partner drove to the rear of the building.

Inside, four or five terrified office workers were screaming and pointing to a parking area in back. I ran through the office and out the rear door with my weapon drawn. Outside, a suspect dressed in a police uniform stood next to the passenger's side of a new red Cadillac about 40 feet away. The other robber held a gun and was crouched behind the open door on the driver's side. I shouted to the standing robber to drop and crawl toward me. When he was about five feet away, I told him to lie face down and spread his arms. The remaining robber pointed his gun at me. I fired three shots, aiming at his head, but at the same time trying to keep my shots low, lest they go astray. Two went through the front of the vehicle and one through the windshield, close to the top of his head.

Meanwhile, sirens ripped through the air, the robber behind the door was screaming, and the robber on the ground kept babbling, "You're going to hit Mr. C—." I realized that the gunman at the car had a hostage. A uniformed beat officer appeared, and he handcuffed the guy on the ground. I ran up until I could see behind the car door. The gunman was pressing his pistol to the upper neck of the hostage, who was crammed onto the floor, clutching the pedals with both hands. Blood covered both men, and I wasn't sure if I had hit one or both. I started talking with the gunman while trying to determine if the hammer on his gun was drawn back. I told him repeatedly that if he would put down his weapon, I would holster mine, which was about three feet from his head. After a couple of minutes, a uniformed officer armed with a shotgun ran up and stood next to me, and we both pleaded with the gunman to give up. Just when I thought he was going to surrender, the local community relations sergeant bellowed onto the scene, followed by the Fourth District commander, ranting, "Back off, back off."

I stepped back, holstered my weapon and returned to the real estate office. The scene was turning into a madhouse—helicopters circling, reporters clamoring, and onlookers milling behind the police cordon. I told my partner that the commander was a fool— the gunman was about to give up. One of the Fourth District officers asked if he could have the arrest of the uniformed robber who was now cuffed and lying on the floor of the real estate office. I told him, "It's all yours." We filled out a shots-fired report and returned to the streets.

That evening when I arrived home, the local news was telecasting that the incident had just ended. The hostage and the gunman were fine, though their faces had been cut by glass from the windshield pierced by one of my bullets. The following day, I asked my supervisor if he wanted an internal report on the incident. He said no. "We'll let the district commander have his grand moment."

About a week later, I was at Area 2 headquarters on another

investigation and stopped by to see the lieutenant who was in charge of the real estate office case. He gave me copies of the reports. Apparently, when my partner and I arrived at the scene, the gunmen, who were known to the hostage, were about to take him in his own car to cash a $20,000 check.

The lieutenant said that when he interviewed the victim, the man seemed mostly upset about his car being damaged by my bullets. The lieutenant said he explained to the man that I had probably saved his life—given his knowledge of the robbers, they likely had planned to leave no live witnesses.

"Too bad you didn't shoot the bastard," the lieutenant told me. I said the robber had been about to surrender. The lieutenant replied that he wasn't referring to the robber.

After I graduated from the academy, the department assigned me to Grand Crossing, a rectangular chunk of tough blocks just south of the University of Chicago. I was a beat cop working in a car, which essentially meant responding to routine radio calls—shots fired, burglary in progress, domestic disputes, dog bites, that sort of thing. My partner and I would respond and then write up a report, if necessary. If the call turned out to be "founded," but we didn't make an arrest, our written report would be forwarded through the appropriate review process. Reports of shootings from the dispatcher would usually override other radio calls, and calls of officers needing help, 10-1, would override everything.

I began working the night shift, and almost immediately I started teaching again. Looking back, my schedule seems crowded. School would start at 7:20 in the morning, and the police night shifts ran from 4 to midnight or 11 to 7. The schedule was particularly hard on Mairsey, who now had two boys to care for, our second son, Michael, having been born in 1968. Still, I don't recall us ever being really tired. I arranged my police schedule to use my two weekly days off in the middle of the week. At school, my teaching position was classified as full-time basis (FTB) substitute, which allowed me to take over a program for an extended period—I could teach from a lesson plan and get to know the students. I was particularly intrigued about how a child learns to read and took a number of courses in graduate school that explored the subject.

Overall, though, the '60s were a dreadful time in many Chicago public schools. The students were turning wild, and the experienced teachers were using their seniority to transfer to safer assignments. Most of the new teachers who came in were young and often lacked the skills to keep the classes under control, one reason these rough schools were happy to have police officers as teachers—we could usually maintain some semblance of order.

In those days, the risk of a fire was the number-one danger that worried the faculty and administration. At Calumet High, for example, the fire alarm seemed to go off every three or four days. When that happened, everyone had to clear out. Teachers tried to explain to their classes the grave risks—a fire could roar out of control, students could get burned or trampled. But still the alarms sounded, and frenzy would erupt—kids running, shouting, throwing rocks and bottles, breaking windows.

Meanwhile, outside the schools, street gangs recruited students and intimidated anyone who didn't join. At a number of high schools, Students for a Democratic Society (SDS) got into the act, setting up tables to pull kids into the organization's radical orbit.

Many parents were appalled at what was happening. For example, at Fenger High School, at 11220 South Wallace Street, just east of Halsted, where I taught in the late spring of 1969, the PTA meetings turned into angry shouting matches. Parents would hear what was going on and demand explanation. "What kind of school are you running? Why can't you get rid of these disruptive kids?"

The administration at Fenger tried to take a stand—the principal was strong, and he'd put together an excellent staff, but the chaos overwhelmed. In those days, the school still had a mixed student body, about 70 percent Black and 30 percent white, and the disturbances often had a racial overtone. In May 1969, disruptions broke out regularly, even as parents of both white and Black students patrolled the halls. One day, as students were rioting, I came upon a group of Black students in the hallway beating up a white student, a small, slight kid. I don't know what had ignited the beating. Some of the Black students must have come from shop, because they were hitting him with two-by-fours. I waded into the fracas and covered the boy and managed to grab the leg of one of the offenders. I got pounded myself, and the young victim went to the hospital with broken bones, including a broken jaw. The authorities closed the school for several days to try to calm matters. Fenger suspended the kids who'd done the beating, including the student I grabbed, but a rights organization filed suit to have them reinstated until the criminal cases were adjudicated. The lower court and the reviewing courts upheld the school suspensions.

The troubles weren't limited to South Side schools. The same *Chicago Tribune* article that reported the disorders at Fenger described a riot between Black and white students at Lane Technical High School on the North Side. The article said that the fighting broke out during a speech across the street from the school given by a member of SDS. The activist was arrested and charged with inciting a riot, possession of drugs, and disorderly conduct, the paper said.

I continued to teach high school until 1973, and the experience— along with my graduate study—led me to a glaring conclusion: The majority of the inner-city high school students in Chicago were reading at least four or five years below grade level.

Along with many others, I recognized an imperative need: drastically reducing class sizes, particularly in the early years. At too many inner-city schools, children arrive with none of the skills to ease into education. Many are struggling with poverty and neglect at home. Head Start alone can't manage. The students need intense, personal attention to make the leap into productive learning. A decade later, as an Illinois senator, I tried to establish a program limiting class size to six in kindergarten through third grade and keeping the same teacher with the same group of students over the four years. At first glance, the cost appears prohibitive. But as I worked on the idea with Senate colleagues, we realized that there are ways to make the numbers come around. In any case, compared to the ultimate cost of sending ill-prepared and troubled students into the world, the upfront costs would be minimal. Unfortunately, that sort of reasoning doesn't grip in a society that won't look beyond the next budget, or the next election, and my proposal was rejected as too expensive.

Through 1968, I remained a beat officer in the Patrol Division, but in December, I was informally notified that I would be transferred from Patrol to the Analytical Unit of the Intelligence Division, which was based on the eighth floor in police headquarters at 11th and State. The transfer meant I would be officially classified as an investigator.

At that time, the Intelligence Division consisted of six separate units: Administration; Analytical; Organized Crime, which tracked mob activity in the Chicago area; Criminal Intelligence, which focused on professional criminals, such as robbers, cartage and jewelry thieves, and commercial burglars; Subversive which was sometimes referred to as the Red Squad from the days when the unit tracked communists; and Gang Intelligence, whose mission was to identify and suppress the criminal activity of the city's street gangs.

My unit, Analytical, was the smallest in the division. In a closed room, a small group of detectives would sift through reams of paperwork from various individuals, groups, or law enforcement agencies—internal police reports, the FBI, Army Intelligence, the U.S. Postal Service, prisons, and so on. The reports covered a wide variety of activity, such as rumors of bombings, arson plots, assassination plots, terrorist or radical activity, and the whereabouts of Chicago's professional criminals. Our job was to sort the material, look for correlations and leads, and pass well-founded information on to the appropriate operation. The work could sometimes get tedious.

During the years I served in the Intelligence Division, I had a single encounter with the Criminal Intelligence and the Organized Crime units. About a year after I was there, I requested all the internal files on the killing of my great-uncle, Sergeant Thomas Lynch. I had heard different stories regarding the circumstances of his death. The files indicated that the killing involved a gang called the 42s. The year was 1927, and violent gang wars were in full swing in Chicago, with the most dangerous feud featuring Al Capone against the Aiello family.

In November of that year, following a failed assassination attempt against Capone by the Aiellos, Chief of Detectives William O'Connor issued an order to "shoot to kill" on sight any known gangsters—a rather incredible command even by Chicago's Roaring Twenties standards. The following day, Tom Lynch and his special squad of four officers, all riding in a police car, spotted a car occupied by members of the 42 gang cruising in the vicinity of an Aiello residence. A wild chase with gunfire erupted as the cops pursued the gang through the West Side. During the chase, Sergeant Lynch was shot in the head. Reports immediately went out across the nation indicating gangsters had killed a Chicago police sergeant. An investigation quickly revealed, however, that Tom Lynch had been struck by a shot accidentally fired by one of his own men.

The ancient files also listed a number of people thought to be the occupants of the chased vehicle, and named Sam Giancana, a future Chicago mob boss, as the likely driver. A half century later, Giancana would be assassinated in the basement of his home, just days before he was to testify in front of a U.S. Senate Committee investigating the relationships between organized crime and the Central Intelligence Agency. Giancana's murder has never been solved.

I had been in Analytical a short time when I ran into my former field sergeant from the Third District, Julius Frazier, who was now working in Gang Intelligence. A huge man with a giant head, Frazier appeared even bigger because his pants sagged low below his waistline—the droop caused by the large stash of coins that he carried in his pants pockets. Frazier's hobby was numismatics, coin collecting. Always seeking to exchange currency for coins, he would station himself at the building's refreshment canteen when the vending machine collectors arrived on their weekly routes.

At the time, Sergeant Frazier was recognized as the department's walking repository of knowledge about the Blackstone Rangers, the powerful South Side street gang. As a youth officer, he had dealt with many of the gang members in their early years and often decided whether they would be steered toward a juvenile correction facility or released to a parent, teacher, or minister. He proudly believed that he had changed the lives of many of the kids in Woodlawn, guiding them away from street gangs.

But in 1969, those whom he hadn't changed—many of the youths he had sent to jail—had created the most notorious street gang in Chicago history. The Blackstone Rangers had moved onto the national stage, claiming a membership in the thousands. To some of the young Gang Intelligence investigators, Frazier was a dinosaur, but every policeman who worked for him would recall Sergeant Frazier's wise words repeated without fail at the conclusion of his roll calls: "Anyone put their hand on you, lock them up. You put your hand on anyone, lock them up. Keep the faith, baby."

Frazier told me I belonged on the street, working under him. I asked to think it over for a while. A week later, I was on the street working for Frazier.

The Gang Intelligence Unit (GIU) was set up in 1967 by Superintendent Wilson, who was frustrated by a sharp increase in violent crime by street gangs. Originally a small unit, it had expanded steadily as gang violence continued, and with the most recent manpower increase, it now had more than 100 investigators and detectives working the streets. The mission was clearly stated: Identify and suppress the criminal activities of Chicago's street gangs and any groups conspiring criminally with those gangs. The second part of that stated mission would later create headaches for GIU, as it extended the unit's investigative reach to operations that turned out to be legitimate.

At the time I entered Gang Intelligence, street-gang shootings were being reported in over half of Chicago's 21 police districts, with most of the gunfire occurring around the schools, parks, and the housing projects. Overall, Chicago recorded 716 homicides in 1969, almost double the 1960 total of 372. (By contrast, the city recorded 495 homicides in 2019, then jumped to 769 in 2020, a sharp increase largely attributed to the pandemic lockdown. Overall, the number rose through the 1970s, fell somewhat in the 1980s, climbed sharply in the 1990s, then started a significant decline to a low of 407 in 2014 before rising again.)

The commander of GIU was the seasoned, unflappable Captain Ed Buckney, an African American who had helped guard Martin Luther King Jr. on his famous march through Chicago's Marquette Park.

In its early days, Gang Intelligence acquired a reputation of being overly aggressive. At that time, it was a small, racially diverse unit, and almost all its investigators had been raised and schooled in Chicago's neighborhoods. Most of the African American officers had served in the military during World War II or Korea. They had all lived through a time of discrimination and unfairness. When they first joined the Chicago Police Department, they had been assigned to patrol districts where they were respected and reasonably well liked by most of the community they served. But now that was changing—less respect and little affection. Commander Buckney understood these changes, and he knew that the temperament of his veteran investigators would not allow a physical threat from a 16- or 17-year-old gangbanger to go unchallenged. Over and over, he cautioned against reacting to threats. Nevertheless, in dealing with citizen complaints, he always gave the men of GIU the benefit of the doubt. So the frequently dismissed complaints helped support the unit's reputation for operating unchecked.

Not long after I joined Gang Intelligence, our sergeant, Fred Rice, succeeded Buckney as head of the unit. A veteran of Korea, Rice had a military style, and he was fair, with a good heart, but sometimes blunt to a fault. One night at roll call, he ordered officers on the night shift to stop going into public housing high-rise complexes, especially the Robert Taylor Homes, unless specifically assigned. He said that too many Gang Intelligence cars were being put out of service, not only from sniper fire but from shopping carts and fire hydrant covers being hurled down from the upper floors. At the current rate of destruction, Rice said, we would all soon be walking on the job. One investigator volunteered that the residents in the projects were entitled to the same protection as everyone else. Without missing a beat, Rice fired back, "How about if I transfer your ass back to a blue uniform, and you can give them all the protection you want?" Fred Rice would go on to become Chicago's first permanent African American police superintendent, and we remained good friends throughout his life.

Street gangs have a long history in Chicago. Going back to the 19th century, the gangs usually involved young men, and ethnicity often determined membership—Polish, Lithuanian, Irish, Italian. Sometimes the gangs would form political alliances and join the political process. Over time, the gangs would typically fade away as the particular ethnic groups that populated them assimilated into the mainstream. By the late 1950s, most of the city's gangs were Black, concentrated on the South and West sides; Puerto Rican, in the Humboldt Park area; or Mexican, in Pilsen. Within a few years, those gangs exploded in visibility and violence, and a handful of Black gangs with shifting names and alliances emerged as the most prominent—the Blackstone Rangers, the Vice Lords, the Black Disciples, and the Black Gangsters. The Latin Kings became the most visible Hispanic gang.

In the late 1960s, the Black Panther Party joined this combustible mix with an agenda largely built on confronting law enforcement. Around the same time, radical white groups, most notably an extreme faction of SDS, tried to extend their influence by working with the gangs and recruiting young Blacks. As much as the gangs directed their anger and rhetoric at the larger white society, they also fought among themselves in conflicts that frequently ended in deadly gunfire and threatened entire communities, a nightmarish situation that is echoed tragically today. With 15- and 16-year-olds carrying weapons, these gunfights could be over anything, though often they had to do with turf and ego. Large-scale drug dealing wouldn't become a gang fixture until the 1970s.

From the perspective of today, that era in Chicago and other large cities seems an incredible mixture of hope, naiveté, fury, recrimination, and disappointment. For a time, several of the Chicago gangs actively set up social programs in their neighborhoods— health clinics, youth centers, job-training programs. The federal and local governments steered funds toward many of these programs, and philanthropists supported various efforts with money and favors. Political elements ranging from the Republican Party to local aldermen tried to pull the gangs into their orbits. On the South Side, one of the chief liaisons between the GOP and the gangs was an African American ex-con-turned-preacher named Claude Murphy, who served as Republican committeeman for the 7th Ward and traveled in national Republican circles. Mickey Cogwell of the Black P Stone Nation, a gang leader I came to know well, attended a reception at President Nixon's inauguration in 1969 at the invitation of U.S. Senator Chuck Percy.

Few, if any, of the promising neighborhood social programs survived long, however, and questions came up repeatedly about where the government money was going. The violence, meantime, increased.

In May 1969, Mayor Daley declared war on street gangs. "We can't continue to have these senseless killings in Chicago," he announced. "We must stop the extortion of adults by criminal gang structures in the neighborhoods, and the extortion of school children, and the intimidation of leaders in our communities." After Daley's announcement, Cook County State's Attorney Edward V. Hanrahan convened a grand jury and in the next month indicted more than

120 alleged gang members, including many leaders. A number of the defendants were eventually acquitted for one reason or another. Hanrahan came from the U.S. Attorney's Office, where prosecutors had much more success making charges stick.

Members of Gang Intelligence worked the street in plainclothes, gathering information and responding to calls that might involve street gangs. Although the Black gangs were our primary concern, we increasingly monitored SDS radicals as they expanded their involvement with the gangs. We tried to function inconspicuously. If we attended gang meetings or gatherings of radicals, we wouldn't broadcast our presence, but if asked, we would identify ourselves. Often, when the gang meeting was large, we assumed that at least one participant was somehow involved with undercover law enforcement.

Our purpose at those gatherings was to learn what we could in order to anticipate and prevent violent gang crime. Mickey Cogwell, one of the cleverest gang leaders, thought our preventive approach was ridiculous. "It shouldn't be called the Police Gang Intelligence Unit," he told James Alan McPherson for an article in *The Atlantic* in June 1969. "It should be called the Gang Stupid Unit because they are so stupid. If they really wanted to get us, they would wait until we commit crimes and then arrest us. Instead, they try to stop us from doing anything."

But in those days, Gang Intelligence frequently saved lives by stepping in ahead of time. For example, my partner and I would speak often to Cogwell, delivering messages from our commander. Cogwell always met us on a street near the Robert Taylor Homes housing project. He would listen and never respond, but I believe he acted on what we said. If we couldn't find Cogwell, I would pass the message to his lawyer, John Powers Crowley, who later became a federal judge.

Cogwell stayed connected to the gangs, but eventually worked in union organizing and tried to play a part in Chicago's political game. It wasn't to be. In 1977, after I was off the job, an assassin gunned him down near his home. I was surprised he had left himself exposed. As far as I know, the killing was never solved.

Cogwell was far from the only critic of Chicago's response to the gangs. Many out-of-towners and uninformed analysts have argued that Mayor Daley's war finished off any hope that the gangs could be channeled toward socially worthy ends, such as community organizing. In December 1969, the City Council clashed over a resolution to abolish the GIU. The sponsor, Sixth Ward Alderman A.A. Rayner Jr., argued that the unit was both repressive and a law-enforcement failure. Another supporter of the measure, Fifth Ward Alderman Leon Despres, told the council, "Studies show that any attempt to repress gangs has the opposite effect." The resolution lost on a 40-3 vote. The more outrageous faultfinders foolishly argued that Gang Intelligence—which was 50 percent African American and run by a Black man—was put together specifically to disrupt the growing political power of the Black community.

For the most part, I think the critics had no understanding of what was happening on the streets of Chicago. The same *Tribune* article reporting on Mayor Daley's announcement of a war on gangs noted that in the first 17 days of that May, gang shootings killed nine people and wounded 59 others. Anyone with sense was deeply alarmed, and police officials clearly thought the department needed better information on what was happening in the streets.

Did we in Gang Intelligence sometimes overreact? In retrospect, perhaps, but, if so, it resulted from earnest efforts to tamp down gang violence and save lives in a frenzied and confusing time.

It's also relevant to distinguish between the Gang Intelligence Unit and the Subversives Unit, which had a criticized record in Chicago long before the 1960s. Decades before, the unit—like similar police operations around the country—had acquired the label the Red Squad, because it grew out of American paranoia about communist infiltration. Encouraged by FBI Chief J. Edgar Hoover, Red Squads had a history of overreaching in their tactics and the targets of their investigations. (Under pressure of a lawsuit and revelations of improper investigative behavior from the Church Committee of the U.S. Senate, Chicago disbanded the unit in the mid-1970s.)

In my time in the Intelligence Division, the Subversives Unit and Gang Intelligence had limited interactions. The Subversives Unit had few investigators, and those in the unit worked long hours. I knew almost all the men who were overt, but few of the covert. In my experience, the information the unit passed on concerning the radicals and the street gangs was accurate—particularly information validating the plans that the SDS radicals had for using the Black Panthers and street gangs as cannon fodder against law enforcement. But for the most part, the Subversives Unit was off on its own agenda. GIU had enough to do keeping track of gangs and purported revolutionaries at a time when fists and guns were sometimes turned on us. ■

"No realistic, sane person goes around
Chicago without protection."

Saul Bellow, Humboldt's Gift, *1975*

~~~~~~

Between 1969 and 1970, gunfire killed 16 Chicago police officers, a level of carnage unequalled in the years since and one only surpassed by the violent Prohibition/Depression years of the late 1920s and early 1930s. Those few years from the late 1960s to the mid-1970s, an era before police routinely wore bullet-proof vests, also saw more than 80 policemen downed by nonfatal shootings, often sniper fire.

Sniper shooting at police became common around that time, though dating the sudden rise is hard to track through official department records because many sniping incidents never got officially recorded. Often, a call of "shots fired" went unreported or was deemed unfounded if no suspect was caught or no one got hit. Anecdotal evidence, however, suggests that sniping at police increased sharply following the riots after Martin Luther King Jr.'s assassination. The weapons commonly used also changed around then, from handguns to rifles. At district roll calls, officers were warned about certain locations, including most of the public housing projects in the city.

The sniping most often came from the street gangs or the Black Panthers, whose actions were aggressively provocative toward law enforcement. Though the numbers are difficult to pin down, during this time across the country, at least a dozen Black Panthers were killed in shootouts with the police.

In Chicago, this frequent violence seemed to climax in two deadly incidents—the killing of Fred Hampton, leader of the Illinois chapter of the Black Panther Party, during a raid on his apartment in December 1969 and the sniper murder by Blackstone Rangers of Gang Intelligence officer James Alfano in an unlit South Side alley in August 1970. The violence at that time was overlaid by the tumultuous protests and outright rioting of radical political groups, some of whom tried ineffectually to ally themselves with Chicago's Black street gangs. Add to all this the inept but noisy Chicago branch of the American Nazi Party, led by Frank Collin, and detectives in Gang Intelligence found themselves staring at deep and confusing rips in the city's social fabric.

My first encounter with the killing of several of my fellow police officers came shortly after I was assigned to Gang Intelligence, and the deaths had nothing to do with gang activity. Rather, it was an early example of a type of extreme violence that continues to plague our country—a mentally unstable but heavily armed individual set out to kill wantonly. Frank J. Kulak had lost several fingers while serving with the Marines in the Pacific in World War II, and he suffered shrapnel injuries in Korea. Since his discharge in the late 1950s, he'd become increasingly isolated, living finally in a third-floor apartment at 9521 South Exchange Avenue in far southeast Chicago. There, nursing a rage toward the world at large, he amassed an arsenal of weapons, including guns, grenades, and homemade bombs.

Starting in late 1968, he planted at least six bombs around the South Side, killing two people and wounding 14 others. One of the bombs, placed in a paper bag on a shelf in the toy section of a Goldblatt's department store on the far South Side, killed a female clerk and injured eight people. On April 14, 1969, about a week after the Goldblatt's explosion, four investigators went to Kulak's apartment to question him. After failing to rouse him from the front, they climbed the rear stairs and knocked on the back door. Kulak responded with a fusillade of bullets that downed two of the officers. He then barricaded himself in the apartment and started shooting from windows with a high-powered rifle, targeting people and cars. He also flung grenades and homemade bombs. The police returned fire, and, as one neighbor told the *Tribune* later, "It sounds like Vietnam."

My partner and I had answered the call and gathered with numerous other officers out of the line of fire in the garage of a funeral home behind Kulak's apartment building. From this viewpoint, we could see the legs of the two fallen officers on the third-floor landing. Ordered by supervisors to stay in place, we impatiently awaited permission to storm the building. Frustrations bubbled over as the clock ticked and the order to stand down was reiterated. Most of the police wanted to rush the landing, even at the risk of getting shot— they were desperate to see if the downed officers were still alive. Those in charge said no way. Later, we learned that Kulak had twice intentionally exposed himself to police sharpshooters, but officers wanted to take him alive because of concerns that he may have planted other bombs in the community.

As the standoff stretched through the afternoon and into the evening, a mutiny began, with officers screaming and pushing at the chief of patrol. The authorities brought in Kulak's sister and brother to try to talk him into giving up. Still, he refused. Finally, Deputy Superintendent James Rochford, the second in command of the force and a World War II veteran of the Pacific Theater, climbed to the apartment and traded recollections with Kulak of the assault on Okinawa. As columnist Jeff Lyon of the *Tribune* later put it, "Unarmed, and dressed in his neat blue uniform with the three stars on the shoulders, [Rochford] began slowly climbing stairs, speaking gently to the man training the gaping .45 on him. Higher and higher Rochford went until all emotion seemed to leave Frank Kulak suddenly and he let go of the gun."

By now it was after nine o'clock at night. We moved to the front of the building with other officers. Suddenly, a car with no lights on raced down the sidewalk and came to a quick stop in front of the building. Rochford and Kulak ran out of the apartment building, and Rochford threw the gunman in the back seat. A crowd of police rushed the car, momentarily blocking it. Rochford warned the officers away, and the car took off. It had been a harrowing six hours, but what impressed me at that moment was the anger and sorrow of so many of the cops.

The fallen officers, James Schaffer and Jerome Stubig, had been long dead. Kulak said he had shot each officer in the head three times. Found to be a paranoid schizophrenic, Kulak was ruled unfit for trial and sent to a maximum-security mental health facility. I was told that while he waited in Cook County Jail for his case to be resolved, Warden Winston Moore put gangbangers who had been intimidating others in Kulak's cell. Kulak would bite them.

As for Rochford, he later became police superintendent, a position he held for three years in the mid-1970s. He earned credit for raising the standards of the department and for pushing to bring in more minorities and women.

The Kulak incident proved to be a sad harbinger of the violence that followed in 1969 and 1970—though, unlike the Kulak case, many of the subsequent shootings and deaths involved Chicago's notorious street gangs.

Just a week before the Kulak shootout, a highly respected Gang Intelligence officer, Richard Peck, stepped from his car to question a group of gang members gathered at 62nd Street and Woodlawn Avenue. A shotgun blast greeted him, sending 15 pellets into his chest. The gangbangers scattered, but no bystanders came to help Peck. Badly wounded, he drove himself to a hospital. He recovered, and eventually Gang Intelligence identified the offenders, who were apprehended.

The shootings and police confrontations continued to plague Chicago's South and West side communities throughout that summer and into the fall, but the police frustrations and sorrows coalesced that November with the murders of two beat officers, Frank Rappaport and John Gilhooly Jr., in a South Side shootout. At just before midnight on November 12, 1969, officers Mike Brady and John Gilhooly, working a beat car in the Second District, answered a call of men with guns on the street at 5800 South Calumet—not a particularly unusual assignment given the time and the place.

Responding, the officers followed the gunmen through the gangway by a vacant building. A shotgun blast caught Gilhooly in the face and neck and severed his carotid artery. A ricochet wounded Brady. A call for help went out, and over 20 cars responded. Almost immediately, a gun battle broke out between the police and the shooters in the courtyard of the vacant buildings. "It was a nightmare," said one officer on the scene. "Gunfire poured on us, and it seemed to come from every direction." Several officers were wounded. Nearby, Frank Rappaport and other officers pursued a Black Panther named Spurgeon "Jake" Winter down an alley. Winter shot several policemen before hiding under a porch. From there, he shot and wounded Rappaport. He then emerged and, while standing over the fallen officer, shot Rappaport in the head and killed him. (The Panthers would later describe this act of Winters as a mercy killing.) The police quickly shot and killed Winters. A second Black Panther, Lawrence Bell, was captured alive and later pled guilty to attempted murder. By the time the gunfire stopped, two officers were dead and seven wounded.

The Illinois chapter of the Black Panthers put out a bulletin: "On November 13, 1969, Jake Winters stood face to face and toe to toe, his shotgun in hand, with pig Daley's murderous Task Force. He defined political power by blowing away racist pig Frank Rappaport and racist pig John Gilhooley (sic) and retired 8 (sic) other reactionary racist pigs before he was shot down."

I happened to know several of the fallen officers. Mike Brady, who recovered from his wound, was a friend who sat across from me in our freshman classes at Leo High School. John Gilhooly had been in my younger brother's classes at Saint Sabina and skated in the parish's annual roller skating programs. The son of a Chicago police officer, he was 21 and engaged to be married.

The memorial for Frank Rappaport, who left a wife and three children, gave me cause to reflect. When I first came out of the academy, I was in a beat car with a senior officer, Maurice Ford. While on patrol, Ford told me to pull over in front of a dry cleaner and wait while he picked up his cleaning. A few minutes later, our car got a call about suspicious people in the alley in the rear of 7400 Evens, a few blocks away. I responded "10-4"—the signal to the dispatcher of a two-man car—and drove there alone. When I entered the alley, several police cars were approaching from the other direction. Frank Rappaport, in the first, hopped out and chased the suspicious people away.

Then he dressed me down for not telling the dispatcher that I was a one-man unit. "The most important thing out here is that the communications center always knows where you are and what your manpower status is," he growled. "You can get somebody killed." With his death, all I could think of was how he had tried to reinforce what had been stressed at the academy: "Always know your location and never misinform the communications center." I regret I never acknowledged or thanked Rappaport for his concern.

The story of the shootout that night spread not only across the city but across the country. The description of the execution of Rappaport and the gloating by the Panthers was talked about in every police station in the country.

The Black Panther Party had been founded in Oakland, California, in 1966 by Huey Newton and Bobby Seale, and it came to widespread national attention a year later when armed Panthers walked into the California Legislature in Sacramento to protest a gun control measure. The Panthers insisted on their Second Amendment right to bear arms, principally, they claimed, to protect themselves and their communities against purported police oppression.

In the fall of 1968, the Panthers—whose numbers were never substantial but who were setting up operations around the country—opened a headquarters in Chicago in a two-story brick building, at 2350 West Madison Street, about six blocks west of the United Center, where the Chicago Bulls and Blackhawks play today. The founders of the local chapter, Fred Hampton and Bobby Rush, didn't hold back on the militant rhetoric, but played a more thoughtful game than the national leaders. Rush has gone on to a long career in politics, and he currently represents a slice of southwest Chicago and the southwest suburbs in Congress.

Hampton, 21 when he died, was a native of Maywood. I never talked with him, though I observed him a number of times. As a speaker, he could move a crowd. Once in Grant Park, three or four thousand high school kids had walked out of school and gathered to hear him speak. In the midst of his speech, Nazi Frank Collin and his followers, dressed in their uniform costumes, showed up carrying signs adorned with hateful, racist language. They marched right into the heart of the crowd, and the kids—almost all Black—erupted on them. Without missing a beat, Hampton raised his voice slightly and told the crowd to stop. As if on command, the kids calmed down. Several hundred people stepped back and let the Nazis march through their gathering. Minutes later, police arrived and hauled the Nazi crew away.

Under Hampton and Rush, the Panthers started a free breakfast program and had plans to open a medical clinic. In Chicago and elsewhere, however, none of these social-service operations lasted, and critics said the organizers used the programs to indoctrinate anti-police attitudes in children.

By Christmas 1968, the Panthers counted more than 300 members in Chicago. During the day, members busied themselves recruiting new adherents and selling the Panther newspaper at high schools, colleges, and busy intersections in select areas. Within a few months, they were said to be distributing 10,000 papers a week. But they clashed with Chicago's street gangs, who considered the Panthers the new guys in town and didn't welcome the intrusion. Conflicts often broke out over sales of the Panther paper—gangbangers would chase the Panther sales force off street corners. Eventually, the Panther leadership sought meetings with the street gangs to end the interference, and these meetings had some success—the Disciples agreed, for example. But the Vice Lords said no, and Jeff Fort, leader of the Blackstone Rangers, issued an ultimatum in front of more than 100 armed members of his gang: No Panthers would be allowed on Chicago's South Side unless they joined the Blackstone gang. Fort's embargo remained in place throughout the Panthers' time in Chicago.

The FBI tried to take advantage and even foment the antagonism between the Panthers and the gangs. For example, a document came to light years after the raid, showing someone in the FBI seeking to pit the Blackstone Rangers against the Panthers had sent a false note to Fort warning that the Panthers had put a hit on him.

Initially, virtually anyone could walk in and join the Panthers, one reason it's difficult to establish hard numbers on the group's total membership. Most newcomers were graded on their ability to sell the Panther newspaper, and most were judged competent—a perfect setting for law enforcement to establish a structure of informants.

In 1968, FBI Director J. Edgar Hoover, still the most highly respected law enforcement official in the nation (the toppling of his reputation would come later), stated that the Panthers provided the greatest threat to America's domestic security. In the years following the raid on Hampton's apartment, thousands of documents have come to light showing the vigor of the FBI effort to destroy the Panthers. As Paul Engleman put it in a 1994 *Chicago* magazine article on the 25th anniversary of the deadly incident, "It emerged that Hanrahan and the police were minor players in a larger production staged by the FBI, a secret counterintelligence program—COINTELPRO—designed, in the words of J. Edgar Hoover, to 'disrupt' and 'neutralize' Black groups and prevent the rise of a 'messiah.'"

As part of a nationwide effort, Hoover set up a unit in the Chicago office called the Racial Matters Squad, whose most prominent agent was the determined and effective Roy Mitchell. For Mitchell, the Panther membership policy offered an open invitation, and soon the Black Panther Party in Chicago was loaded with his informants. Mitchell's successful infiltration included the prize recruit, William O'Neal, who became chief of security for the local chapter of the Black Panther Party—always by the side of Chairman Fred Hampton.

Meantime, Cook County State's Attorney Edward V. Hanrahan took a lead role in the city's response to gangs. Hanrahan may be the most misunderstood public official in Chicago's political history, though much of the trouble was his own doing. His manner was brusque, and he didn't suffer fools. He came to loathe the press, which dealt with him harshly.

People who knew Hanrahan beyond his public persona, however, knew a man whose integrity was acknowledged by even his adversaries and who had great compassion for the poor and for the victims of crime in the inner city. As a volunteer with the St. Vincent DePaul Society, Hanrahan would frequently venture out anonymously at night into Chicago's poorest neighborhoods to provide charitable goods or deeds to residents. This picture would likely surprise some reporters who suggested Hanrahan harbored racial bias in the performance of his office.

A Harvard Law School graduate, Hanrahan gained national attention as the local U.S. attorney who successfully prosecuted crime boss Sam Giancana. Hanrahan won the Cook County state's attorney job in a landslide in November 1968 with a vow to crack down on Chicago's street gangs. In keeping his promise, he established an elite squad of 14 men to go after the gangs. Recruits to the Special Prosecution Unit, as it was called, came from the Chicago police, three of them men from Gang Intelligence. They were chosen for their experience, judgment, and honesty—Hanrahan's own Untouchables Squad.

At that time, the CPD's Intelligence Division was headed by Thomas Lyons, a veteran officer who had earned a reputation as a deliberate thinker. In briefings, he always raised the question, "Have you presented all available options to me?" He would always close planning sessions with the admonishment: "Expect the unexpected, because that is what will happen."In early January 1969, an unrelated robbery ended up playing a little-known role in the Hampton case. Based on information from an informant, Lyons's Criminal Intelligence Unit successfully foiled an armored truck robbery at the Bell & Howell plant in suburban Lincolnwood, just northwest of Chicago. Two of the bandits were shot and killed, but one of Lyons's investigators, Oliver Singleton, was critically wounded in the shootout, and in the following months, he was in and out of the hospital. The injury to the officer weighed heavily on the pensive Lyons.

In the late spring of 1969, the Intelligence Division created a special Black Panther squad within the Gang Intelligence Unit. The officers in it—I was not one of them—were assigned to focus on the activity between the Panthers and the street gangs. Now, three law enforcement units were watching over the city's Black Panthers: the Cook County State's Attorney's Special Prosecution Unit; GIU's Panther squad; and the FBI's Racial Matters Squad.

It's important to understand that a gap existed between members of the FBI and police officers—it might almost be characterized as a status divide. Most FBI agents hadn't joined the bureau to go banging on doors in public housing projects or to chase 17-year-old gangbangers through South Side alleys—a typical day's work for many in the police department. So when the FBI agents collected intelligence on street gangs, they would typically pass it on to the police—and often they were selective and even erratic about it.

As spring moved into summer, the Black Panthers in Chicago

made the news often. In June, one Panther was arrested for killing another suspected of being a police informant. Then 11 Panthers were arrested in a car with materials for making explosives. Later, 16 Panthers, including Fred Hampton and William O'Neal, were charged with kidnapping in an internal dispute over possession of a gun. In July, a Panther shooting wounded two beat officers, one in the head and the other in the shoulder. Later that month, a shootout near Panther headquarters on the West Side wounded five police officers and three Panthers.

Tensions continued into the fall, while the SDS, particularly its radical faction, increased efforts to draw the Black Panthers into the so-called Days of Rage protest scheduled for October in Chicago. That recruitment effort largely failed, but November saw the slaying of officers Gilhooly and Rappaport.

The raid that ended in the death of Fred Hampton on December 4 has been investigated, argued over, dissected, and litigated for years. I wasn't on the raid, but I knew most of the men who were. The event has generated many misperceptions—the cruelest by far being the claim that Chicago police set out to assassinate Hampton. The officers I knew on the raid had long police experience and were neither overzealous nor irresponsible. The last thing they would want was to be drawn into a police homicide.

But the facts of the case lead me to another conclusion: that the FBI set the events in motion, and, by withholding information and perhaps hiding the role of the bureau's informant, led Hanrahan's squad into the deadly encounter.

Here's what I think happened:

In November, Gang Intelligence learned that the Panthers were keeping a stash of guns on the second floor of the party's headquarters at 2350 West Madison. At the time, the original source of this information was closely guarded, but GIU Panther squad informants substantiated the report. Seizing the weapons would entail a dangerous operation, possibly a shootout. Knowing this, Director Lyons had no good options. He could sit tight and try to maintain surveillance on the cache, but this left the risk that one of the guns could nonetheless be used to shoot someone. Or Lyons could get a warrant and hope that serving it didn't lead to a shootout.

On November 19 and 20, a series of meetings took place at the Intelligence Division offices, attended by representatives of the three law enforcement groups that were overseeing Panther activity in Chicago. The officers at the meeting studied building plans for 2350 West Madison, focusing on the long, narrow stairwell leading to the upper floor. Everyone familiar with the building recognized that any attempt to enter the fortified headquarters would result in violence.

Lyons eventually formulated a plan to be carried out by a 35-man team. The initial list of 35 included men from the Gang Intelligence Panther squad and two additional squads. Lyons personally pared the list. (I wasn't included in the final roster.)

Over the weekend of November 22-23, Lyons shared his concerns about the risks of the raid with his three designated raid supervisors. As fate would have it, this was also the weekend that Lyons was confirming details of a Thanksgiving dinner he planned for Oliver Singleton, the officer who had been shot in the Bell & Howell robbery. To his great sadness, Lyons learned that Singleton might not live until Thanksgiving. That Sunday, Lyons told his sergeants the raid was off. Singleton died on Thanksgiving.

On Monday, November 24, the FBI alerted Gang Intelligence that the weapons had been moved, though information on when and where was not provided. The following week, the FBI notified the state's attorney's office that the weapons were now at Fred Hampton's apartment, at 2337 West Monroe, just a block away from Panther headquarters. The information came from William O'Neal, though it's not clear that the state's attorney's office—and Hanrahan himself—knew that the tip on the guns came from an FBI informant. Some later accounts even claimed that O'Neal had suggested to the Panthers that the guns be placed in Hampton's apartment. Why didn't the FBI go back to Lyons with the information? Perhaps because Lyons had declined the raid earlier. In any case, informants for the state's attorney confirmed the presence of the guns. Hanrahan was now in the same untenable position that Lyons had been in two weeks earlier—aware of a dangerous cache of weapons that could be used to kill. Whether Hanrahan knew of Lyons's grave concerns over the previous planned raid is unknown.

To this day, there is uncertainty about the purpose of the raid. Was it to seize the weapons? If so, why didn't the FBI notify the Alcohol, Tobacco, and Firearms Division of the Treasury Department, which normally handled federal gun violations (at least two of the suspected weapons, a sawed-off shotgun and a stolen police pistol, broke federal law)? Or was the underlying purpose to place Hampton in the presence of guns, which would have been grounds for arrest? He was out of prison on appeal of a robbery conviction and facing other charges—circumstances that made it illegal for him to be near a gun.

The state's attorney's office drew up a warrant to seize the weapons and developed a plan to serve it, a plan that is similar in almost every respect to the way such warrants are served today. Hanrahan's Special Prosecutions Unit would take on the job. Fourteen men would go to Hampton's apartment in early morning, so as not to arouse the neighborhood or give up the element of surprise. Three officers and their sergeant would announce their presence and enter the front door, four others would wait in the rear; the remaining officers would stand by outside in the front and rear. Just prior to the raid, the local police district would be notified that nonuniformed officers would be in the area of the apartment. The participants on the raid were specifically told that all occupants of the apartment had ready access to the weapons inside. Hanrahan approved the plan with the warning: "Be careful."

At 4:30 a.m. on December 4, four investigators, one armed with a carbine and one with a submachine gun, announced their presence at the front door of the Hampton apartment. When no one came to the door, they knocked it down and were met by a second, inner door. As one officer banged through that door, a shot came at him from within. The officers rushed into the apartment, unloading a volley of fire. After a momentary halt in the shooting, the Hanrahan men thought they'd been shot at again—later, as best they could reconstruct the situation, the shot was fired in a panic by a Panther named Louis Truelock. That opened another round of shooting by the police. Fred Hampton was killed, as was Mark Clark, who probably fired the first shot. Three other occupants were wounded, and four occupants who hadn't been wounded, including Hampton's pregnant girlfriend, Deborah Johnson, were arrested. The raiders left the apartment without securing it, and soon reporters and the public were streaming through the premises.

The action lasted about 10 minutes. Nineteen unregistered weapons were recovered from various locations in the apartment. At the local police station, Truelock acknowledged that he fired a weapon in the apartment, though later he recanted this admission. Despite conflicting accounts, what is pretty well established is that the officers fired around 80 rounds and the Panthers fired two. To those in law enforcement, this disparity, in and of itself, is irrelevant. Fourteen officers participated in the action, and an automatic weapon can fire a burst of rounds in a second. The fact that the raiders left Hampton's apartment open for public scrutiny confirms their belief that their actions were proper.

As the news reports of the raid poured out, Hanrahan and his police came under intense criticism, not just from the Panthers and their supporters, but from the news media. Hanrahan made clumsy attempts to defend the raid and his men to the public, but several of these backfired spectacularly as more facts came out. He was hampered throughout by concern about revealing the identities of the myriad informers and infiltrators who had worked with the police.

As time passed, the raid devolved into a confusing and lengthy series of investigations and court battles. Separate criminal proceedings against both the surviving Panthers and Hanrahan and the police came to nothing. The families of Hampton and Clark and the survivors of the raid filed a $47-million civil suit, charging that the government had used excessive force and violated the civil rights of the people in the apartment. That case dragged on for years amid charges and countercharges and testimony that floated in all directions. O'Neal's role as an FBI informant only came out publicly in 1973, when he was linked to a supposed police hit squad that targeted drug dealers. (I don't think Hanrahan's men knew at the time of the raid that O'Neal was an FBI informant.) In 1974, a radical group stole documents from an FBI office in Pennsylvania, revealing for the first time the scope of the COINTELPRO program.

The lawsuit was finally settled in 1983 for $1.85 million. When asked by the *Chicago Tribune* why a $47-million case was settled for $1.85 million, one plaintiffs' attorney responded that his clients could not have won. Hanrahan denounced the settlement, terming it a "payoff" and saying it "rewards the Black Panthers for their lawbreaking and their irresponsible charges."

By some accounts, the Panthers were already declining by the time of the raid. The death of Hampton finished the group off in Chicago. Beyond that, the raid had a profound effect on the lives of several of those involved.

Though Bobby Rush wasn't present during the raid, as a chief Black Panther spokesman, he condemned it and accused the authorities of murder. As the Panthers faded, he went back to school and entered politics, first as an alderman, then, since 1993, as a representative in the U.S. House. He holds the distinction of being the only person to defeat Barack Obama in an election.

Fred Hampton's girlfriend, Deborah Johnson, now named Akua Njeri, has flirted with politics and works to promote the memory of Hampton. Their son, Fred Hampton Jr., born less than a month after his father's death, keeps the image of the Black Panthers alive through his activist political organization, Prisoners of Conscience Committee.

Roy Mitchell, the FBI agent thought to have as many as a half-dozen informants in the local Black Panthers and the tutor of the infiltrator William O'Neal, continued a successful career with the Bureau.

William O'Neal, who later said that he knew the Panthers were dangerous and regretted his role with the party, ended his life in 1990 by intentionally running into oncoming traffic on a Chicago expressway.

Tom Lyons, the Intelligence Division director who declined the Panther raid, rose through the ranks of the Chicago Police Department, solidifying his reputation for thoughtful competence. In 1978, at the Nazi rally in Marquette Park, he would order a future mayor of Chicago to desist in his provocative protest or face arrest.

Edward Hanrahan lost his re-election for Cook County state's attorney in 1972. He later lost elections for Congress, mayor, and alderman. Some friends believe he only sought those offices in order to settle a score. He remained bitter over the treatment he had received from the press and from his former political allies. He died in June 2009, his life celebrated in a Catholic Mass, briefly interrupted by a protest staged by Fred Hampton Jr.

Throughout 1970, the attacks on police conducted by a small number of Black militants continued in full force. "Let's face it: Parts of Chicago are in a state of guerrilla warfare," the *Tribune* editorialized on August 15. "The police have not been the only victims; dozens of Black youths have been killed by Black terrorists."

The police communications center was constantly putting out calls of shots fired at officers—particularly around Chicago's public housing projects. Fortunately, most of the shots missed or only damaged a squad car. The problem didn't belong to Chicago alone. Around the country, the number of officers killed in the line of duty hit highs in the early 1970s that have never since been exceeded. Many of those deaths came at the hands of militant factions of

Blacks in metropolitan areas, a relatively small number of hard-core belligerents whose anger was nurtured by the fierce divisiveness of the times and by a general antagonism to the police in many Black communities.

In Chicago, police officials tried to improve relations by instituting a number of outreach programs—Officer Friendly, Talk with the Commander, Walk and Talk, and others—some formalized, others suggested. Few of these were effective. The only one I knew that achieved any real results, even if temporary, came in the late 1960s from the West Side district commander George Sims. He summoned 2,200 members of the Vice Lords street gang and told them that he would help any one of them in any way with any problem, personal or other—home, school, work—if they would cooperate with him in making their community safer. If, however, they continued their criminal ways, he vowed to put them away for a long time. For a time, Sims's outreach cooled gang shootings in the Lawndale area, and gang members even helped police in tracking down suspects.

In one of the formalized department programs, Walk and Talk, groups of officers patrolled on foot through troubled neighborhoods and got to know residents. It was hoped that these closer connections would bolster the mood of the community. The well-meaning effort had a sputtering run. The program had already been shut down in several neighborhoods when on July 16, 1970, two officers who had volunteered for Walk and Talk, James Severin and Anthony Rizzato, were shot in their backs by sniper fire while crossing a ball field at Cabrini Green, the sprawling housing project northwest of the Loop. Officers Rizzato and Severin were experienced and street-savvy. They had worked hard to establish a rapport with the residents of Cabrini Green, and they had succeeded, a fact evident by the willingness of so many Cabrini residents to come forth to assist in the identification of their killers. Two gang members were convicted of murder. The Walk and Talk Program was terminated.

Those who understand the situation say no program can be effective without the trust of the community that is being served.

Securing that trust requires a familiarity and a move toward something like friendship—difficult to achieve given the limitations imposed by the dangers of the street. Today as then, because of the danger, the walking beat cop is unlikely to return in a regular way to inner-city neighborhoods.

Over the years, I have come to advocate—with little success—a complete revamping of the Chicago police beat assignment process. Rather than having officers moving in and out of beats in a somewhat haphazard fashion, I think every beat in a high-crime district should be assigned 10 officers and a sergeant who has broad discretion in supervising his team. Every officer would remain on the same beat for 42 months—no transfers, no reassignments. Special incentives would be provided to those successfully working these beats—guaranteed rapid promotion and increased pay. After 50 years of trying, we know what hasn't worked in these high-crime areas. As conservative U.S. Supreme Court Justice Clarence Thomas put it in a dissent to a ruling that invalidated an anti-loitering law: We must find a way to provide comfort to those imprisoned in their own dwellings, fearful to go out because their neighborhoods are so dangerous.

The violence and heartache of 1970 climaxed a month after the Cabrini Green murders when Gang Intelligence Officer James A. Alfano, Jr., was shot in an ambush in an alley off Stony Island Avenue. Alfano, nicknamed Chico, was well-liked in our unit and in the South Side districts. A 30-year-old ex-Marine, a skydiving enthusiast, and the owner of a karate school, he was married with two young children. We had worked a few assignments together, and we would stop and eat at a restaurant owned by one of his relatives on 31st Street. One night, he learned I was a teacher at Fenger, the high school he had attended. Every now and again afterwards, he would ask if so-and-so still taught there, and if so, would I please say hello.

Late at night on Thursday, August 13, Alfano was riding in the back seat of an unmarked car with two GIU detectives, Richard

Crowley and Thomas Donahue, in the front. The officers were patrolling around the Southmoor Hotel, a huge, shuttered building at 67th Street and Stony Island. The Southmoor had once been a jewel in the South Side neighborhood, a 10-story, 500-room residential hotel looking out over Jackson Park. But the Black P Stone Nation had infiltrated the operation, driven out tenants and legitimate businesses, and forced a foreclosure. Though a judge had ordered the building boarded up, gang members had moved in.

At a little after 11 that night, the unmarked car with Alfano in the back seat pulled into a T-shaped alley behind the Southmoor. A large, stuffed couch blocked the route, and as the car nudged the couch aside, rifle fire opened up, hitting the vehicle. One bullet from the rifle traveled through the trunk of the car and split apart. Fragments ripped through Alfano's back and tore up his liver. "Oh, my God, I'm dying," Alfano cried out. Officer Crowley immediately navigated the vehicle through the dark alleys and streets of Woodlawn to Billings Hospital, and Alfano underwent emergency surgery.

Meanwhile, as many as 100 police descended on the scene, and sniper fire erupted throughout a half-mile square around the Southmoor. A *Tribune* writer, Philip Caputo, reported that the neighborhood became a "battleground as dangerous as any in Vietnam. Police crouched behind squad cars on streets that had been blacked out, waiting and watching for sporadic flashes from the muzzles of the guns of unseen snipers hiding in shabby tenements." Caputo had the credentials to make the comparison with the ongoing war in Southeast Asia. He had served in combat in Vietnam as a Marine, and in 1977, he published an acclaimed memoir of his experience there, *A Rumor of War.*

The shooting kept up in darkness until three the next morning. Earlier, gang members had knocked out streetlights to facilitate the ambush, though as the sniping increased that evening, the police themselves ordered more lights turned off in the neighborhood so that officers wouldn't be easy targets. Police went from building to building, searching for snipers and emptying supposedly vacant structures, including the Southmoor. Remarkably, only one other officer, Willie Anderson, was wounded that night, and his injuries weren't serious. Equally remarkable, the *Tribune* reported that though the police brought in heavy weapons, they fired no shots throughout the confrontation.

With the report of Alfano's shooting, all Gang Intelligence officers reported in. I was instructed by our lieutenant to go to Billings Hospital and to stay there until he personally told me differently. I was to call him every hour and to make sure Alfano's family was aware of my presence. It wound up being the saddest assignment I ever had. After undergoing surgery to stem internal hemorrhaging, Alfano was moved to a large room filled with machines to monitor his condition. I sat off in the corner, a lump in my throat, trying to mask my sadness. A team of doctors, including a specialist flown up from Texas, huddled off and on with Alfano's wife, Judy. People came and went, usually just looking and crying.

Officer Alfano was a physical fitness buff, so he had tremendous resilience. But he also had a rare AB blood type. In response to a plea from the authorities, hundreds of volunteers donated blood, and in three days, Alfano received more than 120 pints. From the corner of the room, though, I could see he wasn't going to make it. The Texas specialist, a woman, would confer in small groups with the other doctors, and her body language told the story. After fighting for life for 70 hours, brave Jimmy Alfano died.

In the following days, his last rueful words, devoid of any hope, echoed across every police district in America.

Investigators quickly established that the killing was part of an ambush planned by the leaders of the Black P Stone Nation, a successor organization to the Blackstone Rangers. The day after the shooting, police arrested one of the prime suspects and key figures in the case, 20-year-old Caesarei Marsh, in front of the gang's headquarters on East 76th Street. Marsh was a former gang member himself, and over the course of interviews and in his testimony at an eventual trial, he gave wandering and sometimes contradictory accounts of a conspiracy: Leaders of the gang planned to murder police in retaliation for efforts by Gang Intelligence to thwart gang activities. Marsh said that he and other gang members had placed the couch in the alley and then stationed themselves around the scene armed with rifles and other firearms.

Though the authorities suspected the outline of the conspiracy quickly, the police went through extraordinary efforts in the days and weeks after the murder to nail down details and find corroborating information. Some of the work was terrifying and dangerous. Officers would go into projects to interview people. If the residents lived on an upper floor, the officers avoided the elevators—too easy to get trapped. Someone could put a two-by-four in the door on, say, the 14th floor, then pour gasoline down the shaft and throw in lit matches. Instead, the police would take the stairwell, but that had its own tensions—shouts, doors slamming.

More frightening even than climbing the stairwells was going into the basement of buildings. After the Alfano murder, the police installed a lot of wiretaps, which often entailed going into a decrepit building and putting a device on the phone box. Placing it wasn't bad, but when you went to pick it up, you never knew if someone had found it and was waiting for you in these dark and dirty spaces.

Eventually, though, the police acquired hours of surveillance tapes—not of the shooters themselves, but of friends of shooters and friends of friends. With eyewitnesses, confessions, and the tapes, the police were able to piece together the whole conspiracy, pretty much as laid out by Marsh.

At least 28 gang members had some involvement in the assassination plot. Homicide officers and GIU investigators arrested all but one. Three initially agreed to become state witnesses, but after a defense attorney somehow accessed the quarters where witnesses were being held, two of them recanted.

In the end, prosecutors charged seven men, all members of the Black P Stone Nation. They were represented by a veteran team of defense lawyers, including R. Eugene Pincham, who had a long and fiery career and went on to become a state court judge; James D. Montgomery, who became corporation counsel for the city of Chicago under Mayor Harold Washington; and Sam Adam, an acclaimed defense lawyer, who later teamed with his son to win a mistrial on 22 of 23 counts in the first trial of former Illinois Governor Rod Blagojevich. Throughout the Alfano trial, the defense hammered hard on the notion that the investigation of the crime, headed by Assistant State's Attorney James Meltreger, was deeply flawed. As Caputo put it in summing up the proceedings, the defense lawyers turned the trial into "the entire questions of law enforcement practices, especially as they are employed in the Black community." A quarter century later, that defense was echoed in Los Angeles in the trial of O.J. Simpson.

The trial got underway in late December 1970. In a tactical decision that proved costly, the prosecutors had granted immunity to Caesari Marsh in exchange for his testimony. Some observers feared at the time that Marsh was a double agent, alerting the defense to what investigators were asking and how he would testify.

For 13 days, the prosecutors put on 15 witnesses to make their case. Eyewitness statements, participant confessions, and electronic surveillance tapes confirmed the version of the conspiracy as laid out by Marsh. He played the chief prosecution role, recounting the conspiracy, though he admitted on the stand that he had changed his story and that he had a history of lying.

In addition to Marsh's credibility, other problems plagued the prosecution. A key witness who had known the defendants for years initially misidentified them. The state ballistic expert on the murder rifle testified with limited certainty. The defense rested after only one hour and calling only three witnesses. The jury deliberated for 22 hours before acquitting all seven defendants. Afterwards, the jury foreman, Thomas E. Nolan, one of four Black people on the 12-person panel, said a majority of the jurors at first thought the defendants were guilty. But after lengthy discussions and reading the law, they concluded that the state had not made its case. In particular, he cited the weaknesses of Marsh's testimony.

The acquittal came as a terrible blow to law enforcement officers, who now legitimately wondered whether there was justice to be found in the criminal courts of Cook County. Several months after the trial, Caesarei Marsh was targeted for assassination in a South Side hotel by suspected members of the Black P Stone Nation. Though hit by eight bullets, he survived.

History, however, has a way of running in cycles that are often impossible to anticipate and difficult to dissect even in retrospect. After 1970, the number of officers killed in Chicago started to decline, perhaps in part because the street gangs increasingly turned their attention to selling drugs and ended up fighting among themselves. Nationally, the number of murdered officers started to drop by the mid-1970s.

Over the years, some former Black Panthers and gang leaders have expressed regrets for those times. The coldest killer I ever dealt with, Blackstone Ranger Ed Bey, took to the ministry, renounced what the gangs did, and preached to the young men of Englewood to choose a life of kindness. At the same time, a certain mythology has grown up around the Panthers—that they were a defensive force for the beleaguered ghetto residents against police oppression; that they were turning African American frustration into useful civic programs, such as health clinics. If bits and pieces of that mythology contain shards of truth, they exist beside a larger truth that I'll never forget—one epitomized by the vicious words of the Panther newspaper celebrating the death of Officer Frank Rappaport. ■

"I don't think [Brian Flanagan] ever meant to kill me.
I also don't think he felt sorry for anyone he has hurt."

*Judge Richard Elrod, 40 years after being paralyzed
in a confrontation with radicals*

~~~~~~

In the year following the 1968 Democratic convention, the radical group Students for a Democratic Society remained active in Chicago and worked at recruiting students and trying to partner up with the various streets gangs and the Black Panthers. Many of the radicals—almost all young and white—were sincerely frustrated by the Vietnam War and the persistence of poverty and racism, and they genuinely sought to build their movement. But I've always suspected that the SDS leaders hoped to enlist students and naïve young people generally—Black and white—to be front-line troops in planned protests, the pawns who would take the heaviest blows when the confrontations started.

The SDS involvement with Chicago street gangs originally brought the Gang Intelligence Unit into the world of militant activists, and in the spring of 1969, we started to monitor the overtures by white radical groups to the Blackstone Rangers. By late spring, activists from Ann Arbor, Michigan; Madison, Wisconsin; Cleveland, Ohio; and various Chicago universities were roaming the halls of the city's public high schools and junior colleges, seeking recruits.

At the time, information flooded into the Intelligence Division from other law enforcement agencies—well beyond the capacity of the Subversives Unit to handle. Consequently, information that touched on gangs was referred for investigation to the GIU.

Officers visiting the city's high schools and colleges would pick up pamphlets and book excerpts that explained how to construct and detonate bombs and where and how to acquire dynamite. We also ran a route of hardware stores near schools and colleges, checking for unusual purchases of turpentine, a favorite arson accelerator.

Our primary goal was to disrupt and discredit efforts by the radicals to recruit high school kids into planned protests. The most effective tactic was the one-on-one conversation with teachers and upperclassmen—warning them of impending trouble and urging them to think hard about what was unfolding. I dressed in street clothing and always identified myself. Working covertly wasn't for me, though I appreciated it had its place. Many of the SDS leaders were my age. In fact, I'd enrolled in DePaul University Law School, and some of the radicals were faculty members and classmates. By this time, the Vietnam War was becoming unexplainable, and Nixon had pledged to bring peace.

But as Bryan Burrough points out in *Days of Rage*, his history of the radical movement in that period, the war was growing less central to SDS, though it remained a powerful recruiting tool. Rather, the group fashioned itself a revolutionary force fighting for the "oppressed" generally. To that end, the SDS leadership wanted desperately to align itself with the cause of African Americans. "I think in our hearts what all of us wanted to be was a Black Panther," Cathy Wilkerson, a former SDS leader, told Burrough.

Meanwhile, though, the SDS was starting to tear itself apart with internal disputes and rivalries. Some of the arguments sink into the finer points of Marxist theory and recall Freud's remark about the narcissism of minor differences. But the divide that rattled the world beyond SDS meetings was the choice between legitimate protest

JEREMIAH JOYCE

and militant action. A small cadre of SDS leaders who came to be known as Weatherman pushed for provocative confrontation with the authorities. The cadre included two young radicals with strong Chicago ties: Bernardine Dohrn, a graduate of the University of Chicago Law School, and Bill Ayers, whose father, Thomas, was head of the giant utility, Commonwealth Edison, and played a major civic role in the city's affairs. When Martin Luther King Jr. marched for open housing in the city in the mid-1960s, Mayor Daley appointed Ayers's father to chair a committee to diffuse racial tensions.

Over the first half of 1969, the militant faction of SDS gained control of the organization. After the summer of recruiting and training, the group planned a massive action to be held in Chicago in October, the operation that came to be known as Days of Rage. The demonstrations would coincide with another fractious event then going on in Chicago, the trial of the Chicago Seven, the government's prosecution of the alleged ringleaders of the riots at the Democratic National Convention the year before. Word went out to colleges that by confronting and provoking the authorities in Days of Rage, the movement would draw attention to its cause and might even spark a revolution. In anticipation of this fall event, Gang Intelligence spent the summer monitoring contacts between the street gangs and the radical groups.

Law enforcement leadership at the national level was convinced that the connection would be contagious. In briefings, federal officials cautioned us that the day may come when the chemistry majors join the high school dropouts, a so-called marriage between bomb makers and bomb throwers, and the country would ask: Where were the police when all of this was being hatched?

The SDS offices sat on the West Side, just a few blocks from Black Panther headquarters, and my partner and I occasionally drove there to locate someone. Invariably, the occupants refused to admit the police, so I would wait outside to speak to people when they left. The interactions were usually civil, though brief.

That fall, as radicals gathered in the city, intelligence indicated that bombs set off in the Loop would trigger Days of Rage action. In early October, militants just west of the Loop dynamited and toppled the statue commemorating the seven policemen killed in the Haymarket bombing in 1886—an historically ambiguous spasm of violence arguably instigated when the police tried to break up a peaceful labor rally.

On October 2, I was assigned to a protest rally at an amphitheater at the University of Illinois Chicago staged by the Progressive Labor Party (PLP) faction of the SDS, a Marxist group that had supposedly been expelled from the organization by the Weatherman contingent. The rally of about 150 people proceeded with the usual tedious speechifying when suddenly a large group of Weatherman militants came on the scene and waded into the crowd, swinging and screaming. At first, it was amusing—this wasn't so much a battle as a giant shoving and wrestling match. But then it became clear that the Weatherman group was much more violent than the PLP faction. Several Weatherman began beating up a slight, hapless PLP member. It looked as if they could really hurt him, so I identified myself and told the attackers to stop. With that, the group turned on me—a half dozen pummeling me and striking me mostly in the head. I grabbed one of them, Jeff Jones, a Weatherman leader, by the front of his jacket and held on tight while his cohort continued to pound away. I didn't want to lose my holstered weapon, so I kept one hand on my holster and struggled to stay on my feet. As we edged closer to a large window abutting the amphitheater, several of my assailants suggested pushing me through it. I dropped to one knee and brought Jones to the ground.

After a few minutes, several members of campus security swept in, along with Chicago police. My ribs were injured, and the back of my head banged up, but we arrested Jones and two other Weatherman and took them to police headquarters in the back of our car. (The PLP member who got beaten up was taken to a hospital emergency room.) During the ride to headquarters, the Weatherman trio babbled on about the coming revolution, but my ribs and head ached so badly that I had no interest in trying to question them. I do recall one of them said his father was a U.S. Navy admiral. The three were charged with felony aggravated battery.

A few months later, before going to trial, Jones went underground with a number of other Weatherman. Most of them stayed in this country, but changed their names and took other steps to stay out of sight. Some made it to the FBI's Ten Most Wanted Fugitives list. In the early 1970s, they unleashed a series of bombings and arsons on college campuses and public buildings across America. Jones didn't surface again until 1981, shortly after the Brink's armored car robbery in Nanuet, New York, a collaboration between members of the Weather Underground (as the faction was now known) and a militant Black liberation group. The robbery left three men dead, including two police officers, and led to the arrest of the participants, including Kathy Boudin and three members of the Weather Underground.

Jones was not involved with the robbery, but was arrested in the law enforcement sweep that followed the Brink's killings. He claims that at the time he had been negotiating to turn himself in. Not long after his arrest, the Cook County State's Attorney's Office called me and asked about the felony charges against Jones for the pounding I took in 1969. Did I want to pursue the case? I said it was time to move on—I'd been off the job for seven years, and the incident was long in the past. Jones pleaded guilty to a lesser charge and was fined and placed on probation.

Today, Jones is a political strategist and an environmental lobbyist in Albany, New York. He denies that he caused the injuries to the PLP member in the altercation that day, and he describes his arrest as a "civilized interaction." As for the actions of Weatherman, he commented in an interview for this book, "We said and did enough things that it's obvious that we kind of lost it there for a while .... We had a moment where we became rather extreme tactically."

During Days of Rage, I had another rather unusual connection with a Weatherman militant. An Illinois state legislator, Ray Kahoun, called and asked if I could do him a favor. He said that a friend of his from downstate, a well-to-do banker active in Republican politics, was concerned about his daughter. She had joined the radicals and would be coming to Chicago for the protests. Would I try to keep an eye out for her? Her name was Diana Oughton. I said of course.

Sure enough, she was soon arrested, charged, and taken to the county jail at 26th and California. I met with an assistant state's attorney who basically said: "If she will leave town, the authorities will not press the case." My sergeant and I went to the county lockup, where a matron tracked Oughton down in the women's wing to tell her we wanted to speak with her. The matron returned and said Oughton refused to talk to anyone but her lawyer.

That was the end of that. Five months later, Oughton and two colleagues were killed while constructing a bomb that was intended to be placed at an officer's club dance at Fort Dix. The bomb prematurely exploded, blowing up a townhouse in Greenwich Village. When I learned of the explosion, I recalled the words of a briefing we had received from an Army demolition officer in Evanston: "These brats with the bombs do not understand these instruments."

For the militant radicals, Days of Rage turned out to be a flop. Instead of the thousands of demonstrators who were expected to show up, only a few hundred appeared. All of the unseen efforts to discourage student participation had succeeded. The overheated calls to violence by leaders such as Ayers and Dohrn apparently failed to incite the young—indeed, there's every indication that people of all stripes were appalled at the nihilism that seemed to underlie the words and acts of the militant leaders.

Nonetheless, on the first night of the confrontation, a mass of demonstrators swept out of Lincoln Park and went rampaging down the streets toward the Drake Hotel, the residence of Julius Hoffman, the presiding judge of the Chicago Seven trial. The action never reached the Drake—the onslaught broke into separate confrontations with contingents of police. After two hours of broken windows, smashed cars, and showers of thrown rocks, police restored order and ended up arresting 60 demonstrators.

What remains somewhat unusual about that night was the fact that a number of officers fired their weapons, and the talk among officers was that five or six of the rioters had been shot—not killed, but wounded—yet there was no indication of that in releases from the police department or press reports. To this day, I'm puzzled by it.

Several more days of demonstrations followed, but none of the protests got beyond inflamed rhetoric and noisy marches. On Saturday, October 11, the final day of the operation, I gathered with a group led by militants at the base of the demolished Haymarket statue to begin the march east towards Chicago's Loop. I placed myself so I could focus my attention on a radical known as J.J.—John Jacobs, described to us as someone who will try to hurt you and is physically capable of doing just that. He was wearing a red helmet. I noticed that several of the marchers had flares taped together to resemble dynamite—apparently they had planned to throw them on the route to induce panic.

Right before the march set off, Lieutenant Joe Healy and corporation counsel Steve Zucker showed up and arrested Mark Rudd, another Weatherman militant who, like J.J., had made his activist name in the 1968 protests at Columbia University in New York. I suggested to Healy that the march might get out of hand and asked if the authorities might cancel it. He said he had already advised that, but they would not rescind the permit.

The march proceeded east down Randolph Street. I positioned myself two rows behind J.J, keeping my eyes on his red helmet. When we got to Madison and LaSalle streets, the marchers broke, scattering in every direction, smashing windows, attacking police, beating civilians. I headed after J.J., but he sprinted into the hurling crowd, ditching his helmet. I had barely begun my pursuit when I came upon city attorney Richard Elrod, lying motionless on the pavement. He had been injured in a confrontation with a demonstrator, Brian Flanagan. Elrod would remain paralyzed from the injuries he sustained that day, but he went on to a successful career in government. Congenial and well-respected, he served as Cook County sheriff and later as a circuit court judge.

That Loop riot ended relatively quickly, with the arrest of more than 100 demonstrators. Overall, the *Tribune* reported, the Days of Rage toll included "290 arrested, 48 policeman and scores of demonstrators injured; hundreds of thousands of dollars in property damage." The police department won acclaim for its restraint—training classes on the proper use of the baton, conducted after the convention, had succeeded. Far from winning converts to the radical cause, the chaotic few days seemed to draw nothing but scorn to SDS and particularly its most militant wing. Weatherman basically retreated after the Chicago fiasco. The deadly Greenwich Village townhouse explosion shattered the remnants of the organization and largely ended whatever influence it enjoyed.

I can still recall being struck, in SDS briefings and file readings, by the distinctions between the SDS women and men. The women leaders were far more intelligent than their male counterparts. Additionally, unlike their male counterparts, many of the women had previously been involved with worthy or charitable causes. But the most sinister distinction between the men and women leaders was revealed in the photo files of protest marches. When confrontations erupted, the male leaders seemed to vanish—take off and leave their followers behind. The women stayed.

Few Weather Underground males ever did any serious jail time. Today, with the exception of Mark Rudd and a few others, none have expressed serious regret for the injuries their violence produced.

For Chicago, what seemed to be an annual ritual of rioting in that era wasn't ready to end. In the summer of 1970, one of the worst riots ripped through the Loop, leaving more than 150 people injured, including scores of police officers. This time, the cause had nothing to do with politics or race. Indeed, it's hard to see the uproar as anything but a kind of tantrum—a violent expression of defiance, greed, and brattiness that casts a shadow backwards over the issue-oriented protests of the prior few years.

That summer, the city decided to offer a concert as a gesture of goodwill to the area's young people, an idea that dovetailed with plans by Sly and the Family Stone to give a free concert after canceling several earlier Chicago shows. The music fest would be held on July 27 in the southern end of Grant Park. The temperature that day reached into the 90s. Fans started gathering early in the morning for a show that wouldn't begin until four in the afternoon, and the growing crowd liberally sampled beer, wine, and marijuana. By a little after four, as many as 50,000 people had gathered—whites and Blacks, some of them young teenagers. When a rumor circulated that Sly had canceled again (he had not), someone threw a rock or a bottle on stage, and the riot was on.

The outnumbered police tried to calm the situation, but eventually a crowd of several thousand surrounded 150 officers isolated on a ball field. Rocks and bottles rained down on them. A *Tribune* reporter compared the turmoil to the clash in front of the Hilton Hotel a few blocks away during the Democratic Convention two years before, when the protesters opened up on the police. "But the rain of debris was much more intense this time. And the number of throwers was much greater."

I was present with a handful of other plainclothes officers at round 6:30, and the place was chaos. Police fired volleys into the air, but failed to calm the situation. The rioters charged, and the police could either fire their weapons or retreat. Screaming and yelling, the mob surged past those of us who were not in uniform. The uniformed police, assisted by massive reinforcements, set up scrimmage lines, and when the crowd charged again, some of the police fired. This stopped the rioters for a moment, but then they rampaged into the

Loop, breaking windows, looting stores, overturning cars. The actual physical violence came from a very small group—the rest of the rioters just kept running around downtown whooping it up. No one in Chicago had seen anything like it. The downtown didn't settle down until after 10 that night.

Who knows what the rioters' grievance was? Nothing. It was merely the herd mentality acted out in the extreme, undoubtedly fueled by alcohol and other substances.

The fissures in American society in those years heaved up another group that wanted in on the protest action and subsequent attention. Frank Collin led the American Nazi Party from a shabby office on West 71st Street, surrounding himself with a small group of mostly young men and boys. Collin was in his 20s himself, "the small man with the shrill voice and the hairless upper lip and the pimples," wrote Rick Soll in the *Tribune*. Collin liked to dress up in his Nazi uniform. His mother told a reporter that Collin's father was Jewish, though Frank denied it. In the overheated racial antagonisms of the late 1960s and early 1970s, Collin devoted much of his focus to denigrating Black people. Among my assignments in Gang Intelligence was to monitor Collin and his cohort.

One time, my partner and I were observing a protest at Logan Monument in Chicago's Grant Park. As usual, Collin and 15 or 20 of his brownshirts made a commotion with blatantly ugly and racist language. Finally, Deputy Superintendent James Rochford—the hero who had talked down Frank Kulak—decided that this had gone on long enough. He told us to get rid of those nitwits.

We approached Collin, and I told him, "Time to go." He said he wasn't finished demonstrating. We told him he would be arrested for inciting and we would process him through the Cook County jail in his present uniform. He understood what that meant, and he quickly acceded. But his car was parked 10 blocks north on Wacker Drive. I told him we could take him and his crew there in a paddy wagon. He refused the ride, so my partner and I marched a troop of Nazis through downtown Chicago. It was so demeaning—we were in plain clothes, and people responded to us as if we were part of Collin's unit.

Toward the end of the 1970s, Collin made a national commotion by attempting to stage a march through Skokie, Illinois, a heavily Jewish community with many Holocaust survivors. Represented by the ACLU, Collin won a U.S. Supreme Court case earning his group the right to march. Shortly after the case came down, I received a call from Cal Sutker, a Democratic political leader in the Skokie area, who said he'd heard of my past dealings with Collin. I told him my former sergeant, Dominick Frigo, knew about Collin's secret life. I set up a meeting with Sutker and Frigo, and a few days later Collin changed the location of the march from Skokie to Chicago.

Several years later, Collin was convicted of molesting young boys and sent to prison. Today, under the name Frank Joseph, he's the author of oddball histories, among other things, claiming that Old World people settled North America long before Columbus. Were it not for that Supreme Court case, Collin would probably only be a noxious footnote in Chicago histories of the time—and an example of how social disruptions can open doors of opportunity for the troubled and misguided.

Meantime, the Gang Intelligence Unit was on its way out. As part of the outcome of the lawsuit against the Subversives Unit, the police department scattered the GIU officers to various areas of the city, where the focus became more tactical than intelligence gathering.

Throughout much of my time as a policeman, I'd also been enrolled in DePaul University Law School, and I graduated and joined the Illinois Bar in 1973. On leave from the police department, I served an interim period as a prosecutor in the Cook County State's Attorney's Office and a brief time on the Judicial Inquiry Board, which investigates complaints against judges. I rejoined the police briefly in 1974. By that time, my two youngest sons, Kevin and Jerry, had been born. Mairsey and I were living with our four boys in a house at 114th Street and Washtenaw Avenue in the 19th Ward, and I was teaching criminal law at St. Xavier University.

One evening in the fall of 1974, I went to a neighborhood meeting and ended up speaking out at a presentation on community stability. I didn't realize it at the time, but I was about to take a sharp turn into the world of politics. ◼

7

"Anthony d'Andrea, defeated candidate for alderman
of the 19th ward, ... holding an automatic pistol in
his hand, backed gingerly up the steps."

Ernest Hemingway, The Toronto Star *May 28, 1921*

In 1970, we moved to a two-story Georgian in west Morgan Park, a neighborhood on the far southwest corner of Chicago, just over 10 miles from the Loop. A century before, Morgan Park and its neighbor to the north, Beverly, had been prairie farmland, and the two communities sprouted originally as suburban enclaves. The Rock Island Railroad anchored the connection to Chicago, and Beverly and Morgan Park joined the city separately in the first decades of the 20th century.

For a variety of reasons, the two communities each acquired a somewhat distinct character, now largely muddied by time and change. Morgan Park, with its curving streets and spacious homes, enjoyed a slightly English air and most of its early residents were well-off, white, and Protestant, though a settled Black population—many of them descendants of workers for the neighborhood's first rich white families—lived on its eastern edge. Beverly served as the commercial heart of the area, with a lively business district along 95th Street and a range of housing, almost all of it single-family.

Though Beverly and Morgan Park didn't welcome Irish Catholics at first, Irish Chicagoans moved to the area in growing numbers through the 1950s and 1960s, and Beverly in particular became a center of Irish life in the city, with a celebrated arts facility and a handful of churches and schools. The area remained distinct, yet connected to the Loop. Today the Metra Rock Island Line has eight commuter stops in Beverly and Morgan Park.

A third neighborhood, Mount Greenwood, just to the west, developed somewhat later, bordered by suburbs on the west and a line of cemeteries running down its eastern boundary. Until the late 1970s, Mount Greenwood featured the last working farm in Chicago. Firefighters, police officers, and other city workers gravitated to the neighborhood's smaller homes. The three communities (along with small slices of Roseland and Washington Heights) combined to make up the 19th Ward.

Our house sat in the St. Cajetan Parish, and the boys enrolled at St. Cajetan School. We had moved to accommodate the larger family and also because of an incident at the apartment we had been renting on 93rd Street in the Brainerd neighborhood, just east of Beverly. At the time, Brainerd, like many South Side neighborhoods, was undergoing rapid and unsettling change that followed the pattern of the last few decades, with white people fleeing and Black residents moving in. On a warm May afternoon in 1970, Mairsey was upstairs putting the three boys down for their naps—the youngest, Kevin, had yet to arrive—when a neighbor noticed that someone had broken into the apartment. The neighbor called the police and banged on the back door to alert Mairsey. The burglar fled—he was never caught—and everyone was fine, but the incident encouraged us to move when the lease came up.

Having lived through the turnover of several neighborhoods, I knew that Beverly/Morgan Park potentially faced the same challenge, but I never had an interest in getting involved in politics. Early on, in fact, I didn't have a preference between the political parties. My family had strong connections with unions, traditionally a

Democratic stronghold. But because Lyndon Johnson was considered anti-union, in my first presidential election, 1964, I voted for the Republican, Barry Goldwater. One summer Sunday, I'd come out of Mass at St. Sabina, and a woman was handing out copies of Phyllis Schlafly's book promoting conservatism, *A Choice, Not an Echo*. At the time, I thought her arguments made sense and pointed me toward Goldwater. (For the record, the only other Republican presidential candidate for whom I've voted was George H.W. Bush in 1992— and, as I'll explain later, that was because I admired the way he responded with federal help after Chicago's disastrous underground flood in April that year.)

We'd been in Morgan Park a few years when a young assistant state's attorney named Marty Russo asked me to help in his race for Congress in the 3rd District, encompassing a handful of suburban towns and a small chunk of Chicago's southwest. A Democrat running against a popular Republican incumbent, Russo thought I could help win support from important union leaders. Pat Gorman, the revered head of the Amalgamated Meat Cutters, was a close friend and protégé of my grandfather; my cousin John Joyce was on his way to becoming president of the International Bricklayers' Union; and a family friend, Stan Johnson, had become head of the politically active Illinois Federation of Labor. I agreed to help, and Russo won, joining the Watergate class of new representatives. He went on to serve in the House for almost two decades and in 1991 sponsored a comprehensive—though doomed—single-payer health-care plan.

In the course of the Russo campaign, I attended a meeting at St. Cajetan School at which the Beverly Area Planning Association discussed its efforts to hold the community together. BAPA, as it is known, was and is a well-regarded group made up of a dozen or so local organizations. Founded in 1946, BAPA's focus in recent years had been to halt the falling domino effect that saw South Side neighborhoods turn from white to Black almost overnight. Despite BAPA's efforts, the people of Beverly/Morgan Park remained anxious, in part because many of the area's white residents had moved there from neighborhoods that had turned over in recent years.

As BAPA's leaders made their presentation that night, a number of questions came up. The organization's plans were worthy, but inadequate. When the opportunity came to comment, several of us in the audience pointed out that we had heard all this before at St. Sabina and in other parishes. We argued that to create a stable, integrated community, BAPA and the government had to be far more aggressive in managing the future.

In the aftermath, small groups gathered to discuss what was to be done. Many of us recognized the familiar pattern starting to unfold in the 19th Ward: new real estate offices opening up, unwanted solicitations to sell your home arriving, house prices stagnating, increasing transfers out of the public high school, Morgan Park High. The meetings led to the conclusion that we would find a candidate for alderman who was not necessarily the choice of the dominant political force in the ward, the 19th Ward Democratic Organization, the local branch of the power network known as the machine.

Anton Cermak, a tough, Bohemian immigrant originally forged the Chicago machine in the 1920s to break through against the city's political establishment, which was both Republican and Democratic and dominated by the Irish. Cermak combined Polish, German, Czech, Jewish, and other ethnic and immigrant groups into a Democratic coalition that elected him mayor in 1931. But Cermak was Protestant at a time when a majority of Democratic voters in the city was Catholic. To show his Catholic bona fides, he strongly supported Al Smith, a Catholic, when Smith ran as the Democratic contender for president in 1928. Concerned with the Irish Catholic vote at home, Cermak remained cool to FDR, even when Roosevelt made a celebrated appearance in Chicago in 1929 to address the state's Democrats.

After Roosevelt won the presidency in 1932, Cermak, who was hoping for significant federal aid for his beleaguered city, wanted to mend relations with the president-elect. In February 1933, before Roosevelt's inauguration, Cermak was in Florida about to leave for a Havana vacation when he learned Roosevelt would be making an appearance in Miami. The Chicago mayor hurried to join the president-elect and was cut down by an assassin's bullet that most historians say was intended for Roosevelt. (A faction continues to believe the Chicago mob targeted Cermak.)

Before his death, Cermak had built his organization—which soon included many Irish—using patronage and constituent services. African Americans, who had long voted Republican, the party of Lincoln, switched to the Democratic side. Since that time, the Republican Party has almost disappeared in Chicago. The machine thrived as the mayor's office passed from Edward J. Kelly to Martin H. Kennelly, and the machine's power probably peaked during the long tenure of Mayor Richard J. Daley, who presided at City Hall and headed the Cook County Democratic Party.

The machine dominated public life in Chicago along with two other institutional partners: organized labor and the Roman Catholic Church. The city's economy boomed after the Second World War, and 11,000 manufacturers of all sizes operated here. Unions organized tens of thousands of workers in the first half of the century, and by the late 1940s, one out of five workers in Chicago belonged to a union. At the same time, worshippers overflowed the Catholic churches in Chicago's 300 or so parishes, as at least 40 percent of the population was Roman Catholic. Some 450,000 Chicago students attended Catholic schools. Thousands of priests and nuns gave direction to their faithful followers.

Leaders of the three institutions—Democrats, labor, the Church—didn't actively conspire, but for the most part their interests were aligned. They provided services, jobs, order, a sense of community. The tables at a typical annual dinner of a Democratic Cook County

Party organization would be filled with priests and leaders of assorted union locals. Together, the three institutions made neighborhood living seem pretty good.

The 19th Ward historically voted Republican, in line with its original WASP population. In 1935, however, the ward elected a machine Democrat as alderman, John J. Duffy, a florist and the state's chief boxing inspector. He proved extraordinarily popular and established a precedent: For years, the ward elected a Democratic alderman while backing Republicans for state and national offices.

When my family moved to Morgan Park, the local Democratic organization was strong, and the longtime alderman was a machine fixture named Thomas Fitzpatrick, who was personally popular and had a large, well-liked family. As it turned out, though, Fitzpatrick decided to retire and not run in the election of 1975. As a result, the ward's precinct captains voted to slate his veteran aide, Thomas Ryan.

Some of the residents who had been meeting to talk about the area's future were unhappy at the prospect of more of the same leadership, and we started looking for our own candidate. (Chicago aldermanic elections are non-partisan, but party affiliations are known; given the Democratic leanings of the ward, our candidate had to be Democratic.) The group trying to find a candidate even developed a campaign theme: Quality integrated living in an urban environment.

We approached two prospects: Tom Stack, a well-known athlete and decorated Vietnam War hero; and Themis Karnezis, a politically active and respected assistant state's attorney. In the end, neither would agree to make the run, and a number of residents asked me to consider it.

At first, I declined. I was not a public person, and while I could speak as a lawyer in a courtroom, the idea of campaigning—shaking hands and asking people for votes—was unappealing. But I talked it through with my wife and with family members and friends, and it came down to a choice: run for alderman or accept the fact that we would eventually have to leave Chicago.

While I was still weighing the decision, the father of a friend approached me with some advice. He was a former alderman from another ward and now a judge. He pointed out that current residents of the 19th Ward included six former aldermen, not counting Fitzpatrick; two former state senators; a former congressman; and descendants of three Chicago Democratic dynasties, the Nashes, Duffys, and Ryans (my potential opponent, Tom Ryan, was not of that family). All stood strongly with the 19th Ward Democratic organization. More importantly, the current leaders of the organization were popular and included Congressman Morgan Murphy, State Senator Tom Hynes, State Representative Dan Houlihan, and Illinois Secretary of State Michael Howlett (who a year later would run in the Democratic primary for governor and defeat the incumbent, Dan Walker, himself a former 19th Ward precinct worker; Howlett lost to Republican James Thompson in the general election).

The judge cautioned me that residents of the ward represented thousands of city jobs, and the precinct captains brought years of experience to their work. In the parlance of the neighborhood, the organization was known simply as the 19th Ward. The upshot, according to the judge: Everyone will be against you. And at the end of the day, Mayor Daley will lower the boom on you.

The judge's demeanor was friendly. He said he didn't want me—or his son, who was helping me—to be disappointed. But something more important struck me from the conversation: He said that if I somehow did get elected, I would never be able to accomplish anything because I'd bucked the organization. That would be the message that the precinct workers would deliver to the voters.

Meantime, in Chicago as a whole, some groups were already lining up to support a possible challenger to Mayor Daley, running for his sixth term in the 1975 mayoral election. Some police officers were urging Edward Hanrahan to run. Other people and organizations were lining up behind North Side Alderman William Singer, who was positioning himself as a reformer. A young group of African

American residents was looking to support a Black candidate.

All of my proposals for the future of our ward were based on the assumption that Chicago would re-elect Mayor Daley, even though I wasn't clear how my support for the mayor would play in the 19th Ward. Some told me that if I spoke highly of Mayor Daley's administration, the various opposition groups would label me just another "rubber stamp" alderman. Others advised that state Senator Tom Hynes would press his Senate colleague Rich Daley, the mayor's son, to secure the mayor's strong support for the endorsed candidate of the 19th Ward's Democratic organization.

In any case, I was going to say what I believed, and I decided I needed to speak with Mayor Daley directly to determine if the ideas we wanted to implement were pie in the sky. The mayor had gone to law school with my Uncle Vince, and Daley's law firm had represented my grandparents. I asked my father if he could arrange a meeting, and one day in the fall of 1974, I visited the mayor's office on the fifth floor of City Hall.

Mayor Daley sat alone behind a large desk cleared of every scrap of paper save a small, white card with nothing on it. This was a little more than two years before he died, but he looked healthy and happy. He asked about my children, and I told him about my family. I recounted my experience at St. Sabina, and I suggested that despite the turbulent recent history of the South Side, things could be done to manage an orderly integration in Beverly/Morgan Park. Then I ran down some of the issues we wanted to raise in the campaign. The most important concerned dealing with several large tracts of open land on the ward's western boundary—already several large developers were eyeing the properties. One expert had pointed out that if the properties were fully developed, the ward's population could increase by 20 percent. We needed control of zoning at a local level. We also needed to address the racial composition of Morgan Park High School, improve police presence in the ward, and find ways to manage block-by-block the integration of the neighborhoods.

The mayor listened without comment as I raced through my list.

At one point, an aide entered the room, and the mayor waved him off. I did almost all the talking. Finally, he asked if I'd ever had anything to do with any political organization, and I told him no—I knew some of the 19th Ward leaders but only from a distance. He stood up. "You will be fine," he said. The interview was over.

I thanked him and walked toward the door. But I still didn't know where he stood on my issues. So I stopped. "To be frank, I really don't know exactly what you are telling me," I said.

"You have good ideas," he said. "You're going to be just fine."

Hardly anyone in the 19th Ward thought so. I heard the constant refrain: "You don't have a chance. You're up against the 19th Ward." Still, the meeting with Mayor Daley gave me a response for people who said I'd be hamstrung if elected. I'd simply say: "I went over my ideas with the mayor, and he didn't reject them."

A dedicated group of my family, Mairsey's family, and our friends came out to help in the campaign. Almost everyone I had worked with on the police department got involved, including my former commander Fred Rice. Many of my former schoolmates, including 35 members of my eighth-grade class, pitched in. The support was heartening, given that few people in the ward believed it was a winnable election.

The overriding issue I faced was how to maintain a workable mix of Black and white residents—to accommodate and manage integration, to halt so-called white flight. At the time, Blacks made up around 15 percent of the 19th Ward population of around 60,000. (With redistricting, the current population is 51,525.) Most African Americans lived in Morgan Park. Mount Greenwood had almost no Black residents. Neighborhoods directly east and north of the ward, including Washington Heights, Roseland, and West Englewood, had turned almost all Black in the space of two years.

I reasoned that the 19th Ward had a chance to be different for a handful of reasons. For one, the strong housing stock in Beverly/ Morgan Park would be hard to flip quickly. For another, the relative affluence of the residents meant that for many, their homes weren't their prime assets—they wouldn't be as inclined to sell in panic. And I trusted the people. Many of the old-line residents were experienced in the ways of the world—you could easily reason with them, and they formed the foundation of the well-meaning BAPA. The fact that many of the newer residents had young children and had moved in from troubled South Side neighborhoods suggested that they wanted to stay in the city—presumably many of the people who didn't want Black neighbors had already fled Chicago.

Working with neighbors and friends, including African American residents, we honed ideas for stabilization that became elements in my campaign.

- Racial balance in Morgan Park High School. White parents get anxious as the Black student population grows—a significant source of white flight. The area's only public high school, overcrowded Morgan Park, had a student population of around 60 percent Black, 40 percent white. I argued that the Board of Education should establish a quota of students, 50 percent Black, 50 percent white.

- Better police protection. From my years on the force, I knew that the police department used a slow-moving system to assign patrols based on statistical analysis of crime in the area. It relied on six-month increments of crime statistics and didn't respond well to sudden upticks of trouble. I suggested pushing to adopt a more responsive system—at least, in the Beverly/Morgan Park area.

- Crackdown on unscrupulous real estate dealers. Many of my neighbors had already received calls from brokers using scare tactics to urge a quick sale, and storefront real estate offices had opened on 95th Street. BAPA had in place programs to counteract the rumor-mongering, including a hot line. We argued that the effort should be expanded.

- Probably most importantly, we wanted to limit the use of all vacant land in the ward to single-family housing.

The public discussion of race was remarkably candid in that era—at least, in that area of the city. A 1972 *Tribune* article about the future of Beverly/Morgan Park quoted BAPA executive director Philip Dolan: "It is absolutely clear that the community must remain predominantly white, or everybody will run away, the schools will go downhill, crime rates will skyrocket, and the City of Chicago will be nothing more than the haven of the old, the poor, and the Black."

Father Robert E. Mayer, a priest at St. Barnabas, a church in the ward, wrote a long article evaluating Beverly in the Sunday, February 9, 1975, edition of the *Southtown Economist*, the major newspaper covering the South Side and close-in southern suburbs. "The vast majority of whites ... will stay on a block only if the whites clearly remain in the majority in that block," the priest wrote. "Let the percentage turn against the white population, and all but the most liberal white family will pull out. And it is not that the whites feel superior and therefore should be in the majority. It is simply that whites feel more secure with a white majority in a neighborhood and surprisingly enough, so do more and more integrating middle-class Blacks. If there is to be any guarantee, therefore, of stabilized integration at the present time, it must be through control of the ratio of Black to white on individual blocks."

Throughout the campaign, I spoke with similar candor about the situation in the ward. There was enormous public interest. We had at least 15 public meetings, and the halls were packed. I said the same thing everywhere—in the conservative sections of the ward and in the liberal: Beverly and Morgan Park are going to be integrated. If done right over time, the process can be a model for the entire ward all the way to the western boundary at Pulaski Road. If you don't accept that, you should probably look for a house in the suburbs. Some people would yell at me, call me names, but in the end, I think most knew I was speaking the truth.

We opened a storefront campaign office at 103rd and Kedzie, and right away, the organization clamped down on the landlord. He owned a local pub, and waves of inspectors checked out the place.

He told me he hadn't even known I was running against the 19th Ward, but he said don't bother to move the office—the organization didn't worry him.

To devote myself full time to the campaign, I resigned from the police department, which reduced our family income to the small amount I earned as a part-time professor at St. Xavier. I withdrew my pension funds from the police work to help make ends meet. Day after day, I'd go door-to-door, precinct-by-precinct, meeting people and asking for votes. By the end, I had stopped at more than 10,000 residences, though often people weren't home, and I simply left literature. I did that for six months nearly every day.

The race became extraordinarily bitter—the organization resented my opposition, and my campaign was naïve and undisciplined. Many of my supporters and I shared friends with organization leaders who were working hard against me. Fights broke out. At one point, some of my supporters sawed down several billboards put up for Tom Ryan, the organization's candidate. I didn't know about it and had to deal with the media reaction. Meantime, the organization relied on all the old tactics. For example, Ryan's seasoned campaign workers went to nursing homes in the ward and collected absentee ballots after helpfully instructing the old folks to vote for the organization candidate. Some nursing homes voted overwhelmingly for Ryan.

Despite the supposedly non-partisan character of aldermanic elections, the political parties endorse a candidate. Of course, Ryan had the Democratic endorsement. A friend warned that a Republican endorsement would hurt my candidacy, so I didn't appear before the 19th Ward Republicans when they interviewed candidates. The Republicans ended up endorsing a nice woman named Shirley Borhauer, a nurse who brought some civility to the campaign. She later wrote a book about her quixotic battle against the Chicago machine, *Shirley Who?* By her account, it didn't take long to spot the animosity the 19th Ward Democrats held for me. She recalls that on candidates-night gatherings, the organization workers delighted in waiting outside the meeting room until I stood to speak, and then they would noisily enter, moving chairs, causing distractions, generally disrupting my presentation.

The fourth candidate in the race was a good-hearted but oddball electrical contractor named William Stanton, who later garnered a bit of fame by fighting with the state over what to do with his pet skunk named Wishbone. Stanton liked to stand up at candidate meetings and tell how be bribed city inspectors to approve his contracting work. "Money talks, and BS walks," he told a startled woman's civic group.

My campaign was so unschooled in the ways of politics that we were well into the race before many learned that if no candidate won 50 percent of the vote, there would be a runoff between the top two vote-getters. As it turned out, that's what happened. Ryan finished first in the February 25, 1975, election. But Borhauer and Stanton pulled enough votes between them to deny Ryan a majority. He and I would face off in a second round five weeks away.

Throughout the campaign, I was approached by supporters of Singer and Hanrahan, candidates for mayor against Daley, who had set up operations in the ward. Both groups said if I would remain neutral in the mayoral race they would work on my behalf. But from the start I'd made clear that even though I was running against the Democratic organization, I would support Mayor Daley and his programs in the council.

Several times during the election and the runoff, the mayor came to the 19th Ward for a campaign appearance. The Democratic organization threw the first event at the Ridge Country Club, and it produced a big turnout, 4,000 or so people. The mayor spoke and with flourishes introduced a roster of Democrats who shared the stage with him—as the mayor put it, a great congressman, Morgan Murphy; an outstanding state senator, Tom Hynes; a hard-working and popular state representative, Dan Houlihan; a longtime friend who's retiring from the City Council, Tom Fitzpatrick. And so on. But Daley never mentioned my opponent, Tom Ryan. Still, during the close of the runoff, the mayor authorized a piece of campaign literature featuring his photo with Ryan and a quote urging Ryan's election.

As the *Tribune* prepared to make endorsements in the aldermanic runoffs, I went to Tribune Tower for an interview with an editorial writer. The interview seemed to go well, but the newspaper endorsed Ryan, citing his selection by 19th Ward Democrats and his long involvement in community affairs. On April 1, the morning of the election, I was handing out leaflets and shaking hands at a train station when the editorial writer who'd interviewed me stepped up. It turned out he was a resident of the 19th Ward, and he said that he and his wife had voted for me. As for the paper's endorsement? Higher-ups in the editorial department had overruled his choice. I won by a margin of 54 percent to 46 percent.

Afterwards, a staffer for Daley called—the mayor wanted to see me. As I walked into his office at City Hall, he approached with a big smile and an outstretched hand. "I knew you'd do it!" he exclaimed. And then he added something curious: When I ran for sheriff, your Uncle Ed was one of my biggest supporters.

Uncle Ed was my father's older brother, Ed Joyce, who was president of the Bricklayers' Union and had fought a takeover of his local by organized crime (which may have had to do with the tavern shooting I mentioned earlier). In 1946, Richard J. Daley ran for Cook County sheriff and lost, the only election loss of his career. I guess Uncle Ed was an old-school contemporary of the mayor who backed him in that losing cause. ◾

Our neighbors on South Prairie Avenue included Mrs. Alphonse Capone, widow of the infamous gangster, who bought this house in the early 1920s.
Chicago Sun-Times/Daily News Collection, Chicago History Museum

Born in Ireland, grandfather John T. Joyce came to America at 16 and within six years became an integral figure in one of the largest labor movements in Chicago. At his death, the *Chicago Tribune* called him "Father of the Eight Hour Day."

My Uncle John Vaughn worked for the Lion Gas Co., which kept a pair of lions for promotions. Uncle John occasionally got in trouble for walking them around downtown Chicago. Here, he's pictured with my father and two of my cousins.

My father, here with me and my cousin Joyce, followed his own father into a lifetime career in the Amalgamated Meat Cutters union.

St. Sabina Church and its community center were the heart of a South Side neighborhood that fought successfully for orderly integration—until tragedy struck.
Chicago History Museum.

Opposite page: Despite a burly police escort, some protestors pelted Martin Luther King, Jr., with rocks during a 1966 fair-housing march in Marquette Park. King's widow later endorsed Rich Daley for Cook County State's Attorney.
Chicago Sun-Times Collection, Chicago History Museum.

JEREMIAH JOYCE

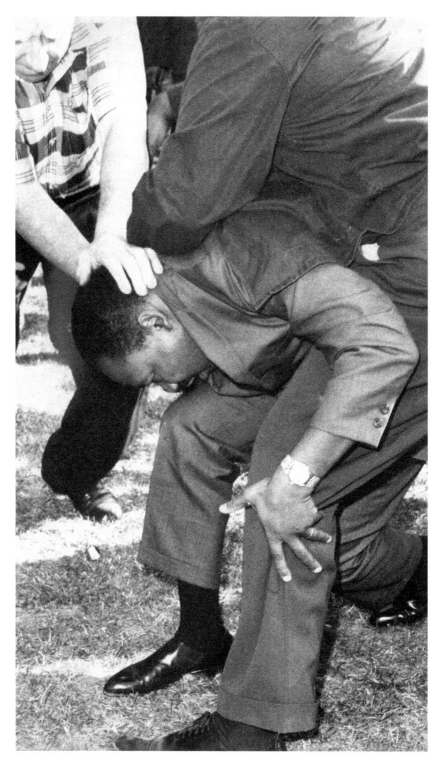

Fred Rice, my commander in Gang Intelligence and a good friend, went on to become Chicago's first permanent African American police superintendent.

Above: Mairsey and I joined the celebration for the promotion of my then sergeant Fred Rice to lieutenant.

Right: Bobby Rush and Fred Hampton held top positions with the Illinois Black Panther Party in the late 1960s. Hampton was killed in a police raid in 1969. Rush has gone on to a long career in politics and remains the only person to defeat Barack Obama in an election. *Chicago Sun-Times, Chicago History Museum*

As a detective in the Gang Intelligence Unit, my job included monitoring efforts by the SDS to join up with the Black Panthers. In this photo taken by the FBI, I'm in the dark T-shirt looking at the camera.

During the Days of Rage strife, I was assigned to join marches (in back, second from right) to keep an eye on the action. Not long after, the Weatherman leaders went underground.

Despite a low turnout of protesters, the Days of Rage street action in Chicago in 1969 led to several hundred arrests, including many young people. One colleague later concluded, "Putting young people in harm's way marked the beginning of the end for Weatherman in Chicago." Working in plain clothes, I'm the fourth from right in this picture. *Photograph by Steve Naegele, ©Steve Naegele*

During the Days of Rage, Richard Elrod (on ground at left), a lawyer for the city, suffered a broken neck in an encounter with a protester. Despite a lifetime of paralysis, he went on to a distinguished career as a sheriff and a judge. *Getty Images*

As part of the Gang Intelligence Unit, my assignments included monitoring the American Nazi Party and leader Frank Collin (pictured here at a 1977 protest). *Chicago Sun-Times Collection, Chicago History Museum*

Before my run for alderman, Mayor Richard J. Daley quietly indicated he supported my agenda. "You'll do fine," he told me, though he endorsed my opponent from the local ward organization.

For five months during my 1974 campaign for 19th Ward alderman, my daily routine sent me door to door.

At the opening of my campaign office for my 1975 run for alderman, my son Jerry Jr. wore a hat that presaged his run for mayor almost half a century later.

My son Kevin found an early interest in politics. We met then President Gerald Ford during his 1976 visit to Beverly.

Patrick Gorman, leader of the Amalgamated Meat Cutters union and one of the most respected labor leaders in the country, was a longtime family friend. He joined my son Jerry and me in my aldermanic office.

Undefeated—on the field: Our strong 1976 city council softball team was captained by Ed Vrdolyak (far right, standing). I'm second from left.

Sargent Shriver had strong Chicago roots and I helped put together an event for him as he vied for the 1976 Democratic presidential nomination. In the end, his candidacy never caught on.

As I watched Ted Kennedy snub Jimmy Carter on the dais at the Democratic Convention in New York City in 1980, I knew Carter had a hard row ahead.

I admired President Jimmy Carter, here in the White House with Mairsey and me, as an honorable man and honest politician. He and his team reached out during the Byrne Administration to try to understand the battling in Chicago politics.

Best wishes to
Mairsey and Jerry Joyce
Jimmy Carter

Contrast in styles: The intense Jane Byrne suffered far more downs than ups as mayor...

... and carried a somewhat confounding antagonism toward Rich Daley—here having a light moment with a photo op—whose father had helped ignite her political career.

JEREMIAH JOYCE

Harold Washington's inauguration as mayor in 1983 pushed a downcast
Jane Byrne out of office and opened a dramatic change in Chicago politics.
Chicago Sun-Times Collection/Chicago History Museum

The pundits and other top Democrats thought Adlai Stevenson III didn't have a
prayer in his 1982 run for governor, but in my own campaign for state senator,
I saw signs that he could win. The day before the election, Adlai's wife, Nancy,
and I hit the trail for him.

Stevenson lost the 1982 race, the closest in Illinois gubernatorial history. He lost again in 1986 in an election fiasco, depriving the Democratic Party of a promising presidential candidate. *Barry Jarvien/Chicago Sun-Times*

The state senate floor in Springfield could be a scene of lively debate and often drew an audience of visitors in the balcony.

As Continental Bank teetered in 1984, I disagreed with my senate colleague Vince Demuzio (shown here) and opposed a distressed sale of the bank.

In the 1986 Democratic primary race for lieutenant governor, I advised my senate friend George Sangmeister (talking to me) to challenge the petitions of the competing LaRouche candidate. Democratic leaders refused, precipitating an election disaster.

In Springfield, Dawn Clark Netsch was one of my close colleagues, and we worked together often on legislation. Running for governor in 1994, she made the right policy choice by calling for a rise in the income tax to fund education, but it doomed her with voters.

Richard M. Daley came into the mayor's office with a vision for development and understood the importance of universities and hospitals to the future of Chicago. *Chicago Sun-Times Collection, Chicago History Museum*

Geraldine Ferraro helped Dan Rostenkowski win his 1994 primary by campaigning in the Italian sections of the district. But a looming prosecution cost him the general election, depriving the city of a wonderful resource who had consistently delivered for the people of Chicago. *AP Photo Archives*

Mairsey's mother, Mary Carey (right), offered advice to then Senator Obama at one of our St. Patrick's Day parties.

During Barack Obama's losing 2000 run for congress against Bobby Rush, Nineteenth Ward Alderman Ginger Rugai coordinated a strong showing for Obama in the southwest corner of the district. Several years later, the U.S. senator spoke up for Rugai.

With the nonsensical Swift Boat attacks on John Kerry during his 2004 run for president, I advised the campaign to counter by naming Bob Kerrey (left), another Vietnam vet, as his running mate. But Kerry ended up choosing John Edwards. *Avalon.red*

Opposite page, bottom: In the crowded 2019 mayoral race, Jerry made a credible showing, drawing particularly well in wards on the Southwest and Northwest Sides. However, he didn't make the runoff, eventually won by Lori Lightfoot.

Over the years, I have remained close to my friends from grade school at St. Sabina, and they actively helped in my campaigns. Before the pandemic, hardly a month passed when we didn't get together.

Cardinal Francis George, the archbishop of Chicago from 1997 to 2014, had a long and close relationship with my family. His cousin was married to my sister Maureen. In 2009, he presented a service award to my son Kevin (to the cardinal's immediate right) and much of the family attended the ceremony.

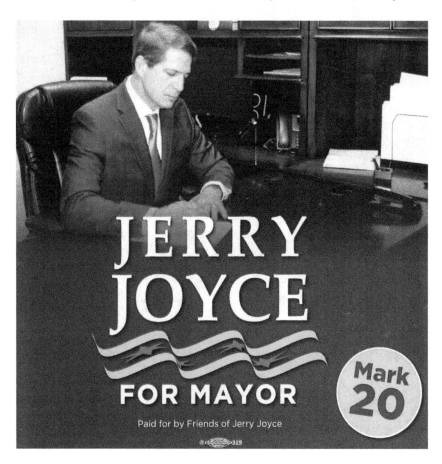

With Mairsey and the boys, from left, Michael, Dan, Kevin and Jerry, around 1979.

The whole Joyce family at the time (around 2013), with Mairsey and me, our four sons, and their families.

Myself with Muhammad Ali and our grandson Jake.

The latest additions (since the group photo): Three of Kevin's daughters.

8

"There is what th papers call a movement on fut to de'crate trees with aldermen, an tis wan that ought to be encouraged."

Finley Peter Dunne's Mr. Dooley

On the day I was sworn in as a Chicago alderman, TV crews, despite our discouragement, followed Mairsey, the four boys, and me from our home to the council chambers—the media's makings of a human-interest story on a fresh political face. One of my newly elected council colleagues, Dick Mell, later complained that I had monopolized the spotlight. Mell went on to a checkered career in Chicago politics, punctuated by his orchestration of the election as Illinois governor of his son-in-law, Rod Blagojevich.

This was my first visit to the chambers of the City Council, located on the second floor of the stolid, block-square 1911 building that is Chicago's City Hall. At council meetings, Mayor Daley presided from a raised platform at the front of the room. Desks for the alderman stood in three semicircular rows facing the front. They were arranged in numerical order by ward—from the 1st Ward, long the domain of Fred Roti, said to be the Outfit's man on the council, through the 50th, home of the outspoken Bernie Stone, who would go on to serve in the council for more than three decades.

With a handful of exceptions—the most notable being Dick Simpson and Marty Oberman, both of whom served on the council with me—almost all the aldermen lined up with Mayor Daley. In fact, in the hurly-burly of council activity, members would sometimes lose track of the vote being taken. In those instances, they would simply look to see how Roti voted. The roll call went by ward, so he was always the first called and he always knew what the mayor wanted. The machine ruled with an iron hand through Tom Donovan, the mayor's chief aide, and the council floor leaders, Michael Bilandic and Wilson Frost. If you pushed back against the script that had been worked out, the leaders would let you know.

It's a myth, however, that the administration would deny basic city services to the ward of the defiant alderman. After all, if residents of a ward lacked services, they wouldn't just blame the alderman— they'd blame the mayor, too. The pressure, if it came, would be more subtle. A permit not denied, but delayed. In instances where official discretion came into play, the discretion would usually be exercised against the defiant alderman. In those looser patronage days, jobs could be an issue.

Even with the support of Mayor Daley, my disagreements with some of the leaders of the 19th Ward Democratic organization persisted. In fact, a schism continued throughout most of my term as alderman. Though I eventually joined up halfheartedly, resentful precinct captains wouldn't forget. The *Southtown Economist* reported: "A local party leader once summed up the situation by calling Joyce an 'embarrassment' to the organization. He and others have expressed the gripe that Joyce often placed working for the ward ahead of strict party loyalty." In the Black neighborhoods on the east side of the ward, machine operatives painted me as a racist former cop. In the white precincts, they called me an integrationist—which, in fact, I was. They simply used my direct language, hoping to tap a bigoted or at least anxious streak in my constituents.

Not every member of the organization tried to thwart me. The long-time superintendent of Streets and Sanitation in the 19th Ward,

Edward Walsh, had worked hard against me in the campaign. Afterwards, though, he came to me and said he'd continue to give the ward what it needed, and he was true to his word. A few years later, Mayor Jane Byrne made him pay for his integrity.

Over time, I was able to capitalize on my experience, arranging to have three extra cars assigned to patrol the ward and place mounted police near the train stations at peak commute times. Mayor Byrne undid both those initiatives.

My home phone was listed, and I was readily accessible to residents. Once during a Mother's Day dinner at our house, a man rang the bell, and when I opened the door, he threw a tire into the living room. He was mad because he'd hit a pothole that had dented his rims.

In Chicago, an alderman is viewed as the person responsible for overseeing basic city services. The 19th Ward took pride in this, and two women who worked in my office became very efficient at continuing this tradition, making sure the streets were plowed, the garbage picked up, and other day-to-day essentials of healthy neighborhoods were being attended to. But basic local services weren't my primary focus. Rather, I devoted most of my office to larger undertakings that could have an impact on the economy and quality of life in the 19th Ward.

One of the first and hardest issues was how to handle Morgan Park High School, in those days the only public high school in the ward. (There were three Catholic high schools—Marist, Mother McAuley, and Brother Rice—and one private school, Morgan Park Academy.) Morgan Park High had been integrated for years, but it had an unfortunate history of racial antagonism. In 1934, white students went on strike to protest overcrowding and to insist that students at the school be segregated. A decade later during another disturbance, Frank Sinatra is said to have come to the school and talked to the white students about the importance of integration.

As alderman, I had no legal control over the schools, but I worked with the PTA and other school groups to come up with a plan to reduce the size of Morgan Park High and thereby create an even mix of white and Black students. I lobbied for a quota system with Mayor Daley, the Board of Education, and the parents of all students. The school was badly over capacity—built for 2,700 students, it had around 3,400 enrolled by 1975. In a school district that was 70 percent white, Morgan Park High was about 60 percent Black. History told a grim story of schools like that in Chicago and elsewhere: When the student population reached a tipping point of Black enrollment, white students left, and the quality of the education dropped. On the other hand, urban schools that maintained a rough racial balance often thrived. The issue wasn't simply about the quality of education. As everyone knew, the schools helped set the future of the neighborhood—when they turned predominately Black, white families tended to move out.

Mayor Daley hated quotas and thought they were un-American, but I requested a meeting with him to explain how a quota system could be crucial for Morgan Park High School. He gave his tacit approval and arranged for me to meet with one Board of Education member, Margaret Wild, who outspokenly supported the plan. The board eventually agreed with her, and a quota plan was instituted at Morgan Park.

To accommodate the change, new African American students were chosen by lottery— the brunt of this was somewhat lessened by the fact that a brand new public high school was being opened on the edge of Morgan Park's school boundaries.

Still, explaining to some Black parents why their children couldn't enroll at Morgan Park was one of the hardest tasks of my four years as alderman. These were parents who cared passionately about education, and a number of the families had moved to the neighborhood to take advantage of the schools. But the harsh equation called for some to sacrifice so a greater number of students—both Black and white—could benefit. Though the quota system made many people uncomfortable, a large number of experts and observers thought it was the most effective way to deal with the pressing crisis. The Washington writer Sanford Unger, for example, wrote favorably about the Morgan Park plan in *The Atlantic Monthly*.

A handful of parents sued, claiming the plan was discriminatory and unconstitutional. Judge Hubert Will of the federal district court ordered the school board to offer to bus any student denied admission to a predominantly white school on the North Side. In the fall of 1977, once the busing program was in place, the judge dismissed the suit, calling the quota system "a very interesting sociological experiment." In court, the judge remarked that during the time his four children attended Hyde Park High School, the school had gone from 10 percent Black to 80 percent Black. The *Beverly Review* reported, "He said he didn't intend the damn 'tipping' process to overtake Morgan Park. The quota system eventually survived all the way to the U.S. Supreme Court.

Morgan Park High School maintained an even racial balance until the early 1980s, when Mayor Byrne's Board of Education knocked out the quotas at Morgan Park and Gage Park, and both schools quickly became virtually all Black. Fortunately, by then, some of the other initiatives to stabilize the ward were underway. Incidentally, NASA astronaut Mae Jemison graduated from Morgan Park High in 1973 and became the first African American woman to travel in space in 1992.

Well before I was on the scene, the Beverly Area Planning Association and other neighborhood groups and individuals had been working to protect buildings in the ward, some of them designed by acclaimed architects such as Frank Lloyd Wright, Daniel Burnham, and Howard Van Doren Shaw. In 1976, the National Park Service placed the Ridge Historic District, an elevated tract that ran down the heart of Beverly/Morgan Park, on the National Register of Historic Places. (The Ridge District also contains the highest point in the city, a whopping 665 feet above sea level, at 95th and Western). Encompassing almost 3,000 homes, the district is among the largest urban areas selected for the Register, according to BAPA. The designation places severe restraints on any changes to structures within the district—which means virtually eliminating the risk of the wrecking ball wielded by ambitious developers.

I heartily endorsed the expansion of landmark status. The advantage was obvious—to make our area financially more attractive and enhance the prestige of the entire community. Later, when I was in the Senate, I oversaw passage of the most difficult bill I ever sponsored. It provided for a 10-year tax freeze on any residential property located in a designated historical district, which, with the Ridge Historical District, included a large section of the 19th Ward. I bargained long and hard with Governor Thompson to get him to agree to sign the bill. The legislation eventually fell victim to the Byrne-Daley political fight of the 1980s. She threatened to use her power to undo the law, and eventually that's what she did. Years later, at a cordial lunch after she was out of office, she told me she regretted what she'd done—she had so many friends in Beverly.

As an alderman, I worked with local businesses to revive and stabilize the commercial strips along 95th Street and down Western Avenue, which were losing customers to new shopping malls outside the ward. Nothing in the 19th Ward comes easily, however, and when I introduced a plan to rezone a section of Western Avenue to keep out tawdry businesses such as porn shops, pool halls, and massage parlors, a group of political opponents and business interests circulated rumors that I owned properties in the affected area—that I was only trying to protect my own assets. The *Southtown Economist* printed the charges and later devoted considerable efforts to investigating them. In a long front-page Sunday article and a subsequent editorial, the paper found the rumors false and printed an apology.

Throughout my term as alderman, we monitored all vacant or significant properties that were changing hands—we didn't want questionable operators to get a foothold in the ward. One of our allies in this regard was the late Arthur Rubloff, the celebrated Chicago developer often credited as the father of the retail-rich Magnificent Mile on North Michigan Avenue. Rubloff didn't live in the 19th Ward, but shortly after World War II, he and 19th Ward resident and drugstore tycoon Charles Walgreen built one of the nation's first shopping centers, Evergreen Plaza, at 95th and Western.

Rubloff owned other businesses in the ward, and several of his employees lived in the area. I could call him when we had a problem, and he'd usually step in. Once, a long-established church was leaving the area and planned to sell its facility. We weren't confident in the buyers, so Rubloff acquired the property and donated it for a youth center. Another time, a longtime funeral home wanted to sell its business to a fly-by-night operation. Again, the sale seemed risky for the neighborhood, so I called Rubloff. He bought the funeral home, and a few years later, the city converted it to a branch library.

By 1976, the 19th Ward had several parcels of large, vacant acreage that had dramatically increased in value, in part because the city had started to enforce its employee residency rule and in part because of the potential to rezone to a higher density. The most contentious battle broke out over a development contiguous to St. Xavier University, where I was teaching. One group wanted to place a senior citizen high-rise there, though the neighborhood consisted of one-story, single-family homes. The neighbors strongly opposed the project, even after the developer dropped the height from 14 stories to eight.

St. Xavier supported the development, but I felt the structure was incompatible with the immediate community. I wanted to limit an influx of new housing units—thereby helping to support the price of existing houses and apartments. The City Council eventually agreed with me and denied the zoning change.

The most difficult and long-running land-use conflict involved plans for a 450-unit apartment complex called University Square that a powerful and somewhat shady political operator named Bernard Neistein wanted to put onto a 12.5-acre site on the western edge of Mount Greenwood. Because development proposals like this involved millions of dollars, the zoning lawyers and their clients would not quietly retreat. Frequently, they would file a lawsuit, and the one filed in this case bounced around for years and eventually resulted in my break with the administration of Mayor Bilandic.

One of the happiest outcomes of our development battles came after I'd moved to the state Senate. From the moment I became alderman, the question persisted of what to do with Chicago's last farm, 72 acres owned by the Board of Education along Pulaski Road. For decades, the board had been leasing the land to a farmer named Peter Ouwenga, who grew tomatoes, corn, peppers, and other vegetables and operated a farm stand on 111th Street. Ouwenga was getting close to retirement, the school board needed money, and a multitude of developers were eyeing the property with dollar signs in their eyes. The Board of Education regularly talked to developers and asked my advice about acceptable uses for the land. My response was single-family residences only.

Over a number of years, I sought possible solutions. As a senator, I had fruitful discussions with the University of Illinois about an agricultural extension on the site, and I made some good progress toward obtaining state revenues. I even reached out to an old acquaintance, Dr. Edward Teller, the famed physicist, to see if Argonne Labs might be interested. In the midst of this in 1985, the Board of Education, prodded by Chicago Board of Trade President Tom Donovan (Mayor Daley's former aide), Alderman Mike Sheahan, and some long-term residents, agreed to open a high school for agricultural sciences on the site. The school reportedly was only the second high school in the country devoted to preparing students for careers in agriculture, from farming to trading in commodities. The well-regarded facility continues to thrive today. It took a decade, but we outlasted the real estate developers.

Sometimes my opposition to development projects opened me to charges of being a racist, working to prevent African Americans from moving into the ward. In fact, a number of my initiatives could be read two conflicting ways—to keep Black people out or to maintain the historical integrity of the neighborhoods while they underwent orderly integration. Several times I was hit with a civil rights suit claiming discrimination, usually based on the denial of a building permit. None of the suits succeeded. My intention was to keep up the high standards of the area, for both commercial and residential properties, and I remained active in my efforts to promote peaceful integration. Working with BAPA, my aide (and future alderman) Ginger Rugai focused on assisting people interested in 19th Ward neighborhoods with finding good homes. The service was available to anyone, but African Americans were its principal clients. When a Black family moved in, we would greet them and ask them to let us know if they had any troubles with anyone or if they needed anything from the city.

The neighborhoods continued to integrate—by 1980, according to one estimate, the Black population of Beverly/Morgan Park had reached 20 percent, most of the growth coming in the last five years. But the process moved in an orderly way. By BAPA's account, the new Black families were coming into neighborhoods in a "salt-and-pepper" fashion, occupying a few houses on a block, in contrast to the pattern elsewhere on the South Side, where entire blocks turned around. In all, we ended up having relatively few unpleasant incidents.

During my first two years or so of running for alderman and serving on the council, I had around a dozen private meetings with Mayor Daley, sometimes to discuss particular issues, sometimes simply to talk about how things were going in the 19th Ward. At the conclusion of some of these meetings, he would encourage me to speak up in the council, but I remained largely silent throughout most of his term. Once, shortly after I had been elected, he asked if I wanted to consider becoming committeeman for the 19th Ward, a party post in the local Democrat organization. I told him no, because I didn't envisage a political career, and I think that surprised him a bit.

I don't believe I knew Mayor Daley, and I don't think any of my council contemporaries did either, even if they claimed to. Only his family knew him, and maybe a few pals left over from the old days and some long-time political allies—Vito Marzullo, Dan Rostenkowski, not many more. All the people who worked for him at City Hall were employees—he made sure they were well treated, and they loved him, but to him they were first and foremost workers for the City of Chicago. On the other hand, he wouldn't have fashioned being called a boss, the title of Mike Royko's celebrated biography. He would call himself a political leader, and he brought an incredible apprenticeship to that title.

Early on, he worked as a clerk in the City Council, where he observed city government firsthand. Then he served in both branches of the state Legislature, where he had an intimate view of Illinois government. Next he worked as Governor Adlai Stevenson's revenue chief, gaining an expertise on government budgets. He headed up the Cook County Democrats and served as county clerk, a role that helped him master the complicated relationship between Cook County and Chicago. Over time, he developed a firm though rarely spoken theory of Chicago government—let some other entity pay, whether it be the state, the county, a regional body, or the federal government.

During the time I served in the council under him, I think I came to understand how he viewed council members, how he evaluated and categorized the aldermen he knew.

If you were there to move up in politics and promote yourself, that would be okay—ambition was good. If you were there to make money for yourself through law, real estate, or insurance, that was okay, too—just don't break the law. If you were just along for the ride, the system could accommodate that, also—it was all up to the voters of the wards.

I was in my ward office on December 20, 1976, when a fireman phoned to report an emergency call had just come in, and it might involve the mayor. Ten minutes later, the phone calls flooded my office. The mayor had been stricken with a heart attack at his doctor's office. I turned on the TV, and soon reporters broke in with the news: Mayor Daley was dead.

It came as a blow to many of us who had worked with him and an emotional blow to the city—he'd been mayor for 21 years. The council was basically unprepared for his death; the law of succession in those days was unclear. Wilson Frost, a Black South Sider who had been Daley's hand-picked president pro tempore of the council, argued that under the city charter he should serve as acting mayor until a special election could be held to fill out the final two years of Daley's term. Frost immediately drew support from Black colleagues on the council (in those days, 14 of the 50 alderman were African American) and from assorted leaders in the Black community, including Congressman Ralph Metcalfe, state representative Harold Washington, and Jesse Jackson, the founder of Operation Push. Meanwhile, several top Daley loyalists, including corporation counsel William Quinlan, insisted that the law didn't provide for an acting mayor.

After several days of bickering and meetings, the council's most ambitious leaders masterminded a compromise: Frost would move up to the powerful post of chairman of the council's finance committee, and Michael Bilandic, from Daley's own 11th Ward, would become acting mayor. One key to the deal was Bilandic's promise that he wouldn't run for mayor in the special election in six months—a promise that no doubt cheered other prospective candidates. Another key to the deal was that any prior agreements with Richard J. Daley would be kept. (Interestingly, in a 2010 interview for the Chicago History Museum, Frost said that while the situation was in limbo, he met with Tom Donovan, William Quinlan, and the president of the First National Bank, among other city leaders, and they talked of a deep concern that the city's finances could be jeopardized by a prolonged battle over who would become acting mayor. Frost said he agreed to withdraw for the best interests of the city.) The council overwhelmingly endorsed the deal, but the dispute served as an ominous harbinger of conflicts to come.

Years later, I was told by someone who knew that if Mayor Daley had made a long list of those qualified or likely to succeed him, Bilandic's name would not have been on it.

Only once did I get involved in a meeting of the inner circle deciding how the succession would go down. I was called into a gathering that included Donovan, Bilandic, Roti, and a few other aldermen, including Edward Vrdolyak, an ambitious lawyer from the 10th Ward on the city's far southeast side. They were putting the final touches on Bilandic's ascension, and I just listened. But I got a telling insight of the real power hierarchy as the meeting broke up and the participants prepared to face the gaggle of reporters: Tom Donovan stepped in front of the others and grabbed Bilandic by the back of his suit, pushing him out first.

Anyone who followed a mayor like Richard Daley would suffer by comparison, and the jockeying after the mayor's death suggested that ambitions would likely rattle the machine. Within two months of Bilandic's rise, I knew he was in trouble. Under Mayor Daley, I'd been able to get almost anything done for the ward. The lines of authority were relatively straight.

Bilandic was a genial, smart, and somewhat simple man, but when he became mayor, he operated with an air of vagueness that made him particularly hard to deal with. Talking with him now was very difficult. I would present him with an issue, and he would respond in a soft voice, "Oh, yes, you have lots to do."

He was surrounded by a tight group of advisors and supporters, some involved in real estate matters in the 19th Ward, and soon they figured in the lawsuit between the city and the University Square project, which was backed by the well-connected lawyer Bernard Neistein. After I filed to intervene in the lawsuit as an interested party, the city's lawyer, William Quinlan, asked me to withdraw. He told me the city would strongly oppose the multi-unit apartment building and my appearance might confuse the matter. Truth was,

Quinlan and Bilandic never meant to oppose the developer. They had intentionally misled me, and that obliterated any trust I had in the new mayor. (After Bilandic's mayoral defeat, he joined Neistein's law firm.) Following some extraordinary legal procedures, I ultimately did intervene and prevented the development from going forward. Ultimately, Jane Byrne, at my request, ended the project—a positive occurrence before our political parting of the ways.

What I found most disappointing about all of this was that nearly a year before, in a long lunch with then Alderman Bilandic, I had explained my theory and strategy for maintaining my ward as a desirable and integrated community.

Once Bilandic sat down in the mayor's chair, it didn't take him long to renege on his promise not to run in the special election. The Democrats slated him, and he won easily in an April primary and again in the June general election. But his honeymoon with voters and even with some of his Democratic colleagues didn't last long. It was clear he didn't have a strong grip on the wheel, and the unity in the council started to crumble. I joined a group of around 10 aldermen— dubbed the Reluctant Rebels—who challenged administration policies, particularly in matters of education policy and the budget. Most importantly, we backed the right of the aldermen to get notice of applications for building permits three days before the permit was issued. On this question, we succeeded, though the City Hall press failed to report it.

Over the years, the Chicago City Council has earned an unhappy reputation as a fount of public corruption. The story goes far back, but has hardly abated. One paper issued in 2012 by the University of Illinois at Chicago reported that since 1973, 31 aldermen had been convicted of one corruption offense or another—a figure that represented almost a third of the aldermen who had served over that time. None of my fellow aldermen were charged with any wrongdoing during the time I served in the council. At one point, Jane Byrne, then consumer sales commissioner, claimed Bilandic had participated in a scheme to fix a taxi fare increase. Bilandic later passed a lie detector exam on the claim, and the accusation went nowhere. The dispute led to Jane Byrne being fired, however, which led to Jane Byrne running for mayor—and becoming the best-known mayor of her time. Corruption of any sort is disturbing, but during my term, I didn't see evidence of dishonesty by my colleagues. (Later, some of the men who served with me on the council did indeed run afoul of the law.)

The only time someone approached me about what might have been construed as a bribe involved a highly regarded presidential advisor who was representing a proposed development in the 19th Ward. He talked vaguely about offering the use of a Florida condominium if I would support the project. I immediately declined, and I later somewhat uncomfortably took to the microphones in the council chambers and revealed what I deemed the impropriety of his conversation. That disclosure ensured the defeat of the project.

In Illinois, news stories to the contrary, it is acceptable and legal for a committeeman to ask a resident or a businessman to make a donation to the ward organization or to buy an ad in the organization's ad book. But you cannot require a campaign donation in exchange for a government job. That being said, I believe patronage has a place in politics. If an elected official knows someone who is capable and needs a job and one is available, why not hire him or her? After all, if the employee slacks off, the elected official may be better positioned to tell the employee to shape up. The problem comes when patronage is abused—and incompetents get the job.

After Bilandic became mayor, I grew increasingly worried that the city that claimed to work didn't. One obvious example: I saw that the city was having problems in the winter of 1977-1978 with snow removal—the trucks weren't getting out; too many streets remained unplowed for too long. This bordered on disaster—for the city, for a mayor, or for an alderman. My colleague William Lipinski, alderman of the 23rd Ward, which encompasses Midway Airport, noticed the same thing. We warned the mayor's aides, but they just passed us off, insisting that they had the situation under control. So Lipinski and I decided that we would acquire or borrow trucks and plows, hire help, and clear our own streets. We'd worked it all out: We could buy the Park District's used equipment from a company in Elmhurst, and Lipinski had mechanics in his community who could keep the machines running. If necessary, we could hold fundraisers to help with the purchase price. Everything was set, and then Bilandic got wind of the plan. His commissioners raised a number of issues, including our lack of insurance. They threatened to seize any equipment we put on the street, and we dropped the plan. The next winter, the snow fell and fell, burying Bilandic. Lipinski later went into Congress and ultimately became a power on transportation matters.

I knew Jane Byrne when she was Mayor Daley's commissioner of consumer sales, and I liked her. Several times I went to her with ward issues, and she was always responsive. But she seemed to have a penchant for making political enemies. Perhaps it was her blunt manner. For some reason I've never established, two of the most prominent aldermen, Ed Burke and Edward Vrdolyak, despised her. As we'd gather for council meetings, she'd be sitting in the front row as part of the mayor's cabinet, and Burke and Vrdolyak would stand close by and speak insultingly of her at a volume she could hear. In any case, she soon clashed with Mayor Bilandic, and five months after he fired her, she announced she was running for mayor, promising to oust "a cabal of evil men [that] has fastened onto the government of the City of Chicago."

In December 1978, the Democrats nominated Bilandic, and no one doubted that he'd win handily. By then, though, I was so fed up with him over the University Square lawsuit that I started telling friends and some colleagues that I was going to vote for Byrne. When the regular Democrats learned of my talk, they asked if I could tone it down. Still, I told friends and supporters they should vote for whomever they wanted; I was voting for Byrne, even though I thought she had no chance of winning.

Then the furious one-two punch of snowstorms and severe cold hit Chicago in the weeks before the February 1979 primary. As Lipinski and I had anticipated, the city responded ineptly. Worse, as the public's mood turned from collegial to sullen, Bilandic kept announcing breakthroughs on clearing the streets, only to be contradicted immediately by news crews whose films told a far different story. The machine's grip on Black voters then slipped badly when the Chicago Transit Authority—desperate to keep up service—ordered some train lines to skip underused stations in Africa American neighborhoods, leaving riders stranded.

Byrne's upset triumph in the Democratic primary arguably dealt a mortal blow to the staggering machine, and she coasted into City Hall with an easy victory in the general election. I was out of the council by then and commuting to Springfield as a new state senator. But my dealings with Jane Byrne were far from over. ◼

9

"Richard M. Daley is a person of great integrity."

Coretta Scott King, endorsement in 1980 state's attorney race

~~~~~~

By early fall 1977, I had decided to leave politics. In three years, we had created a solid network in the ward that involved hundreds of talented and willing residents. Now all applications for liquor licenses, building permits, and rezoning had to be approved by local resident committees. The large community organizations, the Beverly Area Planning Association and the two large Mount Greenwood community organizations, had enlisted an influx of new members and were involved in numerous community activities.

Senator Tom Hynes, now the president of the state Senate, and Representative Dan Houlihan had crafted a solution to the flooded street problem, which had long plagued Mount Greenwood. The PTAs at our local schools were energized, and Morgan Park High was creating a curriculum to attract parochial grade-school graduates, a project supported by the construction of a Catholic Youth Ministry adjacent to the high school campus.

Just before I took office, the local police station had been reopened, and I had arranged to add three patrol cars to the beat. We had instituted an evening community watch program manned by over a hundred volunteers, many of whom were off-duty police officers.

The leaders of the Catholic and Protestant churches were meeting regularly to discuss 19th Ward matters. And, importantly, the two women staffing the alderman's office were among the best in the city. So things were in good shape.

Overall, I thought the ward was well positioned to remain a vital, thriving integrated community.

The other reason for moving on was the realization that it was just a matter of time before I would be at odds with Mayor Bilandic. In a recent meeting with the mayor and Planning Commissioner Lewis Hill, I tried to explain a matter about which they had no knowledge. Mayor Daley and I had discussed a project to widen 95th Street, where businesses were suffering from suburban competition, and relocate viable stores from the north side of the street to available properties on the south side. We had plans and a mockup, but Commissioner Hill interrupted my presentation with the comment, "Mayor Daley is no longer with us." That ended the discussion right there.

I felt that out of office I could retain a voice on issues that affected the ward. I also knew that I had the political leverage and relationships to choose my successor, and the person I had in mind would be well received. Everyone who knew Mike Sheahan liked him. He was a teacher, coach, and Chicago Police youth officer. He'd been recommended to me by his father, Joe Sheahan, a respected ex-policeman, shortly before he died.

But before I announced my plans, Tom Hynes decided to run for assessor, and the local Democratic organization asked me to run for Hynes' Senate seat in the November 1978 election. Given my history, I must have been a painful choice for some members of the organization, but a number of them wanted to block State Representative Emil Jones, a savvy, African American politician, who had his eye on the Senate seat. Jones had recently been hostile to the 19th Ward, particularly on racial issues—among other things, he led the fight against quotas at Morgan Park High School. Still, Jones could arguably claim a right to the Democratic endorsement. He had strong party credentials—he'd been working for the machine for years, and his father had been a precinct captain in the 19th Ward. What's more, the Senate district at the time (the 28th) was moving toward majority Black, encompassing a section of southwest Chicago, including several wards (among them, the 19th and Jones's ward, the 34th) and a handful of contiguous suburban towns, including Blue Island and Oak Lawn.

When Hynes approached me about running, I didn't know that Jones was interested. But at the slating meeting at Graver Park, after I'd given my presentation to the packed audience, I asked Jones if he wanted to make the case for himself. He didn't come up, and I was tapped. (If it had come to that, I could have defeated Jones in a primary because of the size of my turnout, but I probably would have stepped aside to avoid the racial antagonisms.)

The machine's bypassing of Jones generated some resentment. Robert McClory, the St. Sabina priest who had counseled Mairsey and me at our Cana Conference before our marriage, had since left the priesthood and married the principal of St. Sabina school, an event that caused considerable discussion. He later became a reporter. In an article for the venerable African American newspaper *The Chicago Defender*, McClory charged that the Democratic Party had denied Jones a slating that rightfully belonged to a Black person. (If resentment lingered among African American voters, it wasn't reflected in the November election.)

I didn't face a challenge in the primary, and in the general election, my Republican opponent was a businessman named Gerald Maher. The campaign turned ugly. Someone from the Maher camp floated a rumor that if I won the Senate seat, I would promptly resign, thus allowing the machine to handpick a senator. Then, according to the rumor, I would run for re-election as alderman. The timing of the elections made the scenario possible—the state Senate election would be held in November, and the city aldermanic election the following spring. But the idea never crossed my mind. The rumor reached the *Southtown Economist*, and the paper ran a long story about me and my denial. But Maher's campaign edited the article selectively to produce a flyer that made it appear that I indeed intended to resign. The newspaper reacted furiously ("We are angry. We have been used and abused....."), and Maher didn't help his case by waffling about his role in the matter when confronted by news reporters.

I won the election handily that fall. In virtually all my other campaigns over almost two decades, I eventually became friends with my opponent. But not so with Maher.

That January, though my aldermanic term still had a few months to run, I headed to Springfield, where the state General Assembly meets on an intermittent schedule for the first half of each year. For the first session, I stayed in a hotel. Later, I stayed in an apartment with several colleagues, including Rich Daley. During my 14 years as a senator, I usually arranged to take at least one of my sons to Springfield with me. They would stay with me in the apartment and hang out on the Senate floor. They could usually follow what was going on—sometimes they would tell *me* what was going on. Their teachers never objected. Like Mairsey and I, they thought the experience counted toward a good education.

As I recall, a senator's salary when I started was about $26,000 per year, plus a small per diem. You could take the train to Springfield or fly, but I usually drove. My occasional flights ended after I returned to Chicago once with six or so other legislators in a small plane. In those days, we had a choice to fly into either Midway Airport or Meigs Field, the tiny airport on the lakefront, which was convenient but offered a somewhat harrowing landing. The weather was rough that day, and the pilot asked us to choose which airport. My colleagues voted Meigs, and as the ride got rougher, I vowed never to take that flight again. Thereafter, I drove.

I assumed that I would serve out my four-year Senate term and then leave politics. At almost the same time I joined the Senate, I joined the Board of Trade. Some of my friends who were traders introduced me to Fred Brzozowski, the head of Chicago Grain and Financial Futures, one of the biggest operators at the board. (He was also a part-owner of the Chicago White Sox.) Brzozowski helped train me and signed the note for my purchase of a board seat. For a few months in 1979, I spent several days a week in the bond pit, alternating my time with the Senate sessions.

It took me a while to adjust to the style of the Senate. For a legislator, the emphasis is on issues, not service to the neighborhoods, a prime function of an alderman. And compared to an alderman, a senator has much less contact with constituents. Many of the measures that come up will have little or no impact on the people at home. In the city, at least under Mayor Daley, the votes were straightforward, though occasionally some horse-trading behind the scenes was possible. The Senate floor, in contrast, was a venue for speechifying and endless debate. Work that could have been accomplished in four weeks stretched out over six months or more.

With 59 senators, it took 30 to pass a bill. The Democrats held a 32-27 advantage when I arrived, though some of those 32—including me—had an independent tilt. (The House—in those days with 177 members—held an even narrower Democratic majority.) Just after I arrived, we elected the Oak Park Democrat Philip Rock Senate president, and he served in the post for my entire 14 years in the General Assembly. For the previous few years, the real power had been vested in Rich Daley, who controlled a bloc of a dozen or so Chicago senators, some of whom worked for the city. The old machine still had influence, but its loyalties were fracturing.

Shortly after I went to Springfield, the *Southtown Economist* spoke with me for a story on moving from the City Council to the Senate. In the course of the interview, I suggested that the new mayor, Jane Byrne, offered the promise of more openness in City Hall. Within months, that compliment washed away, as I was swept into one of the most bitter political feuds in Chicago history.

Jane Byrne grew up on the North Side of Chicago. As a young widow—her first husband, a Marine pilot, died in a plane crash—she joined the 1960 Kennedy presidential campaign, where she met

Richard J. Daley. He admired her spunk and intelligence and hired her as one of the few women in his administration. She professed undying loyalty to the Daley family, so the origins of her war with the mayor's oldest son are somewhat unclear.

Rich Daley had backed Bilandic against Byrne in the mayoral primary, though without great enthusiasm—he thought Bilandic should have followed his advice and asked the governor to call out the National Guard during the snow emergency. After Byrne won the primary, Daley led the resolution among regular Democrats unanimously backing her in the general election. But given Daley's name and his power base in the 11th Ward, Byrne apparently saw him as a potential rival. And, as the world quickly learned, Byrne could be ferocious in attacking enemies, real and perceived. As best I could figure it out, she had been conditioned by her experience around City Hall to believe Chicago politics was a man's game and had to be played with utter ruthlessness.

Rich Daley didn't hide from the conflict. To the surprise of some people, he could be very tough and hard-core determined. He would persist.

I saw the signs that things were getting off to an odd footing with Mayor Byrne early on. After she'd beaten Bilandic in the primary, but before she officially became mayor, Bill Lipinski summoned me to a meeting with her and Dick Mell, a noisy and posturing alderman from the Northwest Side. I was headed for Springfield and ready to wash my hands of council politics, but I made the visit. The meeting, held in an office in the Monadnock Building, the landmark brick high-rise in the Loop, involved just Byrne, Lipinski, Mell, and me. Puffing on cigarettes, Byrne talked a mile a minute, and she asked all sorts of questions—who's with whom, whose side is he on, how does so-and-so get along with so-and-so. She said Mell and Lipinski would run the show for her in the council. I looked at them, and the two were all for it. The meeting went on for about an hour, and when it finally ended and we stepped outside, a crowd of reporters and TV crews had gathered. As we pushed through the throng, Mell and

Lipinski went ahead while Byrne continued talking to me through the side of her mouth. Finally, she nodded toward the aldermen and whispered to me, "These two are going to be just fine."

With that, I knew there was trouble ahead. Byrne had been elected on the premise that she would bring transparency to city government, sweeping away the shadowy back-room intrigues. I had no idea she would approach the job from a cynical, almost-devious side. What's more, I liked Lipinski, but there was no way he and Mell could muster the power to manage the City Council. There were just too many savvy players on the council with years of experience, institutional knowledge, and long-standing relationships. If Byrne believed Lipinski and Mell could manage the operation, she had a fatally weak grasp on the sources of power.

The portents for Daley were also ominous. He had already earned a reputation for arrogance among some senators and some of the aldermen. Two of the most ambitious, Ed Burke and Ed Vrdolyak, disliked him, in part, I think, because they simply didn't understand his personality. Daley could be short with people in a political context. Outside of politics, he was fun to be around—funny, smart, and politically perceptive. But he was cautious about saying something that could get into the papers. As a result, he was guarded and terse outside of his circle. That's how he'd been raised—don't do anything to embarrass the family.

Byrne and Daley seemed to get along fine at first, but a few months after her election, she came to Springfield to meet the legislators. I noticed that she cold-shouldered Daley, as if she were angry at him. Not long after, the war between them broke out over a complicated tax issue. The Republican James Thompson, the former U.S. attorney in Chicago, was halfway through his first of four terms as governor, and he wanted to keep an existing sales tax on certain food and drugs. Byrne sided with him. Daley wanted to eliminate the tax. The governor eventually came up with a compromise that reduced the tax by a fractional amount, but not before Byrne had publicly derided Daley on the issue. In announcing her position and chiding

Daley, she also took the occasion to cite a completely unrelated news report questioning Daley's integrity.

It was becoming quite clear that Byrne was playing a brand of hard-nosed, vituperative politics that echoed the style of the old machine—brooking no opposition and firing or otherwise retaliating against city workers associated with perceived enemies. In an article in late October that year headlined "As 'reformer,' Byrne fails to measure up," a young *Tribune* political reporter named David Axelrod cited this example: "Although as a candidate [Byrne] denounced the 'power seekers in City Hall' for patronage abuses, she has presided over the purge of more than 20 allies of state Sen. Richard M. Daley, whom she views as a prospective rival."

With threats and retaliation, she seemed determined to take over the very machine she had denounced during the campaign. In early November, she muscled the Cook County Democratic Central Committee into endorsing her choice for the party's nomination for president, Edward Kennedy, over the current president, Jimmy Carter. The move—the start of a harsh fight that would last though the convention the following summer—came over the strong objections of several committeemen, who said the endorsement was premature and disrespectful. After all, she'd earlier told President Carter she'd support him, and he'd been celebrated as a guest at a Byrne fundraiser less than a month before. (Carter later told me: "I've never had anyone look me in the eyes and lie so convincingly as when she told me she'd be with me.") Among the committeemen who stood up to oppose the Kennedy endorsement was Tom Hynes. Shortly after the meeting, one of his political aides was fired from a job at City Hall, obviously in retaliation.

Daley, meanwhile, had been considering a run for Cook County clerk, a move that would have pitted him against a popular, longtime machine incumbent. Several old-line Democrats advised him against it—loyalty to the machine and the man would prevent them from going with Daley.

I was both a friend and ally of Rich Daley, and as we explored the possibilities, he decided to run for Cook County state's attorney. The post had been held through two terms by a Republican, Bernard Carey, who had beaten Edward Hanrahan in the bitter aftermath of the death of Black Panther Fred Hampton. I think at that point, Daley was running to survive. Byrne obviously had him in her sights, and if he couldn't mount a response, his political career might be put on hold. But, as I said before, he was tougher than people thought, and he announced that he would run whether he got the machine's endorsement or not.

He didn't get it. Byrne made clear immediately that Daley wasn't her candidate. She shuffled potential contenders for a week or so and then made a choice that epitomizes the curious alliances that permeate Chicago politics: Ed Burke, the 14th Ward alderman who had openly mocked her just a few years before. Burke was more of a talent in his own mind, but the Democratic slate makers, steered by Byrne, endorsed the alderman. With that, the crack in the machine opened wide.

Daley campaigned on his solid record in Springfield, and he assailed Burke as the mayor's "hand-picked" choice. An impressive roster of independents, including state Senator Dawn Clark Netsch, declared for Daley, even though some of them had opposed his father for years. The regular Democrats campaigned hard for Burke, but they were up against the formidable Daley name and a growing wave of anti-Byrne sentiment. A veteran committeeman later told the *Tribune's* Axelrod, "The pro-Daleys and the anti-Byrnes got together, and there was nothing we could do."

I was closely involved in the campaign, and by early in 1980, well before the March primary, Daley was running far ahead. To keep our campaign workers interested and to temper an increasingly mean tone, we decided to inject a little fun into the campaign. One carefully choreographed event provided our camp with a particular measure of delight. The Democratic precinct captains—pushed by Byrne to support Burke—were scheduled to hold their annual lunch that winter in a ballroom of the Bismarck Hotel. One of my uncles worked in electronics, and I borrowed a tremendously powerful speaker from him. The day before the lunch, we hid the speaker in the balcony of the ballroom and connected a recording of Mayor Richard J. Daley. Then we set the device on a timer. The next day we assembled a crew of campaign workers, each equipped with Daley signs, and we blew up a hundred or so balloons with helium. Just before the lunch started, the workers slipped into the ballroom and released the balloons with the Daley signs attached. The Democrats who were there saw what was happening and ran around furiously trying to catch the balloons. Their efforts were mostly in vain, as nearly all of the balloons floated away and drifted to the lofty ceiling, each trailing a Daley sign, visible but far out of reach. The regular Democrats on the scene were apoplectic. At that point, we walked out. But leaving the hotel, we ran into Mayor Byrne coming in with several of her aides. She told one of them, "They must have just done something."

The luncheon went forward under the balloons. Burke gave a speech, but rather than just ignoring the Daley signs, he talked about them and pointed, which led to a photograph that appeared in the papers the next day. Then Byrne got up, and as she spoke, the booming voice of the late Mayor Daley cascaded over the ballroom from the hidden speaker, singing the virtues of the great Democratic Party of Cook County, the party he had built. It's doubtful that the leaders of that party—meeting there to end the political career of the late mayor's eldest son—appreciated the humor.

After eight or 10 minutes, someone finally found the speaker, and Byrne took it back to her office. She sent word to me that I could come around to reclaim it—the equipment was actually quite expensive. But someone else close to her warned that she might try to have me arrested for disturbing the peace or some such infraction, so I left it with her. I don't know whatever happened to the thing, but the ploy had the desired effect—much of the bitterness in the campaign subsided.

As expected, on the day after St. Patrick's Day, Daley trounced

Burke in the primary, a defeat that was considered a serious blow to Byrne and the old machine. That did nothing to throttle the mayor, however, and she continued to fire or transfer city employees she thought were against her. Among them was Edward Walsh, the 19th Ward Streets and Sanitation supervisor and organization Democrat who had been so helpful to me. After Walsh defied her by supporting Carter in the presidential race, he was summarily transferred to a ward on the far North Side. A number of lawsuits—including one by Walsh—successfully contested Byrne's actions under the Shakman decree, an agreement that grew out of a federal lawsuit challenging the widespread practice of patronage in Chicago. Under the decree, only city workers in policy positions could be dismissed for their political leanings.

As unhappiness with Byrne spread among public officials and voters, my state Senate colleague, Harold Washington, a smart and politically astute Chicago African American, decided to propose a bill allowing the recall of a mayor—a recourse not available to voters in Illinois. He publicly denied that the measure was aimed at Byrne, but no one doubted the inspiration for his proposal. I added a teasing note of my own. After conferring with several mental health officials, I wrote an amendment to Washington's bill, giving voters the right to petition for a psychiatric evaluation of the mayor. The proposal was written in the formal language of psychiatry and the law, and I gave it to Washington while he was reading his bill. As was often the case, sponsoring senators would recite amendments into the record without looking them over beforehand. As Washington started reading the content of my measure, he burst out laughing. I eventually withdrew the amendment, and the bill ultimately failed. Years later, Byrne told me the incident had upset her.

(The issue of recall came up again apropos Mayor Rahm Emanuel, the object of widespread anger over the police shooting of Laquan McDonald, a Black 17-year-old. Nothing resulted, and Illinois voters still do not have the option to recall a mayor.)

The conflict with Byrne and my assistance to Rich Daley tilted me back toward politics and away from business. I spent less and less time at the Board of Trade, and eventually, I gave up my seat with vague plans to re-acquire it a few years hence. As it turned out, that wasn't to happen.

By the time the Democratic National Convention rolled around in early August that year, Byrne was still fighting for Ted Kennedy against President Carter, even though Carter had handily won the Illinois primary. Her efforts seemed to come from an odd combination of admiration for the surviving Kennedy brother and a furious desire to exert her influence over Chicago politics. The Democrats staged their convention at Madison Square Garden in New York City. I was part of the Illinois delegation, which stood 163 for Carter (including me) and 16 for Kennedy. During the primaries across the country, Carter had locked up a winning number of delegates, who in theory were committed to him on the first ballot. But Kennedy introduced a proposal for a so-called open convention—a rule change that would allow delegates to vote for whomever they wanted.

With Carter delegates dominating the convention, Kennedy's self-serving proposition was a non-starter. Nonetheless, Byrne (who was not a delegate) got behind the idea. She sent in a team of city officials to lobby delegates at their hotel. One delegate, University of Illinois at Chicago political science professor Milton Rakove, later told the *Tribune* that the group looked "like a hit squad of heavies out of the Blues Brothers movie."

On Monday, August 11, the day of the vote, Byrne herself flew in with a dozen or so aides and committeemen. While she stood by at a hotel, the group descended on the Illinois delegation on the floor of Madison Square Garden. By a variety of accounts, their methods were heavy-handed and crass, making promises of patronage jobs and other boondoggles to delegates who would vote for the rules change and threatening the careers—political and otherwise—of those who stood by Carter. The lobbying got so intense that I got into a scuffle with one of Byrne's soldiers, Streets and Sanitation Commissioner John Donovan. Donovan was an old-school party loyalist, and we later became friends. We were separated before anything significant occurred, and I thought nothing of it, but the commotion ended up in the media.

Writing in the *Tribune*, David Axelrod called Byrne's lobbying venture "woefully mishandled." Only a handful of Carter delegates from Illinois voted for the rules change, which easily went down to defeat. Byrne flew back to Chicago that night, just hours after she had arrived, having imposed an added layer of bitterness over the Chicago political scene.

For Carter, beating Kennedy for the nomination came at a stiff cost. The next day, Kennedy gave a prime-time speech, ostensibly pledging to support the president and the party in the fall election. I was sitting next to Bill Daley, Rich's younger brother, on the convention floor while the Massachusetts senator delivered the stem-winder. Written by the political consultant Bob Shrum, the speech is considered by many to be Kennedy's greatest. Indeed, the message— hardly hidden—had everything to do with Kennedy and his fight for economic justice and almost nothing to do with Carter. As every stirring phrase rolled out to thunderous applause, climaxing with "the work goes on, the cause endures, the hope still lives, and the dream shall never die," I turned to Daley and whispered, "I think we are dead." Later, when Carter and Kennedy appeared on the dais at the conclusion of the convention, Kennedy made clear where he would be in the campaign, refusing to raise arms with the nominee.

As the Democratic Convention opened, the campaign between Rich Daley and incumbent Bernie Carey for Cook County state's attorney was in full swing. Carey, a rare Republican winner in the modern era in Cook County, had compiled a worthy record in two terms as state's attorney. In the campaign, he emphasized his professionalism and charged that Daley would introduce Chicago politics to the office and use it only as a launching pad for a run against Byrne for mayor.

Throughout the fall, Carey held varying leads over Daley in the polls, and from the start, the race was dominated by the feuding between Daley and Byrne. When pressed, Byrne said for a time that she would support the Democratic Party ticket, but she failed to hide her true feelings. One poll showed that only 11 percent of voters thought she wanted Daley to win. Eventually, the mayor came out fiercely against Daley, claiming that he was "paranoid" and racist. In late October, she issued a misguided accusation that as 11th Ward committeeman, Daley had been part of a scheme with the Building Department to deny permits to Black contractors. (She included the 19th Ward in the alleged plot.) The claim swiftly unraveled, spectacularly so when one of the supposed Black contractors turned out to be a white man with a long history of building violations. Even Carey acknowledged that the racism smear went too far.

In fact, Rich Daley enjoyed considerable support from African American voters, building on the goodwill among that constituency enjoyed by his late father. In particular, many older Black voters thought fondly of Richard J. Daley and transferred the affection to Rich. In Daley's camp, we worked hard to solidify that constituency, and we produced literature and radio ads with endorsements from Mohammad Ali, Andy Young, and even Coretta Scott King, the widow of Martin Luther King Jr. Her endorsement might have surprised some, given the raucous open-housing marches King had led in Chicago in the mid-1960s, but Mayor Daley and Reverend King respected each other. They had shaken hands as negotiators at the time, and during the marches, the mayor made sure King was surrounded by a troop of NFL-worthy police. (Of course, that didn't prevent him from getting hit once with a rock in a march through Marquette Park.)

Curiously, Mike Royko, the iconic Chicago newspaper columnist, who had been a harsh critic of the first Mayor Daley, ended up writing several columns helpful to the son. One day during the campaign, the political insider Phil Krone, who was helping on the Daley campaign, asked me to join him in talking to Royko, who was at the *Chicago Sun-Times* in those days. I only knew the columnist glancingly through softball, but I went with Krone up to Royko's shabby office. He knew we were backing Daley and immediately demanded: How can this guy possibly win this thing? We started to explain, but he told Krone to leave and left it to me to walk him through the numbers. I had no official role in the campaign but was involved in most things of substance. I told Royko, "I'm not promising Daley will win, but here is how it should happen." Then I talked about what the campaign planned and where Daley was going to get the votes, ward by ward and township by township. In the end, Royko said, "Write that down for me," so I did and sent it to him.

Pretty soon Royko started writing pro-Daley columns, often with Krone's help. The columns gave the campaign an added measure of credibility, particularly among the so-called lakefront liberals, many of whom had opposed Rich's father. I always wondered if Royko's columns on the Daley/Carey race reflected some remorse he felt for being so tough on the man he had called Chicago's Boss. His moving obituary of Mayor Daley suggested that the columnist harbored fondness for the longtime mayor. ("If a man ever reflected a city, it was Richard J. Daley and Chicago.") More importantly, I think the way some ward committeemen turned on Rich offended Royko, who always had a soft spot for the underdog.

In every campaign, there is a theme, though often it's not clearly articulated and sometimes even the candidate isn't entirely aware of it. The theme of that state's attorney race, in my opinion, was the betrayal of Daley by many elements of the machine. Some people in the organization waited until his father died and then turned on him. One day Rich was a popular politician helpful to the careers of his colleagues, and the next he was a rude upstart, hiding behind his father, incapable of standing up for himself and totally unfit for the position he was seeking. Many of the old guard Democrats stayed with Rich, but the young crowd, the Burkes and Vrdolyaks and the machine politicians who went with Byrne out of loyalty or fear, attacked Rich viciously.

Royko saw that, and I think a lot of the voting public did, too. In the end, they simply thought: "The father was a good man, he came to our neighborhood, he fixed up this park, he looked out for us, and if the son is anything like his father, he'll be all right."

Two weeks before the election, Byrne outright "unendorsed" Daley, as the *Tribune* put it, withdrawing her support and driving some hitherto uncertain organization operatives to work even harder against him. Polls leading up to Election Day consistently gave Carey the lead, and on the night of the election, both Channel 7 and Channel 2 early on called the victory for the incumbent. In fact, the race remained tight, and Carey didn't concede for a day. In the end, Daley won by 16,230 votes out of 2.1 million cast. He'd run better in the Cook County suburbs than expected, and a broad consensus thought that Byrne's attacks on him had helped his cause. Don Rose, who'd managed Byrne's mayoral campaign and consulted for Carey, said afterwards that Jane Byrne had made the difference.

By the time of Daley's election, I was halfway through my first term in the state Senate. And though I was closely involved in a number of initiatives, two measures that each grew out of special circumstances drew particular public attention. One day, a woman from Oak Lawn named Nancy Czerwiec came to see me. She was a former nun and former primary school teacher who'd been a year ahead of me at St. Sabina, and she had helped in the Daley campaign. With her was a distraught mother who said her daughter, who was perhaps 11 or 12, had been touched or frightened by a local boy who'd shown her pictures in a book that he'd taken out of the local public library. They didn't have the book with them at the time, but the women told me the photographs were shockingly explicit. They said they'd been to the police and other authorities, but no one paid them attention.

I was sympathetic, but I thought the matter would resolve itself. Among other things, I knew Nancy Czerwiec held very tough views on certain matters and was a staunch pro-life advocate. But a few weeks later, more distraught parents came to my office to denounce the book. So I got a copy. And I was stunned. I was looking at child pornography.

The book was titled *Show Me! A Picture Book of Sex for Children and Parents*, by a Swiss child psychologist named Helga Fleischhauer-Hardt and photographer Will McBride. Though purporting to advance sex education, *Show Me!* contained graphic photographs of both children and adults in sexual situations (not together) and an essay for parents by the psychologist about sexual practices and ways to talk with children about sex. A reader review from 1998 on the book's Amazon page perhaps describes the impact of *Show Me!* best: "This is a book that will be considered superb by ultra-progressive parents, children, and by pedophiles. Most parents, even liberally-minded ones, will find this book confronting and offensive."

I didn't realize it at the time, but the book already had been stirring up controversies around the country. It was first brought out in Germany in 1974 by a publishing house associated with the Lutheran Church. After its publication in the United States a year later, prosecutors unsuccessfully brought obscenity charges against the publisher, St. Martin's, in Massachusetts, New Hampshire, and Oklahoma.

When I went to the Oak Lawn Public Library to discuss the situation, the librarian I spoke to was arrogant and confrontational. She accused me of trying to practice censorship and lectured me on the First Amendment. Meanwhile, *Show Me!* was generating a fuss in Oak Lawn, and rumors started flying about shenanigans going on after adolescents got their hands on the book. The sides seemed to be hardening.

I started looking into remedies, and saw that the state criminal statute proscribing the distribution of harmful and obscene materials to minors gave affirmative defenses to certain professional categories, including librarians. A legislative researcher examining laws around the country found that a number of states did not protect librarians, and, as far as I could tell, those states hadn't been the scenes of misguided prosecutions against librarians. So I introduced a bill that simply deleted librarians from the list of protected professions in the Illinois statute. I thought that might get the attention of the Oak Lawn Public Library without causing much additional commotion. But I was wrong—all hell broke loose.

Anti-censorship groups and the media lambasted me. The library associations sent in their lobbyists. I received all sorts of calls. Meanwhile, Nancy Czerwiec was arguing that parents should have the right to say whatever a child can read and how they're taught, that kids are being sexually abused and they don't even know it. She told a Senate panel that sexually explicit books were "explosives for the mind."

In the heat of battle, there was no middle ground. I tried to contain the debate to the legislature, but someone persuaded me to go on the air with Robert Cromie, who had an interview show on WGN-TV. I was told that he was a smart, reasonable guy, and he would provide the chance to explain my point of view. I happened to be babysitting the boys that afternoon, and as we waited at the WGN studios, the boys turned rambunctious, and my temper frayed. When I finally went on air, Cromie cast himself as a great defender of the First Amendment and started attacking me. He'd brought the book onto the set, and I told him, "Hold the book up and turn to page 37." He kept attacking. I said, "Hold it up and turn to page 48. You can't because you'd be arrested." He got nastier and nastier, and so it went.

It took several months for liberals to defeat the *Show Me!* bill in a Senate committee. By then, I was embroiled in another controversy. In late 1980, the President's Commission for a National Agenda for the Eighties, a panel put together by President Carter, released a draft of its report. The recommendations covered an array of topics, but the section on urban issues particularly stood out. It asserted that instead of pouring money into declining cities of the Northeast and Midwest, the federal government should divert some of those funds to assist the unemployed to move to areas of the country where they were more likely to find jobs.

The idea made sense to me and responded to the economic and demographic trends of the last half century. Northern manufacturers had been moving with their jobs to the South, where labor costs were lower and unions rare or nonexistent. A lot of those new Southern jobs reflected federal resources being poured into the South—particularly associated with defense spending. A canny band of Southern senators, led by John Stennis of Mississippi, had come to control the purse strings in Washington, and they steered money into their own states and region. In 1980, the unemployment rate in Illinois was 8.2 percent, while in Louisiana it stood at 6.9 percent; in Texas, it was 5.1 percent. The national average was 7.1 percent.

The State of Illinois could drop money into a range of training and education programs, but they did little good if there weren't jobs available for the people who successfully completed the courses. American society is famously mobile. Why not help people go where the jobs are? With the assistance of Paul Vallas, then a young revenue analyst with the Senate Democratic staff (later schools chief in Chicago and elsewhere and an Illinois political candidate), and Max Ryder of the legislature's research bureau, we crafted a bill that tracked the recommendation of the president's commission. The measure would give unemployed Illinois residents grants of $4,000 to $5,000 to aid them in starting afresh in a region where jobs were more plentiful—in that era, we thought mostly of the Sun Belt. Various controls would apply—for example, an applicant would have to promise to stay away for a certain length of time, so he or she wouldn't just take a two-month vacation and then return, and there had to be a reasonable job prospect on the other end. Illinois would provide advice and assistance.

I submitted the bill in early 1981 with a lot of optimism—this seemed like a smart and workable social policy. And then hell broke loose again. With the Daley/Byrne feud raging in Chicago, the Byrne camp was looking for an opportunity to discredit Rich or any of his allies. The mayor dispatched a team of aides to Springfield to spread the notion that the bill's hidden agenda was to pay a bounty to minorities to leave the state. Even Emil Jones was on the case for Byrne. The measure's opponents started calling it the Marcus Garvey Bill, in honor of the fiery Jamaican who'd advocated for the Back-to-Africa movement, though, aside from the Black caucus and me, hardly anyone in the legislature in those days knew who Marcus Garvey was.

I realized that the burden of unemployment fell disproportionately on Blacks and Hispanics, but in terms of raw numbers many more white people than Black were unemployed. Race had not entered into our thinking when we drew up the measure. Though Byrne had enlisted Emil Jones, several of the Black legislators in Springfield supported it.

Still, the racial angle was too rich for the media to pass up, and the news coverage was harsh. In an effort to defend the legislation, I agreed to go on the *Phil Donahue Show*, then being broadcast in Chicago, and Donahue tore into the idea, hardly providing a chance for me to explain the matter. The whole experience reminded me of the outcry against Daniel Patrick Moynihan's 1965 report on the Black family, in which he argued that slavery and racism had contributed to the breakdown of the two-parent unit. When it comes to race in this country, thoughtful, candid discussion can quickly get drowned out. In the end, my bill went nowhere.

The *Show Me!* and relocation measures were far from my only initiatives in my first term in the Senate. Among other things, I tried to reform the state's tax structure. In particular, I hoped to reduce the reliance on property taxes to fund education, a system that shortchanges many of the neediest school districts. Sadly, that reform battle is still going on today. I sponsored legislation that gave tax breaks to older houses in landmark districts as a way to encourage preservation. I introduced a bill to protect the rights of mentally and physically disabled children, a bill to stiffen child sex abuse laws, and a bill to require jail time for anyone caught using a gun while committing a crime. All became laws. Unsuccessfully, I pushed for a constitutional amendment to require merit selection of judges.

Curiously, the commotions over *Show Me!* and the relocation idea both had odd postscripts. The Oak Lawn library eventually restricted access to the book, and in 1982, the publisher, St. Martin's Press, stopped selling *Show Me!* because of the obscenity prosecutions it ignited. What surprised me, though, was an award I received just a year after I introduced the bill: legislator of the year, from the Illinois Library Association.

And a few years after the fracas over the relocation grants, someone told me they had just heard Tom Hayden, the radical political activist who was then a California legislator, being interviewed on NPR. He'd talked about assisting the unemployed to move to regions where jobs were plentiful. Apparently, Hayden mentioned that an Illinois state senator had proposed that very thing. ◼

10

"He who slings mud generally loses ground."

Governor Adlai Stevenson

~~~~~~

Politics as practiced in Chicago can sometimes be an oddly intimate affair where it seems as if every player is drawn from the same small pool of participants. The connections can come from anywhere—family, schools, teams, religions, neighborhoods. So it was with my 1982 run for Senate re-election. My GOP opponent, J. Theodore Meyer, lived in Beverly and was the nephew of Albert Cardinal Meyer, who had been the brilliant and reform-minded archbishop of Chicago when I was in high school and college. What's more, Ted Meyer's older brother, John, was our family doctor.

Ted himself was experienced and personable, and in more than a decade in the state General Assembly, he'd made a name as a concerned environmentalist. We found ourselves pitted against each other because the state's legislative districts had been redrawn, as required by the state constitution after a census. At the same time, following a state referendum, the number of House seats had been whittled from 177 to 118. Meyer's House seat had been eliminated, so he and I faced off in a new Senate district, the 14th. Compared to the old 28th, the new district was more suburban and included all or parts of nine towns (among them Blue Island, Midlothian,

Oak Lawn, and Alsip). The 19th Ward remained in the district, but several Chicago wards (including the 34th) had been dropped. Two-thirds of the 14th District was new to both Meyer and me, and given the suburban expansion, the voters tilted Republican.

I put together a good campaign, with supporters knocking on doors in every precinct in every community. Drawing on an issue I'd worked on from the start of my Senate career, I emphasized my support for revising the state's flawed system of relying on the property tax to pay for education. The nation as a whole was struggling economically at the time, and Meyer focused on his support for businesses and jobs.

As with almost anything that had to do with Chicago politics in those days, the Daley/Byrne feud took center stage. By then, almost everyone assumed that Daley would run for mayor against Byrne in 1983, and, as a supporter of Rich, I became a prime target for the mayor. She and Governor Thompson, with whom I didn't get along particularly well, arranged for ads to appear arguing that a vote for me was a vote to introduce Chicago Democratic politics into the suburbs. Never mind that Byrne herself was helping to foment those dreaded political conflicts—she wanted to make a point with my loss. Meyer jumped on the theme, and it echoed all over the district. As it turned out, it didn't work. I ran well in both the city and the suburbs and won the seat easily.

That fall, Adlai Stevenson III ran for governor against Jim Thompson, and when I wasn't active in my campaign, I worked with Stevenson in his. From his name to his credentials to his fine record in the U.S. Senate, Stevenson had the makings of a strong candidate. He was the great-grandson of a vice president under President Grover Cleveland and the son of a popular Illinois governor, Adlai Stevenson II, who had twice run for president as a Democrat. Though he lost both times to Dwight Eisenhower, Adlai II still inspired admiration from the liberal wing of the Democratic Party almost two decades after his death. Adlai III came from the same mold as his father— cerebral, witty, and pragmatically liberal. As an incumbent senator in 1979, he declined to run for re-election, later saying he had wearied of the legislative process and wanted an executive role, one where he could actually get things done. Even as he ran for governor, he didn't dismiss talk that longer term he had his eye on the presidency.

I thought that Thompson, running for his third term, was vulnerable. Though I respected his intelligence, I always thought there was something of a showboat about him, something a little bit of an actor. And as both the state and national economies sputtered, I suspected that voters had wearied of Big Jim, as he was known. What's more, Ronald Reagan was only two years into his presidency, and the bad economy had scuffed his image and threatened to handicap Republicans generally.

As a candidate, however, Stevenson had an image problem—one that echoed a drawback that had burdened his father. He was seen as soft. "My father had the 'egghead' problem," Stevenson candidly told a *Tribune* reporter during the campaign. "I've got this 'wimp' thing."

In fact, he was anything but a wimp. Stevenson was tough-minded, even stubborn. He'd served as a Marine in the Korean War, and he liked to hunt. In the Senate, he'd served as head of the Ethics Committee, a job that required common sense and a strong backbone. Still, because his manner was reserved and bookish and his speaking style mild, the image was hard to shake. I volunteered a plan to challenge the perception: Every time Stevenson made an appearance, play the Marine's Hymn, reflecting his military service. That in itself would not change the image, but more than all the coaching Adlai got—and he got a lot—the song would have projected an aura of strength. I was told Stevenson refused to allow it. He thought playing the song amounted to pandering. Just as his father had disdained the crass, new medium of television as a way to reach voters, Adlai III believed in practicing politics with old-fashioned honor and civility, never stooping to the facile ploys.

In the end, a few votes would have made the difference. Though all the polls leading up to the election showed Thompson with a generous lead, I knew they were wrong. I was on the street talking with voters throughout the fall, and I had conducted my own informal polling. In vain, I tried to alert other Democratic candidates, but it was impossible to unravel the understandings many of them had reached with the Thompson campaign. The day before the election, I campaigned with Nancy Stevenson, Adlai's wife, and my requests for other Democrats to join us were rejected.

The contest turned out to be the closest in Illinois gubernatorial history, with Thompson finishing on top by 5,074 votes. The unexpectedly narrow result reflected an influx of new voters, many of them Black, who apparently had been mobilized over dismay at the economic policies of President Reagan.

The Stevenson camp found a significant number of seeming improprieties in the balloting, particularly downstate, and petitioned the Illinois Supreme Court to order a full recount—a precursor to the U.S. Supreme Court battle over a recount in Florida after the 2000 presidential election. On January 8, 1983, more than two months after voters went to the polls, the state high court ruled 4-3 against Stevenson, asserting that his claims of voting improprieties weren't strong enough to justify a long and expensive review. Three Republicans on the panel voted against the recount. Three Democrats voted for it. The deciding vote came from a Democrat— Seymour Simon, a former Northwest Side alderman who had often clashed with the party regulars.

A week after the court's decision, the *Tribune* revealed that when Stevenson was a U.S. senator, Simon had come to him seeking an appointment to the federal bench. Stevenson wouldn't recommend him to President Carter, however, reportedly because Simon was 62, two years past guidelines for the post. Sources told David Axelrod, the *Tribune* reporter, that Simon had been furious and blamed Stevenson. One quoted Simon saying, "Adlai shafted me." Simon acknowledged he'd wanted to go on the federal bench, but he denied holding his disappointment against Stevenson.

To say the least, Simon's denial was unconvincing. Politics, at least as played in Chicago, is personal. And history can pivot on such matters. I believe that if Stevenson had won that election, he would have gone on to be the Democratic nominee for president in 1988, making a far better candidate than Michael Dukakis.

Even before Rich Daley settled into the state's attorney's office in 1981, predictions abounded that he would challenge Jane Byrne for mayor in the spring of 1983. Her mayoralty seemed to stagger from one crisis to another—strikes, fiscal woes, scandals. Sometimes I felt sorry for her. If she had simply shut the door and got down to work, I think she would have been all right politically. But she took advice from scores of people and always seemed to be persuaded by the last person who left her office. She had brought a number of well-meaning managers into her administration, but most of them had no idea how to get something done in the city. And she just had to stick her nose into anything political.

For a time, Daley denied any intention to take Byrne on, and by early 1982, a number of potential candidates had surfaced for the Democratic primary a year away. Among those mentioned prominently was Tom Hynes, then the county assessor. Hynes enjoyed strong qualifications: He had a good public record as a state senator and as assessor, and he had been one of the most prominent organization Democrats to stand up to Byrne. But there was a lot of polling going on, and time and again, the polls indicated that outside the Southwest Side, people didn't really know Hynes.

At least two other undeclared but potential Byrne challengers showed promise: Dan Rostenkowski, the influential congressman with a strong Chicago political pedigree, and Roman Pucinski, a former congressman and current alderman who had long coveted the mayor's office and had made a credible run for it in 1977. But neither was yet willing to commit to the race. Similarly, a number of supporters were urging Harold Washington to run—he'd been elected to Congress by a landslide in 1980.

Meanwhile, when the pollsters lined up Daley in the mix of potential candidates, he knocked it out of the park. His brother Bill opened an exploratory office, and the team hired pollsters and consultants who basically told Rich that he couldn't lose. Finally, with the fall election out of the way, Daley declared he was in the race. Days later, Washington announced that he was in, too. With Byrne seeking re-election, that set the agenda for the most watched mayoral race in years, one that put extreme stress on several of the old political foundations. Regular Democrats were torn between staying with Byrne and the organization or switching to the breakaway faction with Daley. African American voters had long been loyal supporters of organization candidates and equally loyal supporters of Rich Daley's father. But now, in Harold Washington, Black people had a candidate from their own community.

Early polling still showed Daley with a sizeable lead. He had a strong field operation, and he picked up a good roster of endorsements. I was optimistic that Daley could win. So when the talk turned to participating in televised debates among the three candidates, I vigorously opposed the idea. I knew Harold Washington, and I knew he would impress. Washington and I had spent a good deal of time together during the two years we overlapped in the Senate. We would have breakfast together several times a week in the Stratton Office Building, and occasionally we would share a commute to and from Springfield.

He was smart and funny. He loved sports, particularly baseball—first thing in the morning, he'd turn to the sports section of the *Sun-Times*, before the news or editorial pages. That impressed my kids. And Washington knew Chicago. He'd gone to DuSable High School and Roosevelt University, before earning a law degree at Northwestern. He was well educated in Chicago politics: His father had been a Democratic precinct captain on the South Side, a post Washington inherited when his father retired. For almost 20 years, Washington had held public office, first in Springfield and then in Washington. He'd had a brush with the law—pleading no contest in

1972 to a charge of failing to file income taxes for four years in the 1960s. He served 40 days in jail. No one seemed to hold that misstep against him, however. He'd run for mayor once before, in the 1977 Democratic primary against Bilandic—by then, Washington had broken with the organization—but he never got much traction. Indeed, he wasn't particularly well known outside his Hyde Park neighborhood.

I knew that he could be a powerful and emotional speaker, a skill perfectly suited to a TV debate. He and I had battled on the floor of the Senate a few times. You could beat Washington on the merits of an argument because he was casual about his preparation. But once he got rolling with his style and delivery, he was very effective. I used to watch the gallery when he was speaking. Usually there would be a handful of visitors or students listening to a whispering tour guide or a couple of bored lobbyists trying to figure out if their Senate allies were going to show up for the vote. But when Washington started speaking, the gallery would often go silent—the visitors wanted to hear what he had to say.

Daley's other top advisors, including Tom Foran and Dawn Clark Netsch, who was campaign chairman, thought he had to participate in the debates—they argued that it was his civic obligation and his refusal would look defensive or cowardly. The other candidates and the news media were bringing pressure. But the advisors underestimated Washington. I kept trying to explain: He's been through this sort of thing hundreds of times. The debates will introduce him to Chicago, and voters—especially Black voters—will come away thinking he's the most knowledgeable person on that stage.

Senator Netsch, who had known Washington since law school and had served with him in Springfield, just didn't get what I was concerned about. I lost the argument. Wrangling over the number and format of the debates went on for weeks, and at one point, it looked as if the contests might be canceled. In the end, though, there were four. The campaign brought in all sorts of policy wonks with their papers, so Daley would be equipped to answer any question on government that could be imagined. Budget experts pored over the numbers with him. But I knew it wasn't a matter of Daley being prepared—on that front, he would do fine. He knew more about the issues than the wonks. It was a matter of giving Harold Washington a forum.

And Washington shone. As Steve Neal later wrote in the *Tribune*, the televised debates established Washington "as a major contender. He was more articulate, relaxed, and forceful than his two opponents, and most political observers gave him the edge." From the first debate on, Washington closed the gap in the polls, and the three candidates ran about evenly. Byrne drew her support from the remnants of the machine and from lingering backers among the lakefront liberals who had been key to her 1979 election. Daley's support came from people who admired him and the job he'd done as state's attorney. And Washington, campaigning on the slogan "It's Our Turn," dominated the Black vote.

Race was never far beneath the surface. I think Daley was still ahead by a small margin in the last week or so of the campaign. People on the Northwest and Southwest sides were getting phone calls: A vote for Daley is a vote for Harold. Byrne supporters—I suspect campaign chairman Ed Vrdolyak, among others—had put together the operation to make hundreds of thousands of calls designed to frighten potential Daley voters with the prospect of a Black mayor. In the end, the calls didn't make a difference for Byrne, but they killed Daley's chances. The turnout was a record for the time, 1.28 million. Washington, who collected as much as 80 percent of the Black vote in some precincts, finished with 36 percent of the total. Byrne and Daley split the white vote, Byrne running well on the Northwest Side, Daley well on the Southwest Side. She won 34 percent of the total, Daley 30 percent.

The vote was close enough that Byrne didn't concede that night. By midnight, though, Rich Daley told supporters at the Hyatt Regency that it was over. He took it well—he told me it wasn't the end of the world. I wasn't as philosophical. I liked Washington, who would go on to become Chicago's first Black mayor by beating Republican Bernard Epton in the April general election. But I was angry because of the mistakes we had made. Daley could have won.

Not long after the election, Ron Gidwitz, the scion of the Helene Curtis cosmetics and toiletries company and a Republican dabbler in politics, called a meeting of Chicago officials to try to clear the air after the divisive campaign. I assumed it would be a windy affair, so I hadn't planned to go, but at the last minute, my Senate colleagues persuaded me. I was not properly dressed for the occasion, and when I arrived at the building where the meeting would be held, the security guard stopped me by placing both his hands on my shoulders—he apparently thought I didn't look the part of a public official, even though I had presented identification. We exchanged words and shoves. He called more security, and soon I was in a full-scale slugfest with a handful of uniformed men. Eventually, three or four of Harold Washington's advance men came along and identified me. I dusted myself off and continued to the meeting. Washington arrived and had a good laugh. But that small fracas was probably a strong omen of the brawl that would be city politics over the next four years.

Back in Springfield, I went through a lively period. In the spring of 1984, I was chairman of the Senate's Finance Committee, and one day I got a call from Silas Keehn, the chief of the Federal Reserve Bank of Chicago. He asked if I could come see him—sooner rather than later. I had an idea that he wanted to talk about Continental Bank, then the largest bank in Chicago and the seventh largest in the country, with around $40 billion in assets. For most of my life, Continental—officially, Continental Illinois National Bank and Trust Company—had been a monument to stolid Midwestern values. Under a hustling chairman in the 1970s, however, the bank had expanded ambitiously. Over the last few years, the newspapers had been full of stories about Continental's troubles, which included, among other bad investments, a thick portfolio of oil-and-gas loans from Penn Square, the Oklahoma-based operation that collapsed in 1982, shaking the banking business around the country. I thought Continental, which was a financial anchor in Chicago, had largely weathered its crisis, however. The heads of the bank had been offering reassurances.

I went right away to the Federal Reserve's Chicago building, a stunning landmark that happened to be across LaSalle Street from Continental's headquarters. Silas Keehn greeted me in his lavish, second-floor office. He was cautious and bankerly, but candid. He said he didn't know exactly what was going on, but there was apparently a run on Continental—it turned out it came largely from institutional investors in Europe and the Far East who'd picked up rumors and faulty news reports. Keehn said he was worried that because Continental was so big, the panic could spread and threaten the entire American banking system. Of course, that's not exactly how he and other officials put it. Rather, they said something like, "The size of this bank is such that it has major implications for the banking system in the United States." In other words, "too big to fail"—a phrase repeated during the Continental crisis and supposedly coined by Connecticut Republican Congressman Stewart McKinney.

Keehn asked if I were amenable to helping steer remedial legislation through Springfield while maintaining a confidence about the situation, and I agreed.

In those days, the Illinois banking laws were notably restrictive and protectionist. For example, the state limited the number of branch offices a bank could open, which by some accounts had induced Continental to try to grow through speculative out-of-state and international deposits. More to the point in the immediate crisis, though, was the state ban on out-of-state banks acquiring Illinois banks. That obviously limited the number of potential purchasers of Continental and depressed the price. Indeed, several New York banks had expressed an interest in pursuing Continental if the law were changed. But a significant Illinois opponent opposed a change—First

Chicago Corp., the other big Chicago bank, which was the likeliest in-state buyer.

Meetings and hearings occupied the next month or so. So-called "super lobbyists" made the rounds in Springfield. By then, the crisis was well covered, and the papers were full of stories about potential suitors coming and going. First Chicago was interested, then it wasn't, but maybe it would be again. Chemical Bank of New York might take a look, then it wouldn't. Drexel Burnham Lambert had a plan.

A consortium of banks put together a line of credit, and the Federal Reserve Board provided a loan. The Federal Deposit Insurance Corporation infused $1.5 billion. Then the FDIC announced that it would offer protection to Continental depositors beyond the usual $100,000 limit. Still, Continental wobbled. In an indication of how far anxiety had spread, the Chicago Transit Authority Pension Board withdrew its $600-million fund because so many transit workers had called the board offices to complain.

A number of hard-liners argued that the government should back off and just let Continental fail. They made the so-called "moral hazard" argument—that without the discipline of a collapse, bankers will continue to take unnecessary risks, knowing that the feds will step in and rescue them.

At hearings in Springfield and behind the scenes, First Chicago and other Illinois banks lobbied hard for reciprocal rights—if an out-of-state bank could buy in Illinois, then Illinois banks should be able to buy out-of-state. Finally, though, we moved a bill through the General Assembly that essentially applied to Continental alone and would allow an out-of-town purchaser. Governor Thompson signed it at the end of June. By then, though, no bank, in-state or out, wanted Continental.

After a series of conversations with the comptroller of the currency and the chairman of the Federal Deposit Insurance Corporation, I knew it would take a government rescue. In exchange for 80 percent ownership of Continental, the FDIC agreed to take over up to $4.5

billion in bad loans. Bondholders and depositors were spared, but shareholders lost almost everything. The board was swept out, and new managers brought in. The rescue succeeded. The wider economy survived without major disruption, and Continental itself remained intact until 1994 when Bank of America bought it.

For many of us with vivid memories of the Continental crisis, the economic collapse of 2008 raised obvious questions. In particular, why did the government step in to rescue Continental, citing fear that its collapse would have a drastic impact on the economy, and then 24 years later let Lehman Brothers collapse—an event that in fact did have a drastic impact on the economy? Of course, by 2008, the American banking system had changed enormously, with state restrictions largely eliminated by deregulation, giving the banks far more leeway in their investments, enough that they virtually became casinos. Still, in the spring of 2008, just six months before the Lehman bankruptcy, the government bailed out Bear Stearns, another big investment bank. So the question remains: If the rationale for saving Continental had been valid, why wouldn't it be valid for Lehman?

In any case, the whole experience gave me an unsettling lesson in the fragility of the financial system.

Early in my Senate term, a woman who lived in my district came to my office seeking advice on getting a job with the Cook County government. She had been teaching in the Chicago school system for 12 years, and the county job she sought carried a salary only about half of her teaching pay. I asked the obvious: Why take such a pay cut? She said she was worn out. Her students were reading two or three years below grade level, and much of her time was spent controlling her classroom. What most troubled her was that she was starting to dislike her students.

After hearing her story, I began meeting informally with Senate colleagues to explore solutions to the issues facing the Chicago school system. We emphasized the primary grades, in part because educational psychologists hold that children acquire their value systems—honesty, fairness, kindness, selflessness—between the ages of four and eight, and that value system will guide a child's thinking almost into his or her adult years. My colleagues and I met for several months and concluded that the structure of Chicago's inner-city elementary schools was flawed, particularly in the early grades. We agreed on two primary concerns: a failure to inculcate values, and the need for more specialized reading programs that ensured all primary school students learned to read at grade level before middle school age, even if it meant a loss of time and instruction in other subjects, including math.

We came up with a plan that mandated a class size from kindergarten to third grade of only six pupils. These classes would be taught by a specially trained teacher, paid at a premium level, who would remain with the same class throughout the whole four-year term. The program would monitor student progress on a daily basis.

With this preliminary concept, we set off to meet with anyone who might assist—board members, union leaders, university presidents, school superintendents, members of Congress, legislative leaders. None doubted the seriousness of the problem nor contested the merits of our proposal. But everyone had the same response: "Where will you get the money?" As it was, whenever the Illinois Senate sought to increase funds for the Chicago schools, Senate Republican leader Pate Philip would rise in opposition and deliver his "giving money to the Chicago Board of Education is pouring money down a rat hole" speech.

Our timing could not have been worse. The Chicago Board of Education had just avoided a default, and our state universities were facing huge budget cuts. It made little difference to the legislature that while our plan's price in real dollars was no doubt high, the figure would be a bargain under a cost-benefit analysis that included the burdens on society of joblessness, crime, poor health, and heartbreak that results from inadequate inner-city education. Pay now or pay later—that is the stark but simple choice. After two years of failing efforts, however, my concerned colleagues and I couldn't even convince a small school in the south suburbs serving some of the poorest kids in Illinois to sign on to a pilot program guaranteed by the state.

A number of other key legislative issues kept me busy through those years. For one, I stepped out into the charged debate over abortion, and I sponsored a bill that would require doctors to notify both parents 24 hours before performing an abortion on a girl under 18. I had always been pro-life, and this seemed a reasonable balancing of the family unit, the rights of the minor, and the rights of the unborn child. The measure wasn't rock hard—a provision gave young girls the right to go to court to ask a judge to waive the notification requirement.

The legislation passed the General Assembly. Governor Thompson vetoed it, but the assembly overrode the veto. (A companion law, prohibiting abortions because of the sex of the fetus and penalizing doctors who failed to try to revive an aborted fetus that was still alive, did not win enough votes to override Thompson's veto.) Eventually, though, Federal District Court Judge Hubert Will struck the law down as unconstitutional. In my time as a legislator, similar laws that tried to restrict the right to abortion were struck down repeatedly in Illinois and elsewhere.

In the 14 years I was in the Senate, I dealt with many lobbyists. Most would be at it for a few years and then move on, but by far the most persistent and relentless were the people representing the utilities. Any relevant proposals that the utility company itself had not initiated would be resisted, no matter how worthy. So it was with a 1985 law I sponsored that added a small surcharge to phone bills to provide the deaf with devices to allow them to send print messages through the phone. (This was well before wide access to the internet.) The phone company didn't like the idea, and it was all I could do to get the law past the company's lobbying efforts. For some reason, the utility lobbyists stayed long in the job and used their experience to great advantage.

The most irritating lobbying response I experienced in my time came from the pharmaceutical industry, which unloaded a national radio personality, Neil Chayet of "Looking at the Law," against me. I had proposed requiring aspirin containers to feature a warning about Reyes Syndrome, a severe disease that sometimes strikes young children recovering from chicken pox or the flu who have taken aspirin. The measure passed, notwithstanding the lobbyist's threat to use his megaphone to drive me out of office.

Even in those days, the National Rifle Association opposed any legislation affecting gun ownership—the NRA even tried to quash measures that individual members of the organization would support. I pushed through a crackdown on gun possession with a law that required a judge to imprison a felon convicted of a crime with a gun. Gun owners in my district supported the idea.

Also in that legislative session, I brought down the wrath of the auto industry by sponsoring a measure requiring all cars sold in Illinois after 1987 to be equipped with air bags. That measure didn't make it through. But I had better luck while annoying elements of the real estate business by co-sponsoring a bill to crack down on agents who used "panic-peddling" tactics.

Left on hold for future discussion were proposals to restrict public pension fund investment choices and a review of the Illinois corporate income tax. When we concluded the spring 1986 session I had added some heavy hitters to the roster of my opponents—the auto manufacturers, the major utilities, Big Pharma, and the NRA. Soon these were joined by the public pension fund investment community and the State Chamber of Commerce.

Late in 1986, a legislative fracas came close to my heart. The White Sox had been looking for state support for a new stadium, and, as leverage, the club threatened to leave Chicago. The principal Sox owners, Jerry Reinsdorf and Eddie Einhorn, put together a package with Mayor Washington and Governor Thompson, and in a mad rush at the end of the legislative session, the bill got pushed through the General Assembly. The new park was to be built right next to the site of old Comiskey, which would be torn down. A seven-member sports authority would own the park and issue $120 million in bonds to buy the land from the current Sox owners and pay to build the stadium. The bonds would be redeemed with rental fees from the ballclub, a 2-percent increase in the hotel tax, and, if necessary, direct payments by the city and state.

Though the Sox had always been my team, I voted no. I thought the city and state had given up far too much in the deal—in my estimation, Washington and Thompson were playing for votes. The papers were happy to quote me calling Reinsdorf and Einhorn "hustlers" who had manipulated the process, and I warned that the stadium package would redound to the financial disadvantage of the city and state. As it turned out, that prediction was on the mark. Many studies have shown that cities or states that dole out money to hold onto teams consistently get burned—the promised economic payoff to the tax-paying public almost always falls short. Reports have shown that the Sox deal was particularly bad, as the team pays a low rent and gets to keep proceeds from tickets, merchandise, parking, and so on. Fortunately, by the time the Cubs wanted help refurbishing Wrigley Field, the city had learned its lesson.

The Sox vote came after the election that fall, when a conservative Republican named Don Walsh ran against me. In 1982, the *Tribune* had endorsed my opponent, saying I was a "bright, independent gadfly, but some of his legislative proposals have been uncomfortably far-out." By the fall of 1986, however, the paper decided I'd turned into "a thoughtful legislator with wide interests."

I ran virtually no campaign, but easily defeated Walsh in the election. ◼

11

"If a man's handshake is no good, all the [legal] paper
in the world won't make it good."

Mayor Richard J. Daley

In the late fall of 1986, after my third election as senator, I seriously
considered running for mayor the next year as a Republican. The
idea of switching parties had been simmering with me for years.
Among Democrats, I always stood in the center/right, a faction
that often overlapped with liberal Republicans. Early on, during
my term as alderman—officially, a nonpartisan position—I was
approached by members of Ronald Reagan's team, who asked if I
would meet with Reagan and consider being a Reagan delegate to
the 1976 Republican convention. I said no. My respect for Mayor
Daley and my tilt toward organized labor kept me firmly in the
Democratic camp. And this was Chicago—working on a day-to-day
basis as a Republican in the City Council would have been difficult,
to say the least. Besides, I was no fan of the Reagan team. They
had done nothing to defend President Gerald Ford, who was being
hammered for pardoning Richard Nixon, which I thought had been
a courageous move done for the good of the country.

In Springfield, though, some of my closest friends were a group
of bright, young Republicans, including Lynn Martin, who went

on to be secretary of labor under President George H.W. Bush, and Prescott Bloom, an intelligent and popular lawyer from Peoria, who embodied a style of Republicanism that has sadly disappeared from the public forum today—conservative on fiscal matters, liberal on social policy. (Bloom's tragic death in a house fire in 1986 robbed the state of one of its brightest political lights.)

It occurred to me that I could be Republican and remain a strong advocate of labor, though it would be a difficult balance to maintain. On and off, I'd suffered disillusionments with the Democratic Party. When Cal Sutker became state Democratic Party chairman, he asked me to serve as counsel to the party, and out of friendship to him, I agreed. In 1983, the national party appointed me to the committee to consider planks for the 1984 Democratic platform. Chaired by Geraldine Ferraro, the Queens congresswoman who went on to be the Democratic candidate for vice president the next year, the committee held hearings around the country to gather input from assorted interest groups. After a few hearings, I viewed the committee as a hopeless cause. I liked Ferraro, but it was clear the whole exercise was a pageant designed to give voice to the extremes of the party and to hot-button social issues, such as the right to abortion. I wanted the party to run to the center and focus the platform on key economic ideas—jobs and fair opportunity. But I was definitely out of step. I explained my concerns to Ferraro and told her I would be a hindrance to the committee. She understood, and we parted friends.

My next efforts to move the party to the center came with Senator Dennis DeConcini of Arizona and my old City Council colleague William Lipinski, who was now a member of the U.S. House of Representatives. In 1985, they had helped form something called the Democratic Council on Ethnic Americans. In addition to reaching out to ethnic groups, the council supported an agenda to the right of established party thinking. The effort never got far, and the party had to wait for Bill Clinton to shift toward the center.

The chaos surrounding the Democratic maneuverings in the 1986 Illinois gubernatorial race also discouraged me about the party.

Neil Hartigan, the state attorney general and an established North Side politician, was considering a run for governor, and I agreed to manage his campaign. As in 1982, I knew Governor Thompson was vulnerable, and Hartigan—a popular Democratic vote-getter for more than a decade—made an attractive candidate. But Hartigan dithered. He wasn't sure he wanted to do it. He backed out of media commitments and frustrated his staff. He offended David Axelrod— who'd by then left the *Tribune* and was working as a campaign consultant—by confronting him about leaving a meeting early. Axelrod called me at home that night for advice, and I told him to do what he thought was right. He quit and a few weeks later showed up helping the campaign of Adlai Stevenson, who had decided to run again. Soon after, I told Hartigan I was going to step aside, but I would do so in a way that would not harm his campaign. Eventually Hartigan dropped out of the race.

The state Democratic primary in the spring of 1986 turned into an historic fiasco. The party slated a strong roster of candidates, but did little to support them in the face of what was universally acknowledged to be token opposition—a few candidates associated with a far-right, ominously weird political sect founded by a man who called himself Lyndon LaRouche. No one—not the Democratic political leaders, not the precinct workers, not the media—took the LaRouchies, as they were called, seriously. Why would anyone? Their leader believed Queen Elizabeth ran an international drug conspiracy.

Meantime, Stevenson had selected as his lieutenant governor— essentially, the state vice president—George Sangmeister, a popular state senator from Mokena. In those days, candidates for lieutenant governor ran separately in the primary but as a joint ticket with the governor in the general election. (The law wasn't changed to pair them in the primary until 2014.)

Sangmeister was a friend of mine from the Senate, and shortly after Stevenson picked him, he asked to meet with me. He told me that one of his advisors had gone over the nominating petitions of the LaRouche candidates and found that many contained flaws—it was unlikely that the LaRouche candidates had enough valid signatures to qualify. I advised Sangmeister to go to court and challenge them—toss the LaRouchies off the ballot. Sangmeister said he had advocated the same thing, but the Democratic Party leaders—essentially, Stevenson, Hartigan, and House Speaker Mike Madigan—had decided to let it go. They reasoned that it was better to ignore the LaRouchies and not give them any attention. I argued that that would be a big mistake. If you can disqualify your opponent, do it—Barack Obama successfully took that tack when he challenged the petitions of Alice Palmer in his campaign for the state Senate in 1996, the run that launched his political career. The situation was particularly acute with the LaRouchies because it wasn't clear what kind of trouble they could make. I told Sangmeister he should either challenge the cultists or leave the campaign.

In the end, Sangmeister stayed on, and in one of the most flabbergasting outcomes in Illinois political history, two of the LaRouchies won—Mark Fairchild, Sangmeister's opponent for lieutenant governor, and Janice Hart, who was running against Aurelia Pucinski for secretary of state. No one has ever quite been able to figure out how it happened. Some observers theorized that the vote represented a popular revolt against entrenched politicians. Others suspected that Republican leaders had secretly encouraged crossover voting designed to disrupt the Democrats. Certainly, the failure of the overconfident Democrats to expend any effort to promote the slate made a huge difference. Combined with a low turnout, all those factors probably contributed. But I place the primary blame on spelling—the LaRouche names were easy to read and pronounce. The Democratic names were complicated and looked vaguely foreign. Voters who didn't recognize the names went for the simplest.

Several years later, I happened to run into Lyndon LaRouche himself, and I asked about that campaign. He remembered it well—and he was surprised that the Democrat hadn't knocked his candidates off the ballot.

After the election, I participated in some meetings to decide what to do. I suggested that Stevenson go forward as a Democrat, but say that if the ticket were elected he wouldn't give the LaRouche lieutenant governor anything to do—then Stevenson should add that he was in good health and very unlikely to die in office. Whether the tactic would have made a difference, I'll never know. Stevenson decided to bolt the ticket and run as a third-party candidate under the banner of what he called the Solidarity Party. It didn't work—Thompson trounced him in November. The LaRouchies virtually disappeared in the election.

At the same time that I was growing disillusioned with the Democratic Party, I was increasingly dismayed by the condition of the city—its politics and its physical shape. Since his election as mayor in 1983, Harold Washington had been locked in a struggle with an opposition coalition of white aldermen led by Ed Vrdolyak. They blocked virtually anything Washington wanted to accomplish, including his appointments, and he vetoed anything the Vrodolyak faction passed. This was the epic conflict that came to be known as Council Wars. The result was gridlock of a scale and density that rivals any Democrat/Republican divide in Washington today.

Fortunately, Springfield kept me occupied in those days, so I was removed from most of the fracas. The racial element that the solid-white coalition injected into the politics of the situation made me uncomfortable. But Washington played strong racial politics, too. His attitudes worried many of my constituents. At one point, when he scheduled a bus tour that would stop on the Southwest Side, I agreed to stand beside him in Mount Greenwood Park if he delivered a speech renouncing public housing. He planned to say that it had been a well-meaning idea that clearly failed in its execution. Now, public housing had become so stigmatized that it had become synonymous with the destruction of a neighborhood.

But before the tour got off the ground, some of Washington's advisers persuaded him not to make the statement. They told me that he believed what he had planned to say, but he couldn't say it publicly. At that point, I told them I was off the bus.

In that context, I started to think about running for mayor in 1987. Rich Daley was in the middle of his second term as state's attorney, and he said he had absolutely no interest in the mayor's race. Tom Hynes, fresh off his re-election as Cook County assessor, had talked about running, but then told party leaders including Ed Vrdolyak, by this time chairman of the Cook County Democratic Party, that he would not. Vrdolyak himself later indicated that he might run, but it wasn't clear if he would go as a Democrat or an independent or even a Republican. Jane Byrne had long ago declared her plan to run again in the Democratic primary. And Washington intended to seek re-election, though he was hedging about whether he would run in the primary or wait and run as an independent in the general election when, presumably, he would face a divided white vote, the circumstances that had produced his victory in 1983.

With the Democratic field cluttered, and my general dissatisfaction with the Democrats, I explored stepping into the Republican primary. The GOP field at that point looked weak: Don Haider, a management professor at Northwestern University who had served briefly as budget director in Byrne's administration before leaving in a nasty dispute, and Bernard Epton, who'd run an unpleasant and racially tinged race against Washington in 1983. As I quietly explored the idea, a number of people said they'd support me, including Congressman Bill Lipinski. I also got pledges of support from every Republican legislator who had any constituency in Chicago.

As it happened, my son Jerry's football team at Marist High School was marching toward the finals of the state football championship that fall, and I spent many weekends watching high school football. At a game in November, I made the decision: I would run. I called together several hundred friends and supporters, and very quickly we gathered signatures on nominating petitions.

Word quickly got out, and the media started hounding me to comment. TV reporters followed supporters collecting signatures. I tried to stay as low-key as possible. Jane Byrne called me, terribly unhappy. "This is just going to destroy me," she said—she assumed that Southwest Side white voters would defect to the Republican primary to vote for me and draw support from her in her primary battle against Washington. Addie Wyatt, a close acquaintance of Washington's, called and urged me not to run. She was vice president of my father's international union and a friend whom I'd known through labor circles for years. She said Washington was very fond of me and passed on the message that he was happy to accommodate me in any way.

The Republican Party wouldn't slate me because I wouldn't promise to stay in the race under any circumstances, but given the muddled circumstances and the number of potential candidates, I didn't want to make that commitment. If the general election came down to two candidates, each with a realistic chance to win, that would be fine. But I didn't want to be responsible for dividing the vote in any way that elected someone with 40 percent of the turnout. In any case, the endorsement of the Republican Party meant little—the only Republican legislators who had vote-getting ability were supporting me.

When I started exploring a mayoral run, I didn't relish the idea of assuming the responsibility and the refereeing that went with the job. At the same time, I had no doubt that I could win. I intended to file petitions containing 20,000 signatures that could not be challenged (far more signatures than necessary to get on ballot), sending a message to other Republican candidates that I already had enough support to win because so few people voted in a GOP primary. By the Thursday before the first filing date, we had more than 33,000 signatures on more than 1,400 petitions. Over two days, we culled all signatures that could possibly be challenged for one reason or another—the name belonged to an unregistered voter, the address was bad, and so on. We also set aside those petitions circulated by anyone who might be exposed to recrimination from party leaders, such as city employees. The election attorneys reviewed everything, and we bound the petitions for filing the first day.

But nothing is simple in Chicago politics. On Saturday, Lipinski asked me to meet him at his office to talk about the race. He had been outspoken in his support for me, which was going way out on a limb, because he was a Democratic committeeman. On important meetings involving politics, I always liked to bring someone else along just to make sure I understood what was being said. I told Lipinski that I'd bring Mike Sheahan, my successor as 19th Ward alderman. The two of us shared an office on 10231 South Western Avenue. Lipinski insisted I come alone. So late that afternoon, I arrived at Lipinski's office on Archer Avenue. He and I chatted for a few minutes, and suddenly the door popped open, and in stepped Ed Vrdolyak, who by then had announced he would run as a third-party candidate. Vrdolyak went into a presentation—how he and I differ on many things, but he never disliked me; how we can agree to disagree, but he could support me as mayor. After a few minutes, he bid us goodbye. He didn't say it directly, but he left the impression that he might drop out of the race and throw his backing to me.

Now I was in an awkward spot. I had planned to campaign on the premise that I would be open, operating without the intrigue and maneuverings of the last few years. But with the meeting, I didn't know if I had been dropped into some kind of a closed-room deal. Lipinski had my best political interests at heart, and he kept saying, "You'll be a winner, this will work." But I left very uncomfortable because of the way the meeting could be portrayed. In fact, I enjoyed Ed Vrdolyak—he struck me as a Chicago version of New York's famous Jazz Age mayor, Jimmy Walker. He was lively and inventive, and though in many instances he didn't volunteer significant information, he never lied to me outright.

The next day, Tom Hynes threw a party before the Bears game at Soldier Field. On the way, I stopped at Rich Daley's house in Bridgeport to talk strategy with him and to be absolutely certain he didn't want to run. He told me to go ahead. Despite the Lipinski meeting, the path ahead looked clear. But at the Bears game, Hynes pulled me aside. He now said he was still thinking of running as a third-party candidate, and he asked me to hold off filing for a day while he decided. He and I would draw voters from the same base, and because of that, if he ran, I wouldn't—again, I didn't want to divide the vote. So I agreed to hold off.

Hynes had run the assessor's office without the taint of scandal, not an easy accomplishment in that office, where money and politics often intersect. Over the years, he had also acquired a reputation for caution, and it's easy to see how he earned it. The next day, a Monday, he told me that he would run. On Tuesday, he said he wouldn't. I waited. Finally, on Wednesday, we had a long meeting at his house. He had changed his mind once again: He was about to announce that he would be a candidate for mayor. I wasn't longing to be mayor of Chicago, and at that point, with all the finagling, I decided to hang it up. I agreed to be Hynes's campaign manager.

But I regretted all the effort my supporters had gone through— hundreds of them had worked to circulate petitions and organize a campaign. I invited everyone to a ballroom at the Holiday Inn on West 95th Street and gave them the news.

Jane Byrne put on a spirited campaign in the Democratic primary, but Harold Washington beat her by a margin of 52 percent to 43 percent. The vote broke down almost entirely on racial lines, and one of Washington's supporters raised race in offensively hostile terms. The well-known lawyer Eugene Pincham, by that time an Illinois appellate judge, told a rally that any man from the South Side who didn't vote for Washington "ought to be hung." Still, Byrne and Washington seemed to avoid the raw, Black-and-white antagonisms of the previous four years—or perhaps Chicago in general was just worn out. In any case, the newspapers congratulated the candidates and the city for putting on a basically responsible contest. One headline in the *Tribune* appropriately summed up the city's thin moral victory: "A contest no more unpleasant than races elsewhere."

The general election pitted Washington against three opponents: Hynes, running as the candidate of his invented organization, the

Chicago First Party; Vrdolyak, running on Adlai III's makeshift Solidarity Party ticket; and the Republican contender, Don Haider.

From the start, I knew that the only chance for Hynes was if Vrdolyak dropped out. I fully expected he would when he saw he didn't stand a chance, but Vrdolyak stayed in, even as he trailed in the polls. Meantime, while Hynes would have made a good mayor, he was an uninspiring candidate. He was meticulous and articulate, but it was as if he were arguing in front of a federal appeals court or playing a senator from Connecticut. His style had no spark—he couldn't ignite a crowd. The polls showed Washington leading by a substantial margin, and in a move designed to force Vrdolyak out of the race, Hynes accused Vrdolyak of having held a meeting with a mobster. The accusation back-fired—it was loose and out of character for Hynes, and it undermined the effort to paint him as the man in the race above the fray. The campaign was doomed.

Two days before the election, Hynes called me and told me he was dropping out. I told him I thought that would be a mistake. He said he'd talked it over with his wife and kids, and this was the decision. To this day, I'm not certain of his logic. I think he genuinely didn't want to put himself and his supporters through the dispiriting ritual of losing on Election Day. But I disagreed with the decision.

On April 7, 1987, Mayor Washington swept to victory with 53 percent of the vote, trouncing Vrdolyak and Haider largely on the strength of his overwhelming majority among Black voters, though he did get some support from whites along the lake. Vrdolyak, who'd given up his seat on the council to run for mayor, graciously congratulated Washington and wished him "the best of health, success in the next four years."

It wasn't to be. Though Washington had tightened his grip on the council and begun to reach out to white voters—he endorsed Richard Daley for state's attorney that fall—he collapsed in his office and died of a heart attack on November 25, only 65 years old. I happened to be driving past City Hall just after it happened. Several officers ran across the street, and I stopped to ask what was going on.

They said they thought the mayor had died. A few minutes later, the news came over the radio.

Washington's death left a power vacuum in City Hall that soon imploded into chaos. (If Vrdolyak had remained in the council, he would have become mayor.) All the scheming and maneuvering of the Council Wars era broke out again. I was getting calls about this alliance and that faction, about tactics and strategies. This time, one of the serious splits came within the African American contingent. Tim Evans, a friend of mine and a veteran South Side alderman and close ally of Mayor Washington, seemed a likely choice to fill out the remainder of the mayoral term. But, as Dominic A. Pacyga points out in his history of Chicago, some Black politicians had chafed under Washington's domination and hoped for more independence. The choice of interim mayor was up to the City Council, which broke into endlessly spinning and shifting factions. I went down to City Hall on the long night that finally saw the election of Eugene Sawyer, a mild and reliable alderman. I was in the council chambers, but it was so crowded and the air so heavy that I left and drove home.

Despite my dissatisfaction with my Senate role, I returned to Springfield, hoping again to make progress on several issues, particularly the school funding formula—the endless quest to improve opportunities for schools with a poor tax base. A staffer on the Senate Revenue Committee, the tireless Paul Vallas, helped produce a major rewrite of the Illinois corporate income tax that would steer money to the schools. The proposal earned me the enmity of the state Chamber of Commerce, and, sadly, the measure was never called.

In Chicago, interim Mayor Gene Sawyer was proving a credible caretaker of the office. A reserved and modest man, Sawyer was more acceptable to many white voters than Washington had been, but he hardly qualified as a dynamic leader. The former alderman Tyrone Kenner once told me a story that summed up Sawyer's unflappability.

Several people were sitting around Sawyer's living room at his home in the 6th Ward on the Southeast Side. Kenner stood up to introduce himself to someone and just then a stray bullet crashed through the window and hit the sofa right where Kenner had been sitting. Everyone dove for the floor, except Sawyer. He sat there as if nothing had happened and didn't even bother calling the police.

In taking the job of mayor, Sawyer had embittered Tim Evans and a substantial number of Blacks, who unfairly labeled him a sellout to whites. Soon, rivals started circling. In addition to Evans, several aldermen and even Jane Byrne were among those who either indicated an interest in making a run for mayor or became the object of speculation.

The starter's gun fired in November 1988 when the state Supreme Court ruled that there was enough time left in Washington's unexpired term to require a special election, set for the following spring. Throughout the fall of 1988, Rich Daley had been preoccupied with running for re-election as state's attorney. After he won handily, he joined the mayoral race that December.

He certainly knew what he was getting into. Until the mid-1960s, running the City That Works had been demanding but fulfilling for Richard J. Daley—building O'Hare, the McCormick Place convention center, and the University of Illinois at Chicago; watching award-winning high-rises go up; steering the country's most powerful machine; helping place John F. Kennedy in the White House. Daley had been celebrated on the cover of *Time* magazine in March 1963. But the job grew burdensome as the city started to fracture along racial lines, and the chaotic Democratic Convention of 1968 badly damaged Daley's public image.

His son Rich was a careful and astute political observer who kept his own counsel. At age 27, he served at the 1970 Illinois Constitutional Convention, on his way to a seat in the state Senate. Over the years, I have listened to all the pundits go on about the father wishing for his son to succeed him. The few who really knew both—such as Earl Bush, a longtime advisor to both—dismiss this as pure speculation. Most often circumstances dictate choices, however. In this case, circumstances—the death of his father, the paranoid attacks by Jane Byrne, the resentments of some old-line machine Democrats—pushed Rich Daley in another direction, and he never recoiled from a political challenge.

Daley's entry in the race scattered the contenders. Alderman Ed Burke quickly withdrew, as did several other people toying with a run. Mayor Sawyer and Tim Evans, battling over who carried the banner of Harold Washington, looked headed to divide the Black vote. Evans eventually dropped out of the Democratic primary in favor of running as an independent in the general election under what he called the Harold Washington Party.

Daley set up a campaign organization that included David Axelrod, David Wilhelm—later a top operative in Bill Clinton's 1992 presidential campaign—and a young up-and-comer named Rahm Emanuel. When it quickly became apparent that Emanuel didn't understand how Chicago politics worked—didn't know who could deliver votes—he got moved over to fundraising, which became his forte.

Both the primary and general elections turned out to be relatively easy. After 10 years of political feuding and brawling, Chicagoans were fed up, and the figure of Daley recalled a time when the city enjoyed some peace (though Daley didn't invoke his father's name). And just as a split in the white vote in 1983 had helped hand the mayoralty to Washington, the split in the Black vote in 1989 helped tilt the scales to Daley. In the primary, Evans's people told Black voters not to vote for Sawyer. Daley won. In the general election, Sawyer's people told Black voters not to vote for Evans. Daley won again, overwhelming Evans by a 56-41 margin. In both elections, Daley fashioned his victories on a coalition of whites and Hispanics, and in each instance, Black voters failed to come out in Washington-era levels. When someone asked him about plans for the next election, just two years away, Daley said, "First, I start governing."

I originally intended to leave the Senate at the end of the 1990 session. I'd grown tired of the political wrangling. Though I'd learned how to move my programs forward—in part, it involved confronting Phil Rock and House Speaker Mike Madigan so much that they didn't want the fight any more—but I hated being away from home. I'd already missed so much—including the elementary school graduations of two of my sons. Still, with some Chicago matters lingering, I decided to stand for re-election, though I had no intention of campaigning. Meantime, Harry "Bus" Yourell, a Democratic committeeman hack from Worth Township who griped I didn't pay enough attention to the suburbs, decided to play a bit of election trickery on me. Yourell collaborated with the local GOP to put a Democrat-turned-Republican in the Republican primary. I countered with my own Democrat-turned Republican (for this race), Tom Walsh, who was an old friend. Tom won the Republican primary, but from then on, he had as little interest in campaigning as I did on the way to victory in November.

During my last term in Springfield, I focused on Chicago issues. The city's needs weren't popular with Republicans generally and with some downstate Democrats, but I had friendships with a small group of Republicans to whom I could turn when a Chicago project required a few extra votes. For example, the city planned an expansion of McCormick Place, a $1-billion project to help keep the facility competitive in the trade-show business, a major piece of the city's economy. Las Vegas, Atlanta, Los Angeles—a number of cities were going after Chicago's share of the business, so the city came up with a plan to almost double McCormick's exhibit space, adding a 2-million-square-foot exhibition hall to the complex. Bonds to fund the project would be paid with hospitality and entertainment taxes that would largely fall on out-of-towners.

The expansion seemed an obvious and necessary boost for Chicago, but for some reason, Senate President Phil Rock wanted to kill the bill. He pretended to be for it, but I could see that he was working against it. He decided to call the bill when there weren't the votes to pass it—we were five or six votes shy. I asked him to wait, and still he went ahead. I roamed the floor, seeking help from Republicans and some downstate Democrats, and finally the bill squeaked by. The expansion went forward.

I couldn't figure out what Rock's game was. But around that time, the Las Vegas Convention Bureau opened an office in Chicago. A few years later, I happened to be talking to an acquaintance who worked there, and she told me that Phil Rock was always hanging around the office. I meant to ask Rock about this, but never had the right moment (he died several years ago). In the end, I just chalked it up to President Rock being Rock—politically very smart, but often with an unknown agenda.

I stayed in the Senate until the following spring, cleaning up a few matters and working on another important issue—comparable-worth legislation that would have required Illinois to equalize the pay rate for women employed by the state. Unfortunately, the new Republican governor, Jim Edgar, vetoed the bill as too expensive.

By May 1992, I arranged for my staff assistant, Tom Dart, to succeed me as state senator. (He is currently the Cook County sheriff.) I spent a few weeks in Springfield, thanking staffers and seeing old colleagues. Then I gave Phil Rock a simple resignation letter, packed up the files and notes I wanted to keep, and went home to Chicago, my years as an officer-holder over. It would be a decade before I was at the capital again—to see our youngest son, Kevin, sworn is as a member of the Illinois General Assembly. ◼

12

"There are fish swimming in the basement
of the [Merchandise] Mart."

WMAQ Radio News

On Monday, April 13, 1992, I was in my legislative district office working on the details of my resignation from the Illinois Senate. I had been in elective office for nearly 18 years, and I had wanted to leave for over a decade. Twice I had announced that I would not seek re-election, but something always came up to forestall the move. Now I was working on securing house sponsors for my pending bills that had passed out of the Senate. I was also trying to lock up a commitment to appoint my staffer Tom Dart to replace me in the Senate, a decision that rested with Democratic committeeman Tom Hynes, who had some reservations about Dart.

Earlier that morning—at around six o'clock—someone had called to tell me that a flood had overwhelmed the basement of the Merchandise Mart, the enormous commercial property then owned by the Kennedy family. I didn't give it much thought, but as the day moved on, radio reports came pouring in.

A construction crew adding a piling beside a bridge across the Chicago River at Kinzie Street had opened a hole in a tunnel that ran under the river. Water was draining out of the river into a network of tunnels beneath the Loop—an antique and abandoned system once used to deliver coal and goods and now sewn with telephone lines and electric cables. The tunnels connected the basements of buildings that housed Chicago's major businesses. Loop workers had been evacuated, and electricity shut off, but the river water could damage inventories, gas and electrical systems, and even the foundations of the buildings. An underground flood was threatening to drown the city's economy.

At a little after noon, a staffer for Mayor Richard M. Daley called and asked if I could stop by City Hall. The mayor's office is on the fifth floor. After entering through the main door into an outer reception area manned by security, a visitor sits until cleared to enter. He or she is then escorted by a mayoral aide to the inner reception area, a large, tastefully decorated room with three desks occupied by the mayor's secretaries. At the other side of the room are rows of chairs where visitors—rarely more than two or three—again sit to await the meeting. Conversations, if any in the room, are carried on in hushed tones, almost whispers. Beyond this reception area is the mayor's large office and a small conference room.

When I arrived around two o'clock, both the outer and inner reception areas were jammed with people—department heads, city commissioners, retired commissioners. Many hadn't known until that morning that the tunnel network even existed. Several groups of four or five were engaged in noisy discussions. Consultants started to arrive, one loudly claiming that he had experience dealing with flooded systems around the world. He had gone down to the site and was covered with mud. He insisted that he had a solution, and as he lectured, he paced around the reception area tracking mud all over the carpet. One of the mayor's guards pulled me aside and told me the little guy had come with two bodyguards who were carrying badges of some sort and Uzis under their coats. That was the kind of day it was.

By evening, no clear answers had emerged on how to plug the leak. Trucks had dumped tons of gravel and chunks of concrete into the swirling water above the hole without stopping the flow. Someone had suggested dropping in a steel plate. Another suggestion led to a barge loaded with mattresses nosing into position to sink mattresses over the hole. Neither of those options was finally used. The water was too murky for underwater cameras to get a good look, and the suction was too strong for divers to go down.

Throughout all this, the mayor was in his office on the phones. Daley was well known to the press for his tirades when he saw something amiss on his travels around the city—downed street signs, potholed pavement, abandoned buildings; any of these might set him off. So when I entered his office I assumed he would be livid. He wasn't—he was as calm as could be. I asked what the plan was. "Don't ask me," he said. "I don't know anything about fixing flooded tunnels." He must have sensed that his response startled me, because he quickly added, "We will just get it fixed."

Congressman Dan Rostenkowski and Governor Jim Edgar arrived. Rostenkowski, by then the long-time chairman of the House Ways and Means Committee, was considered the most powerful member of Congress. Over the years, he had been responsible for bringing millions of federal dollars to the city. The mayor asked that I join them in the small conference room, where Rosty telephoned President George H. W. Bush to explain the problem.

Rosty put the call on speaker phone, and from the onset, it was clear they were friends. The President called him Danny, and Rosty went from addressing him as Mr. President to Georgie. The conversation ended with the congressman saying, "This is no bullshit, George, we really need help," and the president answering, "Danny, anything you need." Within a few hours, 88 members of the Army Corps of Engineers arrived, accompanied by the Federal Emergency Management Agency.

By the end of the day, Kenny Construction, a company based in Wheeling, Illinois, had started to plug the leak using quick-setting concrete. But the question remained how to get rid of the 250 million gallons of water still sitting beneath the Loop. Over the next several days, the Army Corps of Engineers put together a plan to dig another hole and drain the water into the Deep Tunnel system that had been built for more conventional flood control. But a million details needed to be worked out and decided.

The mayor set up a command center in a building near the leak site. He worked out of an interior office and stationed a trusted employee, Valerie Jarrett, outside the office to ensure that nobody got to see him without authorization.

Those who knew or had worked with Rich Daley were aware of a unique talent he possessed: If he didn't want you to know his thoughts on a matter, you could never discern it from anything he said. In the state Senate, when he was the chairman of the Judiciary Committee and spoke on a measure, the other members often asked whether he supported or opposed the proposal. He answered always: "You will know after the vote."

He soon displayed this talent to the director of the Federal Emergency Management Agency. When FEMA is sent to a declared disaster, the agency requires the local government to relinquish authority over the situation, basically delegating decision making to FEMA. The local officials are required to sign a mission statement.

Daley had made up his mind he was not turning over local control—not to FEMA or anyone else. He knew of FEMA's dismal performance during Hurricane Hugo in 1989. As the Loop flood operation proceeded, the FEMA director continued to press for his mission statement, and Daley continued to evade him with his mumbo-jumbo conversation.

This went on for several days. Finally, the FEMA director and the general from the Army Corps of Engineers edged past the outer office gatekeeper, Valerie Jarrett, and confronted Daley with an ultimatum: Either sign the statement, or we are leaving tonight. I sat watching as the mayor and the officials went back and forth for about 30 minutes, and then Daley excused himself from the room. Nearly an hour passed, while the FEMA director shuffled through his papers and the general tried to make small talk. Eventually, I was summoned outside to a phone call. It was Daley. He had left the building. "Are they still there?" he asked. When I said yes, he hung up. I went back and told them Daley would not be returning to the meeting. The director exploded, but then suggested perhaps I could sign in my capacity, whatever it was. I told him I didn't work for the city, and he again became agitated. "Why are you here?" he demanded. I said I was a legislator and a city resident. Raging, he warned: "You tell the mayor, if this contract isn't signed tonight, all of us, including the Army engineers, are leaving Chicago tonight." Then he stormed out. I relayed the message, and the mayor replied, "They aren't going anywhere."

For the next few days, Daley worked furiously coordinating the cleanup with the Army Corps of Engineers—an excellent unit that went about its business with efficiency. The agreement to put the operation under FEMA wasn't signed until Saturday night, six days after the flood, and by then, the way forward had been settled. Thirteen years later, watching the television coverage of Katrina, the hurricane that devastated New Orleans, I realized how wise Daley had been in Chicago's flood crisis.

I saw Daley a lot and talked to him often in the first years, when he was mayor and I was still in the Senate. He had a clear vision for the city. He thought about it a lot, read a lot, and called on a wide circle of civic and business leaders for advice. Those who don't know Daley vastly underestimate his knowledge of urban affairs.

Early on during his first term, I saw a model of his vision. On his office floor, he unfolded a huge map containing plans for development all over Chicago. Most of it was tied to universities and hospitals—institutions that depend heavily for revenues from special sources, government, and philanthropy. The city neighborhoods could be renewed and buttressed by thriving medical centers and renowned institutions of higher learning. Much happened on Daley's watch. DePaul, Northwestern, the University of Illinois, Loyola, and the University of Chicago all expanded. Columbia College became an anchor of the South Loop, and St. Xavier University bolstered the Southwest Side. On the east side of downtown, Northwestern Hospital rebuilt and expanded, while Rush Hospital did the same on the west.

A couple of big early proposals—the third airport on the far Southeast Side and the Central Area Circulator, a trolley system around the Loop—were abandoned as expensive and problematic. Daley has a personal dislike of gambling and opposed bringing a casino to the city. But with the economy flowing, the mayor kept building new police and fire stations and new libraries. Residents flocked to the South Loop, which builders had started targeting back when I was in the council.

Development stretched into the West Side, with the construction of the new Chicago Stadium, the home of the Bulls and Blackhawks, on Madison Street. Downtown, Millennium Park became an architectural jewel and the city's tourist magnet. With 100,000 new trees and flowery planters, Daley helped refresh the concrete landscape. And he kept the city clean, even in some of the roughest areas. If a house was abandoned and decrepit, it would come down rather than languish for a decade as an eyesore and possible hideout for criminals.

Some argue Daley was lucky—that he was in the right place at the right time to ride the surging economy and a renewed enthusiasm for urban living. It's true that other big cities, including New York, rebounded in the 1990s, but the opportunities presented had to be managed well, and Daley focused relentlessly on building a better Chicago. In some instances, he did it at considerable political risk—for example, taking charge of the city's broken-down school system. A front-page story in the *Wall Street Journal* in August 1996, just before the Democratic Convention returned to the city for the first time since the disaster of 1968, called Chicago "America's urban paradise."

In the final years of his administration, Daley faced tougher times, as the American economy collapsed and he was forced to find additional revenues. He responded by leasing city assets to entities that would derive most of the supporting fees from non-Chicago residents—the Skyway toll road deal and a parking meter concession transaction, for example. In retrospect, some critics say the parking deal looks bad—the $1.16-billion price tag could have been far higher. Daley went all in on an effort to land the Olympic games. The games would have created thousands of jobs and renewed depressed neighborhoods, but even with the help of newly elected President Obama, the politics of the choice was far beyond their efforts.

He ran for re-election five times—1991, 1995, 1999, 2003, and 2007. (The mayoral election became nonpartisan starting in 1999.) I conferred with people working the campaigns, but none of the contests were serious, Daley's opposition was weak. While he largely ignored the crumbling Democratic machine, his support included all the major factions—ethnic whites, lakefront liberals, Hispanics, a sizeable proportion of African American residents. He won over many of the South Side ministries, and that brought many Black voters into his camp.

As for campaign funds, Daley never wanted. A long roster of successful Chicago businessmen raised whatever was needed. Pat Ryan of Aon Insurance and real estate developer Neal Bluhm led many of the fundraising events.

Outsiders used to imagine that the mayor was concerned about potential competition. When Barack Obama first came to see me in 1999 planning to run for Congress, he told me I could assure Daley that he had no plans ever to run against the mayor. I told Obama: "Believe me, Daley has no concern about facing you or anyone in a re-election."

After I left the Senate, assorted reporters claimed that I had some kind of political line into the mayor. One columnist repeatedly called me the mayor's "political brain," which was not true. The misconception about my role may have originated with the people who would go to Daley seeking his encouragement to run for office. Rather than wasting his time, the mayor would often tell them to go see me. Some of the office-seekers interpreted that as a tacit endorsement by the mayor, but I would caution that they would rise or fall on their own. On some high-profile campaigns in which I participated (not involving Daley), reporters and others would ask how Daley felt about an issue, and the question tended to float to me. But I didn't bring any particular inside knowledge—just a long association.

Mayor Daley didn't enjoy the media. At best, he was indifferent and didn't even learn the names of some reporters who covered him. The stories that appeared about him varied between the celebratory, citing his careful management and the blossoming of Chicago under his direction, and the critical. One principal criticism claimed that a circle of friends and advisors received favored treatment in business deals with the city. I was swept up in this criticism, too.

During my Senate career, I was never much concerned about money. My family got by largely on my Senate salary, which was about $30,000 annually in the late 1980s, and what I received for part-time teaching at various universities and law schools. In the mid-1980s, I invested with a group of my grade school friends in the purchase of a company that distributed waterproofing materials. Because of my position, we all agreed going in that we would not sell any product to any public entity. Throughout the time I held office, my complete tax returns were available in my district office for any constituent to read.

Twice in my Senate years, I tried to get into the practice of law. But I had too many commitments and distractions, and after a couple of months, I gave up on that idea. When I left the Senate in 1992, I received several offers from Chicago law firms and decided to join Lord, Bissell & Brook (today Locke Lord) with the understanding that I was not going to be a rainmaker or a lobbyist.

While at Lord Bissell, attorneys representing McDonald's Corporation sought to retain the firm in a case involving the City of Chicago, and that eventually led to criticism of me. Here's how that played out: The city had issued a request for proposal (a so-called

RFP) to manage the retail concessions at O'Hare's new International Terminal. Two responses came in, one from a partnership group headed by McDonald's, the other from a partnership headed by Marriott, an experienced food and beverage concession operator. Though both sides represented widely respected international corporations, the McDonald's proposal clearly guaranteed a substantially higher financial return for the city. After the filing deadline passed, one of the members of the McDonald's group was bought by the competitor, which then argued that the McDonald's response was no longer in compliance with the city's proposal request. McDonald's claimed it had been the victim of an unethical business practice. The competitor responded that when you choose a partner, you assume the risk of its actions. (Years later, I heard strong evidence that the purchase was specifically intended to knock out the McDonald's bid.)

While the city was reviewing the matter, Marriott announced that it was restructuring into two separate corporations, each to be listed on the New York Stock Exchange. This caused a wave of protests from the shareholders and bondholders, with threats of lawsuits. The city decided to issue a new RFP.

With the second round of proposals, the guaranteed rent from the McDonald's group was again substantially greater, and it won the contract. Sometime during this process, the McDonald's partnership group sought to hire me as a full-time employee as part of a plan to expand into nationwide airport retail. The offer was not conditioned on any decisions made on Chicago.

Concerned about the public perception because of my association with Daley, I went back and forth. I vetted the arrangement with teams of lawyers and sought the advice of a local newspaper editor, laying out my concerns over the appearance of impropriety. He acknowledged that I had no conflict of interest, but on the more vexatious question of appearances, the editor pointed out that the term "conflict of interest" was ambiguous and often depended on who was framing the issue and why. He said my reputation for integrity would not be controlling if someone had an ax to grind.

I was also aware of the political complications for the mayor. While I had always avoided discussions of city business, I assumed Daley was knowledgeable on matters such as the new O'Hare contract. His attitude on city business was a little different from that of most elected officials. Though he valued his personal reputation and understood the political ramifications of his decisions, he would not allow his judgment to be dictated or controlled by outside critics. His standard was forthright. If an application was without a direct conflict of interest and it was the most qualified and provided the largest financial return to the city, that application would be selected. Applying his standard often resulted in his present and former political opponents being selected to provide goods or services to the city. He would not disqualify anyone from doing business with the city based on his personal dislikes, no matter how much it might pain him. Given the breadth of Daley's relationships stretching back through the decades, this pragmatic approach may have been the only realistic way to go. Critics of Rich Daley still refuse to accept it.

The development of the internet has opened potentially new avenues for the system of selecting public contracts and business. One calls for qualifying bidders on the basis of experience, recent performance, and financial ability. Qualified bidders would then compete in a transparent public auction with the contract going to the highest bidder. People opposed to this procedure claim it would discriminate against recently formed businesses, many of which are minority owned.

The accusations of contract favoritism in Chicago certainly didn't end with Daley's departure from office. Indeed, his successor, Rahm Emanuel, was dogged by similar criticisms. And, in fact, donations, friendships, and public business overlap at virtually all levels of government. Eliminating that overlap would be impossible, in my opinion, and I'm not persuaded it would always be a good thing. In my mind, performance should be the overwhelming measure of success.

In the end, I accepted the offer to work for the McDonald's group, and, as the editor predicted, I did come under criticism. But I remained actively involved in airport retail and duty-free sales for two decades, working in some way in every major airport in the country.

In September 2010, Richard M. Daley surprised the city by announcing he would not seek re-election the next year. His wife, Maggie, was in the middle of a long and ultimately losing battle with cancer. I suspect he was wearying of managing the conflicts in running a big city—increasingly the City Council had been pushing back against him. And by the next election, his term would stretch 22 years. "It's time," he told reporters. "Everybody is replaceable in life; no one is here forever."

Richard M. Daley came to the mayor's office in 1989 with a template for the future growth of Chicago and a belief that the city is a global asset and hence, when possible, Chicago taxpayers should not overwhelmingly bear the costs of operating it. With a population of around 2.7 million, the city features 1.2 million private-sector employees—obviously, many of them live outside the city. Before the coronavirus pandemic hit, the federal Bureau of Labor Statistics reported that the Chicago metro region contained 4.7 million private- and public-sector employees and generated an annual gross regional product of $635 billion.

Daley ended up accomplishing much that was on his template. He helped grow Chicago's great universities and medical institutions, with the attendant advantages to adjacent neighborhoods. He bolstered Chicago's place as a tourist destination with marvelous magnets like Millennium Park, the Museum Campus, and a nationally admired lakefront. He worked to preserve the city's ethnic communities and renew abandoned areas in the South Loop, Fulton Market, Wicker Park, and Bucktown. The resurgence brought an influx of new residences, restaurants, businesses, and talented workers.

Prior to taking office, Daley had compiled a list of possible future crises with the planned responses: power failures, terrorist attacks, transportation disasters, earthquakes, weather-related emergencies, health epidemics, and mechanical failures. A tunnel flood and a worldwide financial collapse weren't on his list.

As it turned out, the Loop flood of 1992 was handled smoothly enough that it became not much more than an expensive inconvenience. That wasn't the case with the 2008 financial crisis. It resulted in blocks and blocks of foreclosed and abandoned homes, increased poverty, and an enormous disruption of Daley's plans to rehabilitate many of what are now the most crime-ridden and dangerous areas of the city.

Unlike his predecessors, the mayor served during a period when the traditional practices of political compromise were changing and Congressional earmarks were out of favor. Political patronage was under scrutiny, as was Chicago's funnel to federal funds. Ways and Means Chairman Dan Rostenkowski, a Chicago treasure, left Congress. Even the value of having a president from Chicago was changing, as evidenced by the city's failure to be chosen as the site for the 2016 Olympics.

When Daley started his first term, the Chicago hierarchical street gangs controlled and terrorized the high-rise public housing projects. The projects are now down, and the big gangs are largely broken up, but modern technology—cell phones and social media—has allowed fractured, warring remnants to bring massive waves of violence to troubled city blocks.

From an historical perspective, it is too early to define the long-term impact of Richard M. Daley, even though for two decades he was consistently acknowledged by the mayors of the nation's other large cities to be the most effective mayor of his time. Daley defined and provided a great vision for the city, and left it in a much better way than it was in 1989. His finest accomplishment was bringing harmony to a city and a government much divided by racial discord.

Today we hear constant talk that Chicago is becoming two cities: one where children are comfortably escorted to high-performing schools, the other where poor kids dodge their way through bullet-ridden streets to arrive at inadequate schools. Truth is, Chicago has already become two cities.

The people of Chicago can't be fooled—with violent street crime, poor public schools, and often cruel winter weather, the city will never become another Silicon Valley. But two of these three Chicago problems, honestly acknowledged, are solvable. The city has proved itself wonderfully resilient over the years—the rapid recovery from the Great Fire of 1871 stands as an iconic historical example. Despite persistent problems exacerbated by the pandemic, Chicago will endure, and Richard M. Daley's 1989 template for the future growth of the city remains valid. ▪

13

"I was there 36 years; they changed the rules 30 times."

Congressman Dan Rostenkowski

~~~~~~

In early February 1994, Dan Rostenkowski called me. He was in a tough primary race, and he asked if I might get involved. The congressman was a Chicago treasure: deep roots in the city, a longtime Democratic committeeman on the Northwest Side, and, as the powerful chairman of the House Ways and Means Committee, an unabashed supporter of Chicago. I knew him as a man who cared for people. A few years earlier, when I faced a non-political problem, he called out of the blue with an offer of help.

But now he had a problem. His name had come up in a prolonged federal grand jury investigation into claims that some lawmakers had continued to exchange government funded stamps for cash with the House Post Office, even after being warned it was illegal. Rosty never had any personal gain from the practice, but he was stubborn and ignored the directive.

Dan Rostenkowski was a product of rough-and-tumble Chicago politics—his family went back nearly a century in the city, and his father had served as an alderman. When Dan was 10, two precinct workers in his father's ward were found dead from gunshots in a parked car in front of the family home. But that was a time long past. Rosty had entered Congress when Eisenhower was president and had served in there with four men who went on to the White House—Kennedy, Johnson, Ford, and Bush. Rostenkowski liked them all, and they all liked him. In Washington, he was known simply as Rosty and considered perhaps the most powerful person in the Congress. To his old political friends in Chicago, he was Danny. After Mayor Daley died, Rostenkowski was recognized as first among equals on the Cook County Democratic Committee, and first among all of Illinois Democrats.

When he called me in 1994, though, ambitious Chicago politicians had their eyes on Rostenkowski's 5th Congressional District seat. He was six weeks away from the primary election, floundering in a race against state Senator John Cullerton; Dick Simpson, a reformist former alderman; and a sitting local alderman, Mike Wojcik. I had actually met with Cullerton on my own the year before and urged him not to run—Rosty was too valuable to Chicago. Now, Cullerton was 20 points ahead in the polls.

Rosty told me he didn't really have much of a campaign organization, so I agreed to get involved. He was right. He had nothing going, though he had rented a huge space near his Congressional office on the North Side. Because of the investigation, FBI agents were always sitting in a car out front, but inside, the place was dead—a few desks and a handful of people who didn't really know what they were doing. Rod Blagojevich was off in a corner, ostensibly to help, but actually plotting how he was going to run the next time out. Blago's father-in-law, Dick Mell, was hanging around, also plotting for Blagojevich. The brother of another high-up campaign worker was sitting at a desk, staring at the wall—he was there so someone could keep an eye on him until his family got him into rehab somewhere. Volunteers kept marching in, but nobody had organized them or figured out how to use them properly. One had caught the attention of a community newspaper by tacking Rostenkowski posters to trees in a park. David Axelrod had made some commercials for the campaign, but they weren't having an impact.

The Ways and Means chairman had been easily re-elected to Congress 17 times. How had things fallen so low? The grand jury investigation had flummoxed and preoccupied him, and for a time, he doubted he would run again. He eventually filed, but he only went through the motions. Then the suggestion apparently filtered out from somewhere in the Clinton Administration that if Rosty won the primary, the charges against him were likely to be limited to misdemeanors, counts that could be disposed of easily. That put the fire back in Rosty, but now he had to ignite his campaign. The 5th Congressional District, which had recently been redrawn, covered a swatch of the far North and Northwest sides of Chicago and several largely blue-collar suburbs. The area had solidly supported Rostenkowski over the years, but recently turned more conservative and Republican.

I spent most of the next six weeks in that big campaign office. I brought in a couple dozen people from my own campaigns and a group of talented veterans of the Rich Daley elections from earlier years. My son Jerry, who had recently graduated from Yale, took a leave from his job and coordinated efforts.

With Rosty's record, finding the theme to trumpet was obvious. Over the years, he brought home federal funds to repave the Kennedy Expressway; dig Deep Tunnel, the flood-prevention system; revamp Chicago's airports; rehabilitate Navy Pier; and build the Blue Line Transit System out to O'Hare. In all, he was behind hundreds of Chicago projects that stretched over both Democratic and Republican administrations. So the theme of the campaign cried out: Above the fray and delivering for the people of his district and the city.

We identified more than 25 subgroups in the district—ethnic groups, occupational organizations, social and charitable interests, and so on—and designed a campaign to reach each of them. We tuned the theme for each group and found strong and respected voices to carry our message. I wrote more than 20 separate mailing pieces—to police, firefighters, Asians, Irish, Italians, tradesmen, teachers, nurses, and others. An enormous number of district residents—more than 25,000—were contributors to four prominent charitable institutions. I asked the head of one of them, Monsignor Ignatius McDermott of the McDermott Foundation, which supports a variety of programs for the down-and-out, to coordinate a letter-writing effort, pointing out all Rosty had done for the city.

The 1992 redistricting had meant that long-time Representative Frank Annunzio and Rostenkowski were competing for the same seat. Rather than face off against Rosty, Annunzio had retired, upsetting some Italians in the new district. I asked Geraldine Ferraro, my friend from my Democrat Platform Committee days, to join us, and she walked the predominantly Italian areas in the 36th Ward.

We suspected that John Cullerton had a substantial lead among woman, so several congresswomen, including Barbara Kennelly and Nancy Pelosi, came in and held an event at Mercy Hospital, highlighting the important breast cancer legislation that Rosty had pushed through Congress. Rostenkowski had exercised a major influence on the tax laws, so for the business community, we brought in several people from Congress's Joint Committee on Taxation to explain Rosty's role in tax issues that impacted the city.

Cullerton's campaign put out a misleading but attention-grabbing flier suggesting a federal weakness on gun control laws, so we reached out to our friend, Jim Brady, wounded in the assassination attempt of Ronald Reagan. His organization responded with a counter piece of literature. In the last three weeks of the campaign, we staged numerous rallies, and well-informed, well-groomed volunteers tried to visit every city doorstep in the district, stressing Rostenkowski's importance to Chicago.

Rosty won going away, defeating his closest opponent by two-to-one.

Apparently, my style in organizing the campaign ruffled a few feathers, and David Axelrod, the campaign's media person, explained the situation to a *Chicago Sun-Times* reporter. "When you're running a two-minute drill, you've got to have a leader who scurries you up to the line so you don't waste time and energy," Axelrod said. "That's what Jeremiah did." Rosty was very happy.

But just two months later, Eric Holder, then the U.S. attorney for Washington, D.C., indicted Rosty for abusing his Congressional payroll. In retrospect, commentators from Mike Royko to ex-President Gerald Ford said the crimes charged were simply the old way of doing things—hiring unmonitored payrollers, exchanging stamp vouchers for cash, and so on. Small-scale things that weren't ever before seen as criminal. As the headline on the Royko column put it, "Rostenkowski's Sin Was Not Changing with the Times." His old-school stubbornness no doubt contributed to the problem. Three times, the Congressional ethics office issued rules on Congressional expenses, and every time he ignored the advice. But there was nothing venal about his behavior. He didn't enrich himself—he'd used the stamp money, for example, to take constituents to dinner. He had been raised with a squeeze-a-buck mentality, and that led him to cut a few corners.

In any case, the indictment deflated him. I called in September to see if I could help again on his campaign, and he said he was just going to let it slide. He lost that November to a Republican, Michael Flanagan, who himself lost in 1996 to Rod Blagojevich. When Blagojevich ran for governor in 2002, Rahm Emanuel won the seat. Today, it's held by Mike Quigley, a considerably lower-profile Democrat.

After two more long years, Rosty pleaded guilty to a handful of lesser charges. He would later receive a presidential pardon from Bill Clinton. I had lunch with Rosty a number of times after it was all over, usually at his favored restaurant, the Gene & Georgetti steakhouse. I think he had made the best of what had happened—he had considered what it was all about and resigned himself. Until his death in 2010, he remained enormously popular in Chicago and impossible to replace. Some Washington insiders think that if George H.W. Bush had been re-elected in 1992, the Justice Department would not have made the case against Rosty. I find it ironic that the Clinton

White House, with its casual attitude on government ethics, allowed it to happen.

Over the years, I participated in as many as 150 campaigns, both local and national, under rules I set for myself. I never volunteered, only coming in if I was asked. I would never accept compensation. I preferred to maintain a low profile in the operation and would not take a title—the one exception being named the campaign manager for Tom Hynes's mayoral race in 1987.

Often people came to me asking for advice or help in running for office. Those requests were pretty evenly split between first-time candidates and existing officeholders. If the person was a parent of young children, I would always advise against running—the burden on the family is too great. And I always asked people eager to run why they wanted to hold office—what did they seek to accomplish and could they accomplish it another way? After listing all the downsides about campaigning and serving, I would encourage the first-time prospect to write everything out and think it over for a week. Most of the time, the final decisions had already been made.

With experience, I developed a number of campaign principles and insights that can usually be applied across the spectrum, from an aldermanic election to a run for the presidency.

THE THEME

Every campaign will have a theme—a point, a motive, a reason behind the arrogant proposition that the candidate can make a difference as a public official. The theme isn't necessarily the campaign slogan, but it can be (Make America Great Again). It can be obvious and proclaimed, such as John Kerry's "courage to speak out" message in the 2004 presidential campaign, or Dan Rostenkowski's "power to help Chicago" in all his Congressional races. The theme may be subtle and not clearly stated, as when Rich Daley first ran for state's attorney and members of his late father's organization turned against him. The campaign didn't talk directly about betrayal, but Mike Royko certainly recognized what was going on and brought it to the attention of voters. If a candidate's campaign lacks a theme, his or her opponent may provide one. When I first ran for office in 1974, I was without a theme, so the local Democratic organization, which opposed me, cooked one up: If elected, Joyce wouldn't be able to accomplish anything. Fortunately, that ignited a theme for my campaign: Even though Joyce is the clear underdog, he's out there trying every day. That idea caught on with voters and probably accounts for my election.

RESEARCH

The internet and technology have made the analytics process much easier. The information a campaign requests is now usually only a phone call away. In a matter of days, a couple of geeks can produce research that once took forever—results contrasted to pre-election projections; correlations among various campaigns in different voting areas or within different voting areas; varying results among different groups and subgroups. The past is often instructive. Old newspaper accounts of campaigns—particularly community newspaper stories—can be great resources for insights into people and former campaigns.

The research process will be the most important part of a successful campaign because it forces the candidate to answer the question: How will I move that part of the vote needed to win? In local campaigns, carefully examining the ballot-petition signatures can also help in analyzing support. I found that if you sit down with an aspiring candidate after this research is completed and the petitions signatures have been reviewed, you can usually project with considerable accuracy how she or he will fare in a campaign.

Chicago and other Northern cities are great training grounds for figuring out voting groups, because they contain so many small, tight-knit ethnic communities. The Roman Catholic Church built many of its parishes to accommodate specific immigrant populations, and in some neighborhoods, the demographic footprint remains— you can see it in the specialty shops, the businesses, the community newspaper, and you can even follow the tracks of the voters who have left for the suburbs.

CHALLENGING PETITIONS

There may be some situations where an opponent who lacks sufficient signatures on the nominating petitions should not be challenged, but in most cases, if possible, strike your opponent from the ballot. I've already discussed the disastrous 1986 Illinois gubernatorial race, when the Democrats failed to disqualify the LaRouche candidates. Though Obama took criticism for it for years, he used hardball tactics in 1996 to eliminate his toughest foe in his first run for the state Senate. The incumbent senator, Alice Palmer, announced she would not seek re-election and instead run for Congress. When she lost in a special election, she reversed course and quickly gathered signatures on petitions to run for re-election to her old seat. By that time, Obama had launched a campaign for the seat. His supporters disqualified enough signatures on Palmer's petitions to throw her off the ballot. To complaints about his tactic, Obama legitimately pointed out that someone who can't get the signatures right on a petition can hardly be assumed to handle government business well. Palmer didn't forgive him—she campaigned for Hillary Clinton in 2008. But Obama saved himself a lot of trouble and money by focusing on the rules.

The petition operation alone can play an important role in the election. The process should be more than a gathering of signatures to qualify for the ballot. To start, a candidate must decide how his or her name will appear on the ballot—use the middle name, middle initial or nothing, for example. Married female candidates in Cook County will often include their maiden and their married names.

In circulating petitions, make sure the circulators are presentable and informed. If given the luxury of choice and the petition effort is door-to-door, older women and college-age girls make the best circulators, as they won't startle or frighten a potential signer. These days, it has become a common practice to hire circulators to obtain signatures. I find this practice troubling for a number of reasons, notably because it lends itself to fraud. What's more, it indicates a certain lack of support for the candidate—strangers talking to strangers about another stranger.

Particularly in local elections, candidates should rely on circulators they actually know. Presumably, those folks will seek signatures from people they know—church members, neighbors, school parents. Most importantly, after the signatures are obtained, the candidate should send a personalized thank-you letter to each signer, clearly acknowledging that his or her signature enabled the candidate's name to be on the ballot. People place a value on their signatures, and this formal recognition can create a sense of pledged support. Finally, if the campaign has the manpower, it should select areas for circulating that analytics show contain an abundance of persuadable voters.

Properly executed, the petition effort should be a campaign within a campaign. It should also provide empirical data on the effectiveness of those you will be relying on throughout. I recall a number of times when a well-executed petition drive determined an election before most people knew a campaign had even started.

THE CALENDAR

In designing campaigns, people sometimes overlook the election calendar, what will happen in the campaign time span—holidays, likely weather, and so on. The best approach is to start with Election Day and work backwards, determine as best you can what will be happening at each point in time and what significance it may hold.

GOING NEGATIVE

I generally believe that it never works to go negative. Unless your opponent accuses you of something unethical or immoral, dismiss other claims as just politics as usual—and respond with humor. When I first ran for alderman in the primary and bumped up against the Democratic organization's candidate, a precinct worker tried to provoke me at a candidate event. He said he'd been studying my resume and saw I'd been a policeman, a teacher, and a lawyer. How could I find the time, he challenged? I told him I could make time because I didn't have to work a precinct like he did.

DEBATES

This is a hard one to defend: Do not debate, unless all else has failed, and even then, never debate a more likeable opponent. I hold to this principle based on harsh experience. In 1983, Rich Daley was well on his way to being elected mayor of Chicago until his campaign got hooked into debating an eloquent but relatively unknown politician named Harold Washington. Daley performed well in the debate, but the event provided a forum that started Washington on his way.

The one exception to my rule: If the candidate is little known and lacks the finances to make an advertising splash, a debate can get the name out in front of voters.

But overall, the roster of costly debate episodes forms a rich vein of American political history: Richard Nixon under the weather and looking gray and sweaty to the television audience when he faced off against John F. Kennedy in 1960 in Chicago (many people who only listened to the debate on the radio thought Nixon had won); Michael Dukakis giving a clinical, unemotional defense of his anti-death-penalty stance in 1988 when asked if his position would change if his wife had been raped and murdered; George H.W. Bush glancing impatiently at his watch when he faced off against the relaxed Bill Clinton in 1992; Al Gore's lugubrious sighs as he confronted George W. Bush in 2000, and Gore's moving in on Bush's stage space (something he had been cautioned not to do and something the Bush campaign was prepared for). The examples could go on and on.

But even aside from the risk of blunders, the drawbacks of a debate stand out. For one, it eats up enormous preparation time—hours that could be spent more profitably campaigning (or resting). The moderator typically has his or her own agenda, usually tilted toward finding a question that makes the candidates squirm. The reporters and commentators set their own expectations and declare their own winners, analyses over which the candidate has little control. And, as the endless GOP primary debates in the 2016 presidential election ably demonstrated, a debate calibrated for TV is basically a clown show—not a probing, sophisticated way to illustrate differences between candidates.

In 1984, the presidential election was all but over after Mondale announced he would raise taxes, but Reagan looked old and lost in the first debate, at times fumbling and rambling. Afterwards, John Reilly, a top Mondale aide, asked me what I thought. I recommended that Mondale cancel the second debate and quietly suggest it was because of concern that Reagan is losing his marbles and Mondale doesn't want to expose the president's condition to the world. Reilly said that was not realistic, and, of course, Mondale didn't do it. He got creamed in the second debate—Reagan unloaded the famous line that he wouldn't make an issue of age: He wouldn't exploit Walter Mondale's "youth and inexperience." It's hard to stand against a remark like that. The image of Mondale's weak smile in response still pains.

Political consultants usually disagree with me on this, but I think it's possible to refuse to debate without damaging a campaign. Of course, it takes nerve and discipline. If you are running far ahead, history suggests you can refuse with impunity. LBJ never debated Barry Goldwater in 1964, and, once burned, Nixon didn't debate in the '68 and '72 presidential campaigns. After Harold Washington in 1983, Rich Daley never debated in any of his later campaigns for mayor, and he won every race in a landslide. If challenged, Daley would simply say he was busy around the city—everyone knew where he stood. Leapfrogging to 2016, I suspect someone advised Donald Trump to review the styles of his Republican opponents. At the GOP primary debate in Iowa, he didn't show up and held a competing campaign event. Still, he finished just behind Ted Cruz in the caucuses, despite having virtually no ground game in the state.

Certainly, if a well-established candidate refused outright to debate today, the media would scream, the opponent or opponents would scream, but I think the voters wouldn't care. The candidate who declined would be better off buying television time—before and after the debate, if one is held—saying that TV debates are a warped and inaccurate way to show where someone stands on the issues. It's one thing to be questioned and challenged on the issues by a serious journalist; it's another to participate in the bizarre performance art that modern political debate has become. In refusing to debate, always let it be known of your availability for any individual appearance at any place, any time.

I haven't even mentioned the sinister dishonesty associated with political debates—stolen briefing books, leaked questions, biased and even corrupt moderators and panelists. Television commentator Donna Brazile, who leaked debate topics to the Hillary Clinton campaign during the Democratic primaries in 2016, wasn't the first and will not be the last to do such a thing. (Everyone involved in conducting the presidential debates should be required to sign an affidavit swearing to no improper conduct or collusion regarding his or her role.) I could care less about the silly responses from the opponent when a candidate refuses to participate: the empty chair on stage, the character dressed as the Cowardly Lion roaming the audience. I dismiss all of that. Of course, if a candidate is so far behind that he or she couldn't possibly win—what the hell, go for it, have a little fun. In 1927, the flamboyant and corrupt Chicago Mayor William "Big Bill" Thompson presented two caged, live rats as his symbolic opponents and debated them on stage. For what it's worth, he won that election but lost the next and still stands as the last Republican elected mayor of Chicago.

TAXES

Never say you'll raise taxes. Never. At the Democratic National Convention in San Francisco in 1984, Walter Mondale gave a stirring speech to kick off his run against President Reagan. "Let's tell the truth," he said. "Mr. Reagan will raise taxes, and so will I. He won't tell you. I just did." The pledge crippled his candidacy from the start. I was at the convention and asked the leading labor leader in the county what he thought. "We are done," he said. When Dawn Clark Netsch was running for Illinois governor in 1994, she recommended a rise in the state income tax to fund education and lower property taxes. She was absolutely right on the policy, but wrong with voters.

Candidates think they are being candid, only telling the truth. And in most cases they are. But voters don't want to hear the truth about raising taxes. In Illinois, Richard B. Ogilvie built an outstanding record as governor, but was turned out of office in 1972 for raising taxes. The highly respected Paul Simon was defeated in an Illinois primary in 1972 for supporting tax increases. I do not like to use focus groups, but I recommend them when a candidate insists on a tax-raising position that guarantees a defeat. If after a focus group confirms defeat and a candidate still refuses to change his position, it may be wise to let him go over the cliff alone.

At the same time, a campaign vow *not* to raise taxes can lead to trouble when the victorious candidate turns around and raises them anyway, even under duress—just ask George H.W. Bush. So what's the solution? An artful answer that skirts the tax issue. For example, if Mondale had a hope of winning the election, here's what he could have said on the tax issue: "There's not an ounce of difference between my position and my opponent's." And that's the line he could have stayed with throughout.

In two of my own campaigns, I have violated my no-tax rule. I won both elections, but saw the margin fall on Election Day, when voters who were typically apathetic became energized by the tax issue and showed up to cast their concern.

ENDORSEMENTS

Campaigns often devote a great amount of time and effort to securing endorsements from news media, unions, trade associations, other officeholders, and various public figures. Sometimes, these are double-edged swords. This is one area where polling may be useful—to answer the question: Will the support of a potential endorser make it more likely or less likely to positively influence a voter?

It's helpful to understand the distinction between an endorsement and an attestation. The latter usually references a specific matter and a past accomplishment or involvement of the candidate, and it is far more effective. The clearest example I know of came in Paul Simon's race for the U.S. Senate in Illinois in 1984 against longtime incumbent Charles Percy. Tom Stack, a highly decorated leader among Vietnam vets and an Agent Orange victim, campaigned for Simon throughout the state, stopping at veterans' halls and events to give speeches. He sent letters to 250,000 veterans, explaining that Percy had failed to help on the Agent Orange issue, despite being asked by Stack and a group of veterans. At the same time, Stack pointed out that Simon had worked hard on the issue. Simon won by only 75,000 votes out of more than 4.5 million cast.

I have been in campaigns where the candidate received an endorsement from the president and from past presidents (Ford, Carter, Clinton, Reagan, and Obama), from world-respected figures (Mrs. Martin Luther King Jr. and Muhammad Ali), and from Chicago sports stars (Dick Butkus, Mike Ditka, and Michael Jordan). While all these endorsements helped, none was as effective as a personal attestation citing a particular issue on which the candidate assisted, such as a letter on gun control from wounded Reagan press secretary James Brady, an ad placed by Congressman Barney Frank on gay rights, and numerous communications from religious leaders addressed to a target audience on a specific involvement in a charitable or worthy cause.

POLLS

The 2016 presidential election illustrated a lesson that should have been obvious: Always be wary of polls. When Rich Daley was running for Cook County state's attorney in 1980, the polls showed him well behind as Election Day neared. The hired political consultant Bob Squier sent the campaign a letter advising it to stop spending money—Daley was going to lose. In one sense, Squier behaved honorably. He stood to make more money if the campaign continued to broadcast his TV ads. But he hadn't seen beneath the polls, which were based on phone calls to households with listed numbers. In Chicago, in those landline days, a lot of people who worked in the city—particularly police, firefighters, and teachers— had unlisted numbers, and a lot of them were for Daley. Fortunately, Daley ignored Squier's advice. (Daley beat Bernard Carey by less than 1 percent of votes cast.)

Two years later, the polls indicated that Adlai Stevenson was on the road to being clobbered by Jim Thompson in the Illinois governor's race. I was running for re-election to the Senate at the time, and I couldn't get any political leaders from my district to appear at campaign events with Stevenson because they were so certain he was a loser. Meantime, the polls gave Thompson an opening to raise more money and solidify support. Yet, I was out on the streets, and I knew the race was close.

So I polled the race, using one of only two polling methods I ever trusted (the other being the old *Chicago Sun-Times* straw poll, when the paper at great cost would send people out on the street with sample ballots). Here's how my method worked in that fall 1982 poll: The responding sample was held static, and the participants were called back at two-week intervals, providing a monitor of voter movement. The poll confirmed what I was experiencing in my door-to-door campaigning: The governor's race was very close. In the end, Stevenson barely lost. If it hadn't been for those bad polls, he would have won. That's hardly the only instance when I have seen bad polls ruin good candidates—the money dries up, the workers lose energy, and the candidate turns listless.

Granted, with advances in technology the quality of polling has improved, but many flaws remain—as the 2016 presidential election demonstrated. For one, people lie in polls or they are confused by the questions. Worse, most pollsters don't have the experience or savvy to look behind the data, to see if there is a discrepancy in the results. When I receive poll data, I always try to find out how the numbers compare with the results in past campaigns. Are there major differences? Do the numbers make sense? If they don't, there is almost always something wrong with the poll. Anomalies in voting are rare. I always suggest to a candidate that the consultant and the pollster come from separate operations. I prefer a distance between them. If they are part of the same outfit, they are more likely to coordinate their thinking—for example, arguing that the candidate is a failure and proving it with polls. One thing to keep in mind: In polling primary elections, if two candidates are basically equally qualified, those polled often respond with their affinity group, whether it is race, sex, or ethnicity.

CONSULTANTS

I have worked with scores of political consultants, a curious guild that has expanded exponentially in recent decades. It's no surprise that the growth corresponds to the huge influx of money pouring into campaigns and the increasing role played by television advertising. The consultant draws a fee based on what he or she can negotiate. In the past, typically, the campaign paid a consultant 15 percent of whatever was bought in advertising time or space. Plus, all production costs of the ads. Plus, expenses. And sometimes an outright salary. The fees can be demoralizing to the volunteers or low-paid workers in a campaign—people who sometimes put in 16 or more hours a day. The consultant breezes in with an hour of work and makes off with an inordinate percent of the campaign funds.

As is probably apparent, I consider political consulting a mercenary trade that offers little of substance to a campaign. Often I've seen the consultant tell the candidate to say something that is inappropriate or immoral—the candidate then takes the hit, while the consultant waltzes off to the next gig.

In promoting themselves, consultants inevitably feature the campaigns that they won. In 1980, for example, Bob Squier, who was based in Washington, D.C., worked on six races—one for Rich Daley and five for U.S. Senate candidates. Daley won (against Squier's expectations), and four of the five Senate candidates lost. Naturally, Squier emphasized the Daley race in looking for other work. And Squier was an honorable guy for the trade.

In national campaigns, the kibitzing among consultants presents a serious conflict problem. The primary candidates compete with each other, but the consultants often regularly confer. It's as if they are the college faculty and the candidates are the students—just another cohort passing through. When a campaign starts to go south, the typical consultant plants an escape narrative: The candidate was weak or wouldn't take the necessary advice. I think consultants have produced far more losses than wins. (One of the most revealing articles on the fraudulent world of political consultants came from

Molly Ball in the October 2016 issue of *The Atlantic* magazine titled, "There's Nothing Better Than a Scared Rich Candidate." Ball carefully quantifies the huge expenditures of money with little or questionable results.)

When asked to weigh in on hiring a consultant for a campaign, I always seek the thoughts of the spouse of the consultant's past losing clients—someone who typically won't hold back on candor. But in general, a losing candidate will give you a much more candid assessment than you'll get from a candidate who won. I also preferred consultants who had personal experience going door-to-door, working the street in a campaign. I like to borrow the comment from the old House Speaker Sam Rayburn. After his protégé, Lyndon Johnson, became vice president, Johnson came back from an early meeting with JFK's advisers, marveling at how smart they all were. "I'd just feel a whole lot better if one of them had ever run for sheriff," Rayburn supposedly said.

John Norris, the terrific Iowa consultant who was such a help to John Kerry in 2004 and whose wife, Jackie Norris, managed Barack Obama's 2008 campaign in Iowa, certainly hit the mark on street-level campaigning (though even Norris lost in the 2018 Iowa Democratic gubernatorial primary).

I knew and admired some of the early political consultants—the huge West Virginian, Matt Reese, who gets credit for helping to refine the trade in the JFK era. On the other side of the aisle, I enjoyed Lynn Nofziger, the witty former reporter who helped engineer the election of Ronald Reagan. I don't believe either of these consultants based their compensation on the number of ads they placed on television.

I worked with David Axelrod on a number of campaigns (and against him on a few others). Today, he's ostensibly out of the consulting game—between appearances as a commentator on TV, he's set up and run a politics and policy institute at the University of Chicago, his alma mater. In Chicago terms, David didn't really understand the average person who was raised in the city, but he worked hard, studied the data, and carried great historical campaign knowledge. His value came from his skill in spinning and dealing with the media and even pushing reporters around. I'm not entirely sure he is out of the game forever, and I would not want to be in a campaign in Illinois without him.

THE MEDIA

Reporters have their own key roles to play in the election process. During my time, I have witnessed the best and, in a few cases, the worst of the profession. Some reporters I came to know well outside of politics. Acclaimed journalist Georgie Anne Geyer grew up a block away from me on 83rd Street near St. Sabina, and the *Washington's Post*'s Ed Walsh and I went to grade school together and were friends. David Broder of the *Post*, long the dean of national political journalists, attended the school at which I first taught, Washington Junior High in Chicago Heights. When he was in Chicago, we would occasionally meet, and he would talk about his memories of his hometown. I considered Robert Novak and a few other national journalists as friends, though I never lost sight of the fact that they were professional journalists.

During the presidential primaries and mayoral elections, the national media would arrive in Chicago, often convening sizable lunches and dinners. I always came away from these impressed by the respect and the deference the country's best-known journalists had for the judgment and opinions of Chicago's political reporters, not only on matters of local politics but also on national and international affairs.

Among the best advice I could offer a candidate when dealing with the press is never lie or try to mislead. If you don't want to talk to a reporter, don't. And with columnists, be cautioned by the wisdom of Mayor Richard J. Daley's press secretary Earl Bush: "Some columnists may love their column more than their wife." I have also seen an unethical side of political journalism. I witnessed a publisher bargain his newspaper's endorsement for a promise of support for his own planned run for the U.S. Senate. Another time, a major paper committed to endorse legislators in exchange for their votes for a sports facility.

The last campaign in which I got involved came in 2015—the contest to elect the mayor of Chicago. A veteran Chicago politician named Jesus "Chuy" Garcia was challenging the incumbent, Rahm Emanuel. I'm not an admirer of Emanuel. I've known him in assorted capacities over several decades, and I've found his confrontational and haughty manner off-putting and counterproductive and his intelligence challenged. I didn't believe he had served Chicago well during his first term as mayor, and I thought he contributed to divisions within the city at a time when Chicagoans needed to pull together.

Chuy Garcia had been an alderman, state senator, and county commissioner over the years, though I had never met him before the campaign. Born in Mexico, he grew up in Chicago and attended St. Rita High School. As a young politician, he had been a protégé of Harold Washington. At the time of the campaign, Garcia lived in Little Village, the heart of a large Mexican immigrant community, and he sat on the county board. My son Michael, a former boxer who created a successful boxing program at Leo High School, had met Garcia through boxing contacts and had been persuaded to help out. He asked if I might lend a hand. By that time, Garcia had emerged from a field of challengers to force a run-off against Emanuel in April 2015.

I thought a Garcia victory was a long shot. In the first tier of the election in February, Emanuel held a 45-33 advantage over Garcia, but more than 20 percent of the votes had gone to other candidates. In theory, those votes were now up for grabs. The Garcia camp hoped to win by reproducing the Harold Washington coalition of Blacks, Hispanics, and liberal whites—and by adding police, firefighters, and teachers, who strongly opposed Emanuel.

After meeting with the campaign staff, I produced several pieces of literature emphasizing the Catholic school educations of Garcia and his wife and highlighting the endorsements of the children of Muhammad Ali and Jackie Robinson. I advised Garcia and his campaign on the importance of getting to early voters and contacting absentee voters, and I urged them to do a mass distribution of the endorsement literature at transit spots around the city as Election Day drew near. For whatever reasons, the suggestions were either ignored or lost in the shuffle. (Some believe the Garcia campaign had been infiltrated at the highest level.) Emanuel won the run-off by 56-44. A strong push by the Garcia campaign in the final days might have won the day—among the two-thirds of voters who went to the polls on Election Day (as opposed to voting absentee or by early ballot), a majority voted for Garcia. Nothing Emanuel did in his second term changed my opinion of him, and I have no second thoughts about helping Garcia, a man with a good heart who I think had Chicago's best interests in mind.

By the spring of 2018, it was clear there was fading support for Rahm Emanuel's re-election in 2019, particularly among the homeowners of Chicago's Northwest and Southwest sides and in most African American neighborhoods. At City Hall, his off-the-record media conversations and leaks critical of Mayor Daley, which had served him well politically for nearly eight years, were wearing thin, as was his self-created façade as Chicago's "tough-guy mayor." In addition, many of the activists involved in the past campaigns of Mayor Daley and Obama lacked enthusiasm for a third Emanuel term.

In this context, a number of names surfaced as potential candidates for the office, including: Paul Vallas, the former head of the Chicago, New Orleans, and Philadelphia school districts; Gery Chico, a prominent Hispanic leader who had been president of the

Chicago Board of Education and a former U.S. Senate candidate; Willie Wilson, an entrepreneur and philanthropic businessman; and Lori Lightfoot, a former assistant U.S attorney and Emanuel appointee to the board that oversees the Chicago police. Over time, others joined the race, including Susana Mendoza, the state comptroller; Toni Preckwinkle, president of the Cook County Board and the chairperson of the Cook County Democratic Party; and Garry McCarthy. the former police superintendent.

For over a quarter century, my son Jerry had worked in mayoral elections in Chicago's Southwest and Northwest neighborhoods. He had frequently been urged to run for office, and in the spring of 2018, he met with a large group who asked him to consider running for mayor. Initially he declined, but over several months he reconsidered, and in early summer, he and his supporters began to assemble a campaign to take on Emanuel. Though I wasn't actively involved in Jerry's campaign, I knew that my friend Bill Daley, the brother of Mayor Daley and former chief of staff in the White House to President Obama, would be supporting Emanuel in 2019. Throughout 2018, Emanuel had stated often that he would seek re-election, but in the first week of September, he unexpectedly announced he would not. A couple of weeks later, Bill Daley formally announced his candidacy for mayor, creating a situation in which he and Jerry would be drawing strength from many of the same constituencies.

Eventually, 14 candidates were certified for the Feb 26th election; if no one garnered a majority, the leading two would battle in a runoff. As it happened, Lightfoot and Preckwinkle finished first and second in the February election, advancing to the runoff. The wards on the Southwest and Northwest sides, where the vast number of Jerry's supporters lived, only made up 12 percent of the total registered vote, but he ran well in those wards. Overall, Daley won more votes than Jerry, but Jerry beat Daley in several of the "homeowner" wards, including handily in the 19th.

In the runoff on April 2, Lori Lightfoot was elected overwhelmingly as Chicago's first African American woman mayor. An already difficult job has only grown more demanding with the onset of the COVID-19 pandemic.

During the campaign and in the aftermath of the February election, political commentators and media offered the whys and the wherefores of the 14 candidates and their campaigns. Reflecting on Jerry's campaign, *Sun-Times* columnist Mark Brown wrote, "Jerry Joyce ran because he believed he could win."

Early on during the 2015-2016 events that were called the Republican presidential debates, candidate Donald Trump touted that he was an "insider," and thus knew more about politics and government than any of his opponents. Surprisingly, he was telling the truth, because for nearly half a century the success of his business ventures required a close attention to political campaigns. In New York, Florida, New Jersey, Nevada, and Illinois, the winning candidate in a local election might end up making a decision on one of Trump's requests for a rezoning, a building permit, a tax abatement, or a casino license.

It is often said that in political campaigns the most obvious choices are the most ignored—I believe William F. Buckley called them psychologically obvious. And so it was in the 2016 campaign. There were two such decisions I will never understand. The first was Jeb Bush's failure to publicly savage Trump for Trump's comments about the physical appearance of fellow candidate Carly Fiorino. Bush's reproach was tepid. He should have used the incident as justification for withdrawing from the debates, which at that point had all the makings of a circus favoring Trump, a reality television star. Bush had the reputation, finances, and party relationships to sustain a long battle to the convention.

The other decision I puzzled over was Hillary Clinton's choice of a running mate. The few times I was around any high-level conversations about selecting a vice presidential candidate, the discussion focused on who would increase the likelihood of winning. For months, Bernie Sanders had run better than Clinton in hypothetical matchups against Trump. The fact that many of Clinton's campaign people disliked Bernie and considered him a goof—evidenced by campaign manager John Podesta's hacked comments—should not have mattered. Historians have documented the feelings the Kennedys had for Lyndon Johnson in 1960. The enthusiasm and intensity of the Sanders supporters was clear, and they were not going to disappear. The argument that they had nowhere to go in a Trump-Clinton election was incorrect. They could stay home or just hang out in their dormitories.

Around the time of the Republican convention, it appeared that Trump's distasteful and crude campaign tactics had finally caught up with him. But in early October at a small luncheon in Chicago, I listened to a group of Big Ten Conference football referees discussing the enormous number of Trump supporters present at the games they officiated in Ann Arbor, Michigan; Madison, Wisconsin; and Columbus, Ohio. All had been refereeing for a long time and had never seen anything like it.

A month later, that ominous observation proved prescient.

I don't have anything to add to the exhaustively chronicled chaos around the Trump re-election campaign, though I was surprised by the strategy of attacking the Democratic big cities in states that would decide the election: Philadelphia, Detroit, Milwaukee, and Atlanta. Using clear and hard language, Trump did his best to demonize the leadership of those cities over the handling of the protests and riots associated with Black Lives Matter. He clearly hoped to excite his base outside the cities, but—whether he realized it or not—he also provided the environment to encourage new voter registration and massive mail-in voting. The Democrats with their base are far more adept at capitalizing on these voting processes than the Republicans. And those votes may well account for Trump's downfall in the 2020 election. ◼

14

"We have not yet at this moment, including the eight years of Obama, had someone in the White House who really cared about the city, and about these problems here in the City of Chicago."

Congressman Bobby Rush, MSNBC Town Hall, February 10, 2017

~~~~~~

In the late summer of 1999, a young Illinois state senator named Barack Obama asked to see me. He was running for Congress in a district that encompassed most of the 19th Ward. Obama's chief opponent in the race was the incumbent, Bobby Rush, whom I had followed since the days when he was a Black Panther and I was a detective in the Gang Intelligence Unit.

I told Obama I'd be happy to talk. I knew who he was, though I'd never met him. At the time, he had served in the state Senate for 2½ years, and friends I admired spoke well of him. A few days later, I was in the yard talking to a neighbor when I saw a slender, neatly dressed Black man poking around on the sidewalk, obviously confused about addresses. Even under those circumstances, he carried himself well, with a kind of dignified strut—head back, stiff posture—that by now has become familiar to many Americans.

He told me something about himself, and we went through his impressive resume. I know what it takes to be president of the *Harvard Law Review*, but he was modest about his accomplishments.

He emphasized his work as a community organizer in Chicago—much of the work paid for by a number of Roman Catholic parishes.

Then he outlined his plan for the campaign and asked what I knew about Congressman Rush. I didn't know Rush personally. As a member of Gang Intelligence, I had read assorted law-enforcement reports on him, and I'd followed him from a distance, but that was a quarter century before and not appropriate to share. I did offer that several of my Democratic political colleagues respected Rush and supported him.

Obama had clearly done his homework. He knew the issues, the political figures, the various neighborhoods in the 1st Congressional District, which took in much of the South Side and stretched into the southwest suburbs. Overall, the district broke down about 65 percent Black and 35 percent white. He admitted that his legislative record through three years in the state Senate was thin—Republicans held control. Stacked up against that, though, stood his community organizing experience, which gave him some good grassroots connections and led to a strong relationship with the Catholic Church. He didn't say it, but I could see that his knowledgeable and articulate manner would play well in the 19th Ward.

I warned that Jesse Jackson could pose an obstacle. In those days, Jesse Jackson Jr. was an ambitious and rising Chicago political star, though his resume couldn't compare to Obama's. I assumed that the Jackson family wouldn't want to see someone like Obama come along. Obama didn't think that would be a problem—he said that his wife, Michelle, was friends with one of the Jackson daughters.

We also discussed Obama's name. I thought "Barack" would be a problem. A lot of voters go into the booth without knowing all the candidates. An unusual and foreign-sounding name could put off some people, particularly middle-aged and older white voters. He told me he used to go by "Barry," but that he'd decided to stand by his real name. His instincts on that front were clearly better than mine.

In all, we talked for a couple of hours. I was impressed. I worry about the future of Chicago and other big cities, and here was someone who spoke directly to many of the urban issues that concerned me. Kids, schools, poverty, gun violence. He could analyze the issues, and he was street smart about them—he was serious, but he had a good sense of fun. Mairsey spent some time with him, and she was also impressed. Toward the end of our conversation, I told him I thought he could go all the way. He said, "Yeah, maybe." He wasn't arrogant, but there was no modesty in his reply.

I said I would do what I could to help in his campaign. When I walked him outside, I introduced him to my neighbor. As Obama left to go to his car, I told my neighbor to remember this day. "Later you will recall it as the moment you met that guy."

I saw Obama in passing over the years, and in late summer of 2006, he asked to meet with me again. By then, he'd been a U.S. senator for a little over a year and a half, but already there had been talk of a run for president in 2008. Publicly, he had been rigorous in denying he would do it.

We met in his Senate office in the Kluczynski Federal Building in downtown Chicago, and we joked about how circumstances had changed since our first meeting in my basement. He'd been calculating his political situation carefully, and he was candid in sharing his assessment, a rare and honest quality I admire. He said he couldn't run for president because Hillary Clinton had the nomination locked up. What's more, he reasoned, she wouldn't want him as vice president because he wouldn't bring anything helpful to the ticket in her general election contest. Then he explained his plan: He would watch what happens. If Hillary got elected, he would leave the Senate and come back to Chicago and go into business. Then he would run for president in 2016. If she lost, he would stay in the Senate and run in 2012.

I reminded him that in the mid-1970s, Illinois Congressman Marty Russo brought around a low-profile Southern governor named Jimmy Carter who was thinking of running for president. At the time, almost everyone thought that a Carter presidential run was far-fetched at best. So I told Obama that politics is a strange business and you never can be certain how things will unfold. If he ever needed help, I said, let me know.

Within in a couple of months, Obama acknowledged that he was considering a campaign for president after all, and he made his run official in February 2007. I didn't know what induced him to change his mind, but later many people claimed that they had influenced his decision.

My first experience with a future occupant or contender for the White House came when I was around 13 and my father took me to the international convention of the Amalgamated Meat Cutters in Cincinnati. Hubert Humphrey, then a U.S. senator from Minnesota, gave a rousing speech, and I remember watching union officials going up to hug him. At one point, he sat on the stage, and people in the audience took turns standing to announce that this or that local was contributing this much to Senator Humphrey's campaign. Someone would collect the check and run it up front to place it in a box while Humphrey raised his arm in triumph. The pageantry was captivating, particularly to a 13-year-old.

Because Humphrey was labor's best friend in the Senate, I read about him regularly in the Amalgamated magazine, and I followed his activities in the same way (though on a far lesser scale) that I followed news of, say, Nellie Fox and Billy Pierce, two White Sox stars of the era. But in 1964, even though Humphrey was on the Democratic ticket as vice president, I wouldn't vote for Lyndon Johnson, in part because he was considered a bitter enemy of labor.

Of course, I voted for Humphrey when he ran for president in 1968 and fell just short. In 1972, Patrick Gorman, the head of my father's international union, took on George Meany, head of the AFL-CIO, and other AFL-CIO leaders over their tacit support for Richard

Nixon. Meany, a Vietnam War hawk, didn't actually endorse Nixon, but he made clear his dislike of George McGovern, the Democratic candidate. Gorman admired McGovern's pro-labor record, and he shared the candidate's strong anti-war position. So I was for McGovern. Seven years later, I happened to talk to Meany at a White House event, just six months or so before he died. I asked him about that election, and he said his stance had been a big mistake that he still regretted.

As the 1976 election approached, I met a few times with candidate Sargent Shriver. Before helping to found the Peace Corps for his brother-in-law JFK, Shriver had headed the Chicago Board of Education in the 1950s and managed the Merchandise Mart in Chicago for the Kennedy family. Though it was widely thought that the Kennedys kept Shriver on a short leash, he dispelled that assumption by tossing his hat into the ring for the 1976 Democratic presidential nomination. He was capable and, to me, quite engaging. I helped put together an event for him, but his candidacy fizzled, and in the end I was a delegate for Adlai Stevenson III—a favorite son—at the Democratic Party Convention in New York City. Richard J. Daley decided the Illinois delegation. By then, Jimmy Carter had the nomination sewn up. Though he beat Gerald Ford in the general election, Carter lost in Illinois, a state he considered key to his eventual re-election prospects. When the Chicago Democrats fell into chaos several years later, and Mayor Jane Byrne led the Cook County Democrats to endorse Ted Kennedy for president, President Carter and his people reached out, trying to understand what was going on in Chicago politics.

I remember sitting in the Oval Office in November 1979, just days after Iranian revolutionaries had taken the Americans hostages. President Carter's advisers were saying that the crisis could impact the 1980 election, and I thought to myself: This seems strange—I assumed the matter would be resolved in a week or so.

I liked President Carter's team—Vice President Walter Mondale, Hamilton Jordan, Jody Powell, Jack Watson—and I greatly admired the president himself, who was an honorable man and an honest politician. In April 1980, after President Carter had trounced Ted Kennedy in the Illinois primary, the White House said it wanted to appoint me to the Commodities Futures Trading Commission, at that time a relatively new federal agency organized to regulate the futures trade in various agricultural products. (Since then, the CFTC's authority has expanded to oversee a wide range of financial, energy, and metals contracts.) The appointment carried a five-year term.

I didn't know much about agri-economics, but I did understand the trading of commodity futures and had some experience at the Chicago Board of Trade. In Washington, the director of presidential appointments accompanied me to meet the Secretary of Agriculture and other relevant people.

All went well through the vetting process, and the administration was prepared to make an announcement. I had misgivings about relocating my family to Washington, but I was told that a CFTC office could be opened in Chicago, so my family could remain there, and I could commute to Washington when necessary. The appointments director offered the position, and I accepted. But when I was back in Chicago the next day, I realized I was going to be tied up that fall on Rich Daley's campaign for state's attorney, a contest shadowed by the bitter feud with Jane Byrne. As a result, I asked that the appointment be postponed until after the fall election.

During the general election campaign that year, the White House sent out a coordinator who tried without much success to patch the schism among the Chicago Democrats. I spent my time working for Daley's election and staying involved with Carter's top campaign aides. The president's debate style wasn't good, and he had been badly damaged by Ted Kennedy, but I didn't realize the deep hole he was in until just a few weeks to go in the election. On the way to losing the White House to Ronald Reagan, Carter again lost Illinois.

I had come to know Walter Mondale when he was President Carter's vice president, and I worked for his candidacy in the roll-up to the 1984 presidential election. Because the economy was still sketchy, there was speculation that President Reagan might be vulnerable. At first, the Democrats featured a long roster of candidates, including Chicagoan Jesse Jackson, whom I had known since the mid-'60s, but Colorado Senator Gary Hart emerged as Mondale's toughest opponent. I thought Hart was basically a fraud—he'd changed his name and changed his date of birth to lower his age. In Iowa, where I pitched in for Mondale, Hart had some very unpleasant people working for him. But candidates who come out of Minnesota's Democratic Farmer-Labor Party tradition, such as Humphrey and Mondale, have a fundamental political problem: They are polite, too gentlemanly. Humphrey, for example, had let himself be browbeaten by LBJ.

During the Mondale presidential campaign, I suggested a tough approach, particularly toward Jackson's candidacy. But the campaign rejected my suggestions out of fear that Mondale could be perceived as being ill-mannered. In any case, Mondale won the primaries in Iowa and Illinois, but the battle with Hart dragged on through most of the spring of 1984. Mondale eventually secured the nomination, and I was prepared to lead his effort in the general election in a couple of tough states, including Ohio. At the convention in San Francisco, I argued that Mondale and his team should run to the center and forget about all the fringe stuff—leave the pro-life issue to the pro-lifers and the pro-choice issue to the pro-choicers. Just say, "Here's what we stand for: Everyone should have a job, everyone should have a fair opportunity, and everyone should enjoy equal justice." I met with the vice presidential candidate, Geraldine Ferraro, but she didn't think it possible to win with my basic centrist approach. When Mondale told the convention he was going to raise taxes, I knew the game was lost. Out of admiration for the former vice president, I helped out that fall, but it was futile.

I pretty much sat out the 1988 presidential race, which again started out with a long roster of Democratic candidates. Bill Daley backed Joe Biden, and I went to a meeting with him, but his campaign disintegrated after he plagiarized a speech. My cousin

Jack Joyce of the International Bricklayers' Union urged me to get involved with Dick Gephardt, the Missouri congressman. Another cousin, prominent Chicago attorney Ed Joyce, was backing Illinois Senator Paul Simon, whose campaign was being managed by David Axelrod. But by the winter of 1987, I'd decided to stay out of the primary campaign.

Later, after Massachusetts Governor Michael Dukakis won the Democratic nomination, Ed Markey—then a Massachusetts congressman, now a U.S. senator—flew out to ask me to join the Dukakis campaign, but I saw nothing in Dukakis to draw me into an exhaustive undertaking. He was honest and clearly able, but I couldn't quite connect with him. I recalled a story House Speaker Tip O'Neill told a group of us one night: O'Neill had once made a promise to a dying campaign worker who had supported the speaker throughout his political career. Attending to his affairs, the loyalist asked Tip to secure a job promotion for his son from the governor. Tip gave the dying man his word that he would do so. After the man died, Tip went to Dukakis with the request and explained the circumstances out of which it had risen. Governor Dukakis responded by scolding O'Neill for making a promise without first knowing it would be granted. The governor eventually came around, but the speaker was appalled at his callousness.

At the close of our spring legislative session in 1991, one of Bill Clinton's Illinois friends and top advisors asked if I would meet with Clinton to talk about being the campaign manager of his bid for the Democratic presidential nomination. I had watched Clinton from a distance since the 1980 Democratic convention, when he was governor of Arkansas and considered one of the great young hopes of the party. From the start, I was skeptical of his style—he seemed like a candidate who never really stood for anything. (This was well before the women issue popped up.) So I said I wasn't really interested. Would I at least talk to him on the phone? I declined, lest I end up agreeing to get involved in some way. I did talk to New York Governor Mario Cuomo—our sons had been friends in college—who was considering a run for president. I liked him and admired his politics, but after his dalliance with the idea, he decided not to go for it.

Later that year, I was approached about the campaign of Paul Tsongas, a former Massachusetts senator who was also after the Democratic nomination. I didn't know much about him, but he called and then sent me a booklet outlining his positions, *A Call to Economic Arms*. It remains one of the best policy documents I've ever read (and remains in print through Amazon). Tsongas's early warnings about too much debt—public and private—were referenced frequently during the 2008 financial crisis, but his economic argument emphasized the creation of wealth. He called for Democrats to drop their reflective anti-business stance and cooperate with the business world to promote growth policies, and he advocated government investments in industry and science. Beyond economics, his programs touched on major urban problems—bolstering education for the young, recognizing the barriers to African American advancement, finding just ways to suppress crime. Tsongas came to my house, and we talked for a long time, mostly about the decline of the great cities and the disappearance of the old neighborhoods. I was even more impressed. By then, he had scored well in the primaries and was beginning to get some attention.

I told him if he was willing to make an all-or-nothing case in Illinois—invest time and money here—I believed we could help him carry the state. I would provide more than 500 experienced campaign workers. Winning Illinois would give him a big Midwestern victory that could carry him through to a contested convention. But he said he was pledged to go to Georgia, where Jimmy Carter's old pal, Bert Lance, was heading up the Tsongas campaign. I warned that that would be a mistake—Democratic primary voters in Georgia weren't going to support someone from the same state as Ted Kennedy, who arguably cost Carter the 1980 election. Still, Tsongas stayed with his plan. He got soundly defeated in Georgia, and Illinois became an afterthought. He lost and dropped out of the race. We talked once or twice after that as his health declined. He died in 1997.

After the Illinois primary, the only candidate with a shot at overtaking Clinton was former California Governor Jerry Brown. He came through Chicago at one point and asked to meet with me. I had never spoken with him, but I understood he was something of an ascetic. We met during a rainstorm at Eli's restaurant downtown, and he arrived soaking. First thing, he ordered two Manhattans and told the waiter to bring them both at once. Nothing else memorable came out of the meeting. I thought Brown had a slight chance to defeat Clinton, but he made the mistake of naming Jesse Jackson as a potential running mate before the primary in New York, where Jewish voters distrusted Jackson.

I pretty much avoided national politics through the 1990s, but when the 2000 campaign geared up, my friend and attorney John Gearen was helping in Bill Bradley's campaign. The two had been Rhodes Scholars together at Oxford. I'd met Bradley in 1996 when he helped bring Bulls Coach Phil Jackson out for Dick Devine in Devine's election for state's attorney, and I'd long admired the former New Jersey senator. Dan Rostenkowski thought Bradley would have made a good president. Unfortunately, he lacked the persona for campaigning—he was like a brilliant college professor who had been teaching the same course for 10 years, and his campaign faded and died.

A long list of Democratic hopefuls angled for a run at President George W. Bush in 2004—John Edwards, Howard Dean, John Kerry, Dick Gephardt, General Wesley Clark, and Dennis Kucinich among them. I stayed out of the fray largely because my time was obligated to the airport concession business. But in the fall of 2003, Kerry's chief fundraiser, Chicago investment banker Lou Susman, asked if we could meet. We got together at Manny's, a South Loop eating spot and political clubhouse. At the same time we were meeting, David Axelrod sat at a table across the room with the campaign people working for John Edwards—Axelrod was in the process of signing on with the Edwards campaign. Kerry's operation was in disarray at that point. He had fired his campaign manager, and other top staffers had quit. Kerry was lagging behind Howard Dean in the polls, both nationally and in Iowa, where the caucus was still months away. Susman asked me to go quietly to Iowa and see what was happening with the campaign. I agreed to get involved but only in Iowa. The Kerry campaign there turns out to offer a model of how to build a success.

I had only met Kerry briefly in 1984 at the Democratic Convention in San Francisco. Since then, I'd followed his career and viewed him as straightforward. Susman arranged a meeting, and I went to Iowa and had a long sit-down with the candidate at a motel where he was staying. Then I spent a few days traveling around the state, talking to people and trying to get a read on the Howard Dean campaign, which appeared to be roaring ahead. I met people coming out of church, in diners, on the street, and I came to believe that Dean's support was thinner than it appeared.

Later, I went to Kerry's campaign headquarters, and the three people in charge brushed me off. I suspect that at first they thought I had just wandered in off the street. I retreated to my hotel, and a half hour later, the three came to find me—they had obviously done some checking and now they were concerned that I would have them fired. It turned out John Norris, the head of the Kerry operation in Iowa, was on a ski vacation with his family—an arrangement he'd worked out in advance when he'd signed on. He returned in a day or so, and we spent several days together. It quickly became clear that he knew Iowa better than anyone in politics, and he had a solid plan for delivering the state for Kerry. He had endorsements lined up, including the governor's wife; links into the ministry community; seasoned workers enlisted; all bases covered, even my favorite group, the youth programs for wrestling, a cherished Iowa sport. I called Susman and told him that if they followed Norris's direction, Kerry would win Iowa.

I met with Kerry several more times in Chicago, discussing how to respond to the Dean phenomenon and other campaign issues. I agreed to put together the slate of Kerry delegates in Illinois. In one of our meetings, we were sitting alone in a conference room of a big Chicago hotel, and Kerry's daughter popped in and asked her dad for some cash. Hardly missing a beat in our discussion, he took out his wallet and gave her $50 or so. I enjoyed that—seeing such an ordinary personal moment in the hurly-burly of the campaign.

I made several trips back to Iowa, once to a mosque in Cedar Rapids, and I told Susman and the campaign that I intended to focus my efforts on the Catholic voter. We reached out to the Catholic schools—colleges, such as St. Ambrose University and Loras College, and several Catholic high schools. Kerry was a Roman Catholic, but there was a wrinkle. While he personally opposed abortion, he supported pro-choice, and the American bishops had an effort underway to tell Catholic voters to oppose any pro-choice candidate. Nevertheless, we went forward. At several Catholic schools, we put together a poll asking the students to weigh in on issues in the campaign. We were interested in the responses, but mostly we wanted to engage the students. We assembled lists of Chicagoans attending the colleges and put together two events in Chicago over Christmas, signing up students who wanted to get involved in the campaign. We taught them how to organize once they were back at school. We held sessions explaining how the Iowa caucus system worked, and we brought in people from Chicago who lived on the campuses of the Catholic colleges. On Election Day, John Norris delivered Iowa—Kerry won 38 percent of the caucus voters, leading the pack. Howard Dean came in third (after John Edwards) at 18 percent, and his campaign was mortally wounded.

I continued to work for Kerry in Illinois over the next few weeks. By then, the primary campaign for U.S. senator from Illinois was underway, and Dan Hynes, the son of my longtime colleague Tom Hynes, was running against a crowded field that included Barack Obama. In early February, though, I got a painful call: My friend Steve Neal, a book author and columnist for the *Sun-Times*, had died. Steve and I had spent hours together talking history and politics, and his death was a blow. He had just finished a new book, *Happy Days Are Here Again*, about the 1932 Democratic Convention. Alderman Ginger Rugai coordinated a memorial gathering for him that summer at the Democratic convention in Boston, but I didn't have the heart to go to the convention myself.

In the late spring, I had learned from a friend who had served on a Navy Swift Boat in Vietnam that an effort was being organized to defeat Kerry. A hard-core group of Kerry critics would claim that his service on a Swift Boat had been concocted or exaggerated. The claim was offensive and outrageous, but it was gaining some traction. To quash the bogus assertions, I advised the campaign that Kerry should name as his vice president former U.S. Senator Bob Kerrey, a Navy Seal veteran of Vietnam. Someone argued that Bob Kerrey had a Mai Lai-type problem in Vietnam, but I pointed out that he'd lost a leg there. A ticket featuring two decorated Vietnam War veterans would have ended the Swift Boat nonsense. But the Kerry-Kerrey ticket didn't happen. John Kerry picked John Edwards. In retrospect, I should have personally carried my suggestion to John Kerry or his brother, who was involved in the campaign. This would be the last national campaign for me.

According to Ecclesiastes 9:11: "... the race is not to the swift, nor the battle to the strong, ... but time and chance happeneth to them all." In political parlance, this means it's better to be lucky than good. There certainly was an element of that when Barack Obama joined up with consultant David Axelrod. Both of them, through different personal experiences, had learned the political intricacies of multi-candidate primary elections. They had suffered losses in elections involving well-supported candidates, had learned the tactical differences between one-on-one elections and races involving multiple candidates—a difference as profound as the difference between checkers and chess. Axelrod had gone through the 1992 Democratic U.S. Senate primary in Illinois representing

Al Hofeld against Carol Moseley Braun and Alan Dixon. Obama had his moment with Bobby Rush and Donne Trotter. What's more, Axelrod had been through two losing Iowa caucus campaigns, Paul Simon in 1988 and Edwards in 2004.

In 1999, after Obama came to see me to tell me he was running for Congress against Bobby Rush in the Democratic primary, I agreed to help. After several years in the state Senate, this was Obama's first substantial election test, and I knew he faced a steep uphill battle. But the year before, Rush had run against Mayor Daley, and Daley received 44 percent of the vote in the Chicago slice of the 1st District, a result that I think gave hope to the Obama campaign.

I committed to working the white-dominated areas of the district, which meant the suburbs and the 19th Ward. I enlisted Alderman Rugai, and she met with Obama and his campaign and then contacted our volunteers from previous elections.

Every year, I hosted a party on the Sunday of the South Side St. Patrick's Day Parade, which fell before the 2000 primary election, in which Obama would face Rush. The party started out for family and friends, but over the years had swollen to more than a thousand guests, many of them interested in politics and many of them residents of the local Congressional district. I decided to highlight Obama at this event. My sister and nephew brought him around to each guest, asking for support, and Obama was well received. Toward the end of the party, Tom Hynes showed up with Bobby Rush, the candidate Hynes was backing in the election. Rush pulled me aside to talk. He said he had no hard feelings over my support for Obama, but I should know that his polls showed he was going to win easily. Rush said that after the election, he wanted to sit down together. I told him that Obama was going to crush him in our area of the district.

On Election Day, we were both correct. Alderman Rugai's operation delivered nearly 80 percent for Obama. But in the African American section of the 1st District, Obama barely got 30 percent. He had greatly underestimated the power and political skills of

Rush and the veteran Black political leaders who supported Rush. They labeled Obama as a late arrival to their cause and, with that message, soundly trounced him. (Bobby Rush and I never did have that sit-down.)

On the heels of that defeat, Obama remained in the Illinois Senate, representing a constituency that had given him weak support in the Congressional race. But luck was coming his way. In 2001, the Illinois Legislature was up for redistricting, and the legislators failed to agree on a map. The rules then called for a drawing—the party whose member's name is pulled from a hat creates the new map. As it turned out, a conspiracy developed between the Republican leaders in the Senate and some African American Democratic senators. In the event that the Republicans won the right to decide the map, Obama would be placed in a difficult Senate district.

At the tie-breaking ceremony, names from both parties were placed in a hat once worn by Abraham Lincoln. The name of Democrat and former Chicago Mayor Mike Bilandic was pulled out. This ensured that Obama could practically draw the boundaries of his new Senate district. He retained Hyde Park and added Chicago's liberal, wealthy Gold Coast under the new map. Afterwards, he continued to build on his reputation as one of the most talented members of the Illinois Senate.

Tom Hynes asked me to support his son Dan in the 2004 Democratic Senate primary, which featured Obama and a long roster of candidates, including the rich former trader Blair Hull. I wasn't active in Dan Hynes' campaign, though—the contest heated up after Steve Neal died, and I stayed away from politics.

As Obama's campaign for president unfolded in 2007, I talked occasionally to Axelrod and others in the campaign, but I was dealing primarily with an illness in the family. Around Thanksgiving that year, Axelrod called to ask for help in Iowa. Because of the health emergency, I took the call at Northwestern Hospital, and I told him I just couldn't go, as much as I would have enjoyed it. Maybe after Christmas. But the caucuses that cycle came January

4—so there would have been little I could do. Of course, Obama did perfectly well without me. Earlier, I'd suggested bringing John and Jackie Norris into the fold to help with the Iowa operation, and Jackie Norris helped run the campaign there and later served briefly as First Lady Michelle Obama's first chief of staff.

After Obama's election to the presidency, I continued to speak occasionally to Axelrod—by then, a senior advisor to the White House—usually at the request of some candidate who wished to know how Axelrod or the president viewed their campaigns. But around 2011, Axelrod's office called to see if we could get together. We met in an office on Chicago's North Side, and after exchanging small talk, he asked what I thought about the Obama presidency so far. I told him it was going well under difficult circumstances, though I was somewhat disappointed that he hadn't been able to do more for Chicago and other big cities.

Axelrod disagreed with that assessment, but asked what I would suggest. Not knowing if he really wanted an answer, I nevertheless rattled off some ideas. One had to do with residential real estate. Following the financial crisis of 2008-'09, millions of homes sank into foreclosure and ended up abandoned, increasing blight, flight, and crime. The problem particularly afflicted Chicago. I suggested a program to create thousands of small residential real estate management companies, comprised of teams of armed services veterans, trained in the rehab, management, and financing of these homes. After a training period for the vets, bundles of neighboring properties would be turned over to these newly formed miniature REITs (real estate investment trusts). The veterans involved would have equity in the firms. Some of the funds to support the program would be derived from the bankers and others yet to be held accountable for creating the financial crisis. If successful, the program would result in the formation of several thousand small REITs, and the communities where they operated would have a serious problem removed.

A second idea aimed at the horrific proliferation of guns in the cities. I proposed hiring another 10,000 ATF agents and putting them on the streets with the sole objective to find and remove guns. Unlike the typical law enforcement officer, they wouldn't make arrests— their only mission would be to retrieve weapons. The officers would work out of satellite offices in high-crime neighborhoods and get trained in ways to persuade those in possession of illegal guns to hand them over. One obvious tool would be to allow the agents to influence prison or jail terms.

I talked through some other concepts, mostly dealing with job creation projects. One called for constructing a series of high-speed, truck-only highways. All the jobs programs I proposed would incorporate the coming technological advances. And all would be partnerships between government and private-sector companies.

Axelrod dismissed my ATF suggestion, thinking it unconstitutional, intrusive, and politically unsound. He acknowledged some of the other suggestions had merit, particularly the one about foreclosed and abandoned residential properties. He suggested I present it to the White House. I wasn't eager, especially because Axelrod had quickly dismissed what I thought the most important idea, the gun-collection operation. But a few months later, my grandson was at my home looking at old photos taken in Washington during the Carter years, and he asked if we could visit the capital. I called the White House and, referencing the Axelrod suggestion, made an appointment.

A week later, on a hot, humid day and in the midst of another Congressional standoff, I arrived at the White House with two of my grandsons, one 11 and one 13, for a one o'clock appointment. Told the meeting had been put back an hour, we were escorted to the Roosevelt Room and soon joined by a staffer who made a presentation and then took the kids on a tour. When they returned, the boys were antsy and sort of uninterested. They asked when could we leave. The president was at the Treasury Department in a meeting with Secretary Timothy Geithner. My grandsons were drifting around, looking into the Oval Office. Bill Daley was chief of staff then, and while I sat in his office, my younger grandson came in and pulled a little camera from his coat pocket and started snapping photos of the communications equipment. Daley jumped up, the Secret Service agent jumped up, and I decided it was time to leave. The boys and I thanked everyone, and we went to lunch.

Politics, as with most of life, is replete with what-ifs. If Obama had defeated Bobby Rush in 2000, would he have given up his office to run for the Senate in 2004? And if he had not been in the Senate in … and so on. In late fall of 2016, a decade after we had met in his office to talk about the presidency, he was on the campaign trail exhorting voters to support Hillary Clinton. Never mind that a few weeks earlier her husband, Bill, had told an audience that the Obama health-care plan was ridiculous. Obama's message was a vote for Hillary Clinton was an affirmation of the Obama legacy.

At the time, I was surprised and questioned the political wisdom of Obama's use of the term "legacy." Few people choose that word when referring to themselves—there's something self-aggrandizing about it, particularly in this situation, delivered at a large event that will be telecast on all media. It seemed especially odd coming from Obama, who was usually good at projecting a sense of modesty. Paradoxically, if Clinton had won, she would have worked to eclipse Obama's legacy in countless ways. Come 2050, bronzes of the first First Couple, Hillary and William Jefferson Clinton, hand in hand, would stare down at visitors in parks and town squares around the country.

As for presidential legacies, I never understood how one is created or defined. I assume that respected historians require a sufficient passage of time to allow for perspective and a review of otherwise unavailable material. In any case, over time a presidential legacy changes—witness Harry Truman—but the who, when, where, and what of the process escapes me, particularly when considering those presidents who are ranked in the middle of the class.

President Obama's legacy should benefit from the fact that he will be stacked against the other three baby-boomer presidents—Bill

Clinton, George W. Bush, and Donald Trump—none with a claim to greatness. Clearly, part of the Obama legacy is forever set in stone. He was the first African American president, and that will be a source of great pride for Americans for generations to come. Beyond that, historians may note that he assumed office at a time of a world financial crisis and responded with his head and not his heart. The historians will consider his refusal to yield to aggressive military advice. And—no matter how the law is amended—he moved America forward on the course for universal health care. In making their assessments, historians may find the mother of a soldier who didn't die in an expanded war or a guy who was able to keep his job in the plant at GM or a previously uninsured patient who received life-saving treatment.

At the conclusion of Obama's term, Congressman Bobby Rush said Obama didn't do much for Chicago. There is truth in that statement, but he did locate his presidential museum in Jackson Park on the South Side, providing hope and pride to future generations of Chicago's neighborhood kids. For Chicago, that may be the most important part of his legacy. ◼

15

"He was still where he had always been. Just hoping."

James T. Farrell

~~~~~~

They had all grown up in Chicago before the Second World War, attended a neighborhood school, played sports in the local park, and now shared a common experience: The communities in which they were raised had gone from white to Black. These men—and they were all men—would gather in city restaurants four or five times a year or, as one of them used to say, "We meet on an irregular basis, at undetermined locations, on unscheduled days." I was fortunate enough to be invited to join them.

Each luncheon was hosted by a personality known to many Chicagoans by a single name: Kup, Father Mac, Abe, Moose, Earl, Saul. All were widely recognized for success in their chosen field—sports, journalism, law, religion, business, literature. None would ever mention his own achievements, only what someone else had accomplished.

The luncheon topics varied from world events to great movies, but always included talk of their days in their old neighborhoods. They would recount incidents unknown, previously untold, or even forgotten by design. A few of the incidents, witnessed by one of the men through some circumstance, touched on a piece of Chicago history: President Roosevelt bargaining with Chicago's Cardinal Mundelein for Catholic support of the president's appointment of Felix Frankfurter to the U.S. Supreme Court. Chicago Mayor Edward Kelly gathering a conclave of conspirators to dump Vice President Henry Wallace from the 1944 Democrat ticket. (The plotters knew Roosevelt would not survive another term, and the vice president would ascend to the White House. Mayor Kelly would fall victim to the same type of plot a few years later.)

The stories may have endured a few inaccuracies, some a result of failing memory, others simply embellished for greater listener appreciation. But when it came to accounts of their days growing up in the old neighborhoods, the luncheon friends could accurately cite the scores of long-past high school basketball games, the word misspelled to lose the public school's spelling bee, the names of the neighborhood grocer's sons who kindly erased the credit debts of large families. Even the paired double feature movies shown on Saturdays at their local movie theaters came to mind. So much information stored for so long.

Every once in a while, someone would tell of having exercised his official discretion to an unaware supplicant because the person had some tie to the old neighborhood, had lived on a particular block or street, had attended a certain school or played for a local team. These were men who fit Alistair Cooke's description of Harry Truman: He came from "the sort of people who despise a man who forgets a favour." A lot of unheralded second chances emanated from this practice.

It begs the question, if the neighborhoods were all so wonderful, why did people like these men and members of the following generations leave? The first to go believed progress represented getting out of a third-floor apartment for a suburban ranch house near a new expressway. Others left for employment—unlike the men of Carl Sandburg's time, the workers of Chicago were no longer butchering hogs or stacking wheat. The reason most often cited for the exodus, however, was the concern for personal safety.

Violence—white against Black, Black against white. At lunch, each man spoke of a specific racial incident that caused the wave of moving vans through the neighborhood. Once started, it became an epidemic, exploited by the block busters, panic peddlers, and other unscrupulous parties all long involved in the ugly process.

The men in the lunch group had for the most part all moved out before the racial conflicts exploded. But they had stayed in touch with people left behind, and, more to the point, they never believed they had left. Their neighborhoods had carved memories so deep.

As these gatherings moved through the first decade of a new century, they became less frequent—replaced now by hospital visits and wakes. When the declining members did get together, their conversations had changed—not as much talk of the old neighborhoods. As memories faded, the men found it increasingly difficult to revisit the schools, parks, and street corners of past times. Then the lunches stopped—someone said they just lost their quorum.

Though these gatherings seemed so special to me, I would guess lunches such as this were held in the other large, older cities of the Midwest. Perhaps, in some smaller ones, too. Old friends from way back, sitting around a table reminiscing about the days of their youth and the particular, familial enchantment of a big-city neighborhood.

A few years after those lunches stopped, I rode through some of those neighborhoods of my youth. It was a bleak Chicago spring day in 2015, the air filled with cold, light rain that didn't seem to hit the streets but just hung suspended. The gloomy weather felt apropos considering my destination—a meeting with Cardinal Francis George at his North Side residence just south of Lincoln Park. By then, the cardinal had resigned as archbishop and announced that he would cease any further treatment for his cancer and await the inevitable.

My grade school friend Bill Nelligan was taking me for what I knew would be a farewell. To avoid the expressway congestion, Bill chose to drive a depressing route through Chicago's South Side, past the Catholic churches and schools that we once knew so well and that now stood at locations in some of the most dangerous sites in the country.

Pope John Paul II appointed Cardinal George archbishop of Chicago in 1997. It was a homecoming of sorts—George and his sister had been raised on the city's Northwest Side in St. Pascal's Parish. He had two cousins, also in that parish, and one of them, Edward, was married to my sister Maureen for over 45 years. Chicago's Catholic community knew little of George at the time of his appointment, but in the world-wide Church hierarchy, he was known and respected as a prominent scholar and theologian. He served 12 years in Rome as the Vicar of his Order, the Missionary Oblates of Mary Immaculate— an order whose primary work was in Africa and Latin America. Prior to that, he taught philosophy at several colleges around the country. He was a devoted disciple of Pope John Paul II and recognized as the intellectual leader of the Catholic Church in America.

Once, speaking with a small group of priests, Cardinal George said, "I expect to die in my bed, my successor will die in prison, and his [successor will die] a martyr in the public square." These words, often taken out of context, were spoken to emphasize the dangers of an increasingly secularized culture in our country. Catholic conservatives around the world viewed him as someone who could possibly have become the first non-European pope.

Cardinal George had a special and unique relationship with my sister Maureen that spanned nearly half a century, and he spoke movingly of it when he delivered the eulogy at her funeral Mass. Over the years, I shared conversations with him at Ed and Maureen's family celebrations, and after his arrival as archbishop, we developed a close friendship.

The cardinal's homecoming to Chicago came as the greatest crisis in American Catholic Church history was about to unfold— the failure of church leaders to respond appropriately to reports of sexual abuse of children committed by pedophile priests. In many cases, this failure—particularly the failure to alert authorities—had allowed the statute of limitations to run out, precluding prosecutors from filing criminal charges. As the head of the American Catholic Bishops, Cardinal George established a policy of zero tolerance, quick government notification, and a clear statement that an innocent victim's right to justice prevailed over all other interests. But even with the cardinal's firm policy, one of those pedophile priests, Daniel McCormack of Chicago, eluded the system. Though McCormack is now in a state facility, the McCormack case of abuse has left a scar on the Chicago Church that will be a long time in healing. Indeed, this case has caused some to abandon the Catholic faith.

Arriving at the residence, I was surprised that the cardinal answered the door, and when we sat down, I couldn't detect if he was experiencing pain—his discomfort being the criterion I would use to determine how long we would meet. Everything considered, his spirits appeared to be okay. He wanted to know how my wife, Mairsey, and our four sons were doing, and he recalled many of the past family celebrations we shared with Maureen and Ed. As always, he spoke of Maureen's strength during her illness. He asked if my son Kevin was satisfied with his decision to resign from the Illinois Legislature to take a position with Ave Maria University in Florida. The cardinal had counseled Kevin about the decision. He jokingly described in detail a recent visit to a Catholic high school in our neighborhood. He had requested the school to summon a student, his nephew Danny's daughter, to the principal's office on the pretense it involved a disciplinary matter.

The cardinal spoke at length about the views of Pope Francis, the current pope, and surprisingly described in detail what had actually happened during the pope's election. We talked of Chicago politics—Richard M. Daley had been mayor for eight years before the cardinal's arrival in Chicago, and though initially their relationship was a bit chilled, over the years it became much better. Regarding Mayor Daley's successor, George agreed with most of what I thought. He expressed a strong belief that the Hispanic community was very important for the future of the Church and the city.

The afternoon passed quickly. As early dark settled in, it was time to leave. Cardinal George walked with me to the door. Almost as an afterthought on his personal checklist, he said I should tell my son Michael, who was a volunteer boxing coach at an inner-city boys high school that received aid from the archdiocese, that he had made provisions for the financial assistance to continue. He added that he didn't know if his successor, Bishop Cupich, would renew it on a long-term basis.

That was it. We said good-bye, shook hands, and as he opened the door, he quietly said, "I always believed I would be more accepting of this."

As I've puzzled over the cardinal's words since then, I've come to believe that it wasn't so much death he had trouble accepting, but his realization, as the end drew near, that he had not achieved all he had hoped. The thought certainly touches a chord in me. I spent a youth growing up in the homes, schools, churches, and playgrounds of Chicago and invested much of my adult life in trying to maintain my community and serve the city as best I could. I take comfort in knowing that the 19th Ward, where I devoted so much effort early on, has remained vibrant and stable. The template for quality integrated living in an urban community is still in place there, having been followed faultlessly by the three succeeding City Council members, Michael Sheahan, Ginger Rugai, and Matt O'Shea.

Yet, today I see a city still plagued by obstacles, particularly the divide between Blacks and whites. That divide is fueled by the unequal opportunities for many African Americans in housing, schools, jobs—an American problem that goes back centuries, but one especially acute in big cities, such as Chicago. None of the potential solutions are easy.

Still, I place the cardinal's comment in a larger context—one that gives me hope that I will be more accepting than the cardinal as my end approaches.

Fast forward from my meeting with the cardinal to one of the annual St. Sabina reunion dinners at Gaelic Park in Oak Forest. In the large banquet hall are tables filled with hundreds of friendships, first formed in the classrooms of St. Sabina, each guided by a cadre of nuns who taught the importance of faith and family, which remains with us today.

Mairsey and I consider ourselves blessed and fortunate. Our parents, our siblings, our extended families—uncles, aunts, nieces, nephews, and cousins—have all been gifts. Our sons and their wives are kind, caring, and generous, which is reflected in the daily lives of their children. As a family, we have shared moments of sadness and difficulty, but these have been overwhelmed by times of joy, and when we go, we will part knowing we have left something of great value. ■

ACKNOWLEDGMENTS

For inspiration, advice and help: Steve Neal, Bernie Judge, Ray Coffey, Richard Babcock, Ginger Rugai, and Monsignor Ignatius McDermott. ◄

INDEX

NOTE: Page references in *italics* refer to photos.

CPSIA information can be obtained
at www.ICGtesting.com
Printed in the USA
LVHW082158250821
696137LV00014B/154/J